CliffsTestPrep®

Praxis II®: Mathematics Content Knowledge Test (0061)

by

E. D. McCune, Ph.D.
and Sandra Luna McCune, Ph.D.

WILEY

Wiley Publishing, Inc.

About the Authors

E. D. McCune is Regents Professor in the Department of Mathematics and Statistics, and Sandra Luna McCune is Regents Professor and math specialist in the Department of Elementary Education at Stephen F. Austin State University in Nacogdoches, Texas. Regents Professor is the highest honor that the university has in its authority to bestow upon a member of the faculty.

The authors wish to thank Grace Freedson for bringing us this project and the editors for their help in making it a reality. We would also like to thank our families especially our children and our two grandchildren, Richard and Rose, for their loving support.

Publisher's Acknowledgments

Editorial

Acquisitions Editor: Greg Tubach

Project Editor: Kelly D. Henthorne

Technical Editor: David Herzog

Production

Proofreader: Christine Pingleton

Wiley Publishing, Inc. Composition Services

CliffsTestPrep® Praxis II®: Mathematics Content Knowledge Test (0061)

Published by:
Wiley Publishing, Inc.
111 River Street
Hoboken, NJ 07030-5774
www.wiley.com

Copyright © 2006 Wiley, Hoboken, NJ

Published by Wiley, Hoboken, NJ
Published simultaneously in Canada

Printed in the United States of America

10 9 8 7 6 5 4

1O/RZ/QW/QW/IN

Library of Congress information available upon request.

ISBN-13: 978-0-471-78767-9

ISBN-10: 0-471-78767-1

WILEY

Table of Contents

PART II: 3 FULL-LENGTH PRACTICE TESTS

Introduction

General Description

The PRAXIS Mathematics: Content Knowledge test (test code 0061, Mathematics CK) is designed to assess the mathematical knowledge and skills that an entry-level teacher of secondary school mathematics needs to possess. As listed in the *Mathematics: Content Knowledge (0061) Test at a Glance* (www.ets.org/Media/Tests/PRAXIS/pdf/0061.pdf), the test addresses five broad areas:

I. Algebra and Number Theory

II. Measurement, Geometry, and Trigonometry

III. Functions and Calculus

IV. Data Analysis, Statistics, and Probability

V. Matrix Algebra and Discrete Mathematics

The test consists of 50 multiple-choice questions. Each multiple-choice question contains four response options. You record your answer choice in the separate answer booklet by filling in the space corresponding to **A, B, C,** or **D**. No penalty is imposed for wrong answers (you merely score a zero for that test question). The test booklet provides a mathematics reference sheet containing information organized under three labels: NOTATION, DEFINITIONS, and FORMULAS. You are given two hours to complete the test.

Calculator Requirements

You are required to bring a graphing calculator to use while taking the Mathematics CK. The calculator that you bring must be capable of the following:

- producing the graph of a function within an arbitrary viewing window
- finding the zeros of a function
- computing a numeric derivative of a function
- computing a numeric integral of a function

Calculator memories will *not* be cleared by the test administrator prior to the start of the examination.

You are NOT allowed to bring computers, including powerbooks and portable/handheld computers, calculators with QWERTY keyboards (for example, TI-92 PLUS, Voyage 200), cell-phone calculators, or electronic writing pads or other pen-input/stylus-driven devices.

Format of the Test

According to the *Mathematics: Content Knowledge (0061) Test at a Glance* (see "General Description," earlier in this chapter for the Internet address), the content categories for the test and approximate number of questions and percentage of the test for each content category are as follows:

Format of the Test		
Content Category	*Approximate Number of Questions*	*Approximate Percent of Test*
Algebra and Number Theory	8	16%
Measurement	3	6%
Geometry	5	10%
Trigonometry	4	8%
Functions	8	16%
Calculus	6	12%
Data Analysis and Statistics	5–6	10–12%
Probability	2–3	4–6%
Matrix Algebra	4–5	8–10%
Discrete Mathematics	3–4	6–8%

In addition to mathematical knowledge and skills, the PRAXIS Mathematics CK assesses five process categories: Problem Solving, Reasoning and Proof, Connections, Representation, and Use of Technology. These process categories refer to the ways through which mathematical knowledge is acquired and used. The first four process categories are adopted from the National Council of Teachers of Mathematics (NCTM) *Principles and Standards for School Mathematics* (2000) process standards and are as described here:

Problem Solving (http://standards.nctm.org/document/chapter3/prob.htm)

- Build new mathematical knowledge through problem solving.
- Solve problems that arise in mathematics and in other contexts.
- Apply and adapt a variety of appropriate strategies to solve problems.

Reasoning and Proof (http://standards.nctm.org/document/chapter3/reas.htm)

- Make and investigate mathematical conjectures.
- Develop and evaluate mathematical arguments and proofs.
- Select and use various types of reasoning and methods of proof.

Connections (http://standards.nctm.org/document/chapter3/conn.htm)

- Recognize and use connections among mathematical ideas.
- Understand how mathematical ideas interconnect and build on one another.
- Recognize and apply mathematics in contexts outside of mathematics.

Representation (http://standards.nctm.org/document/chapter3/rep.htm)

- Create and use representations to organize, record, and communicate mathematical ideas.
- Select, apply, and translate among mathematical representations to solve problems.
- Use representations to model and interpret physical, social, and mathematical phenomena.

The description of the fifth process category as given in the *Mathematics: Content Knowledge (0061) Test at a Glance* is as follows:

Use of Technology

- Use technology appropriately as a tool for problem solving.
- Use technology as an aid to understanding mathematical ideas.

The process categories are integrated into the content questions. This circumstance means that you will not be asked explicit questions about the process categories, but rather you will be expected to use one or more of the processes in answering questions on the test.

The Role of the Mathematics CK in Teacher Certification

The Mathematics CK is one of the PRAXIS II Series subject assessment tests designed by the Educational Testing Service (ETS). The PRAXIS II tests are part of a national teacher assessment program and are used as part of the certification or licensing requirements in about 80 percent of the states. This means that you can transfer your score on the Mathematics CK from state to state for those states that use the PRAXIS II subject assessment tests.

If your state has selected the Mathematics CK to assess secondary teacher candidates' mathematical knowledge and skills, then this *CliffsTestPrep* book will be invaluable in helping you achieve the passing score for your state. Test scores needed to obtain certification vary from state to state because each state sets its own passing score. ETS maintains a listing by state of links to test requirements for those states that require the PRAXIS II subject assessment tests for certification at www.ets.org/praxis/prxstate.html. ETS also publishes the most recent information it has regarding passing score requirements in a pamphlet titled *Understanding Your Praxis Scores,* which you can download at http://www.ets.org/Media/Tests/PRAXIS/pdf/09706PRAXIS.pdf. The following is a list of states that require the Mathematics CK along with the current (in 2006) score needed to obtain certification in each state:

Alabama—118	Kentucky—125	Ohio—139
Alaska—146	Louisiana—125	Oregon—138
Arkansas—116	Maine—126	Pennsylvania—136
Colorado—156	Maryland—141	South Carolina—131
Connecticut—137	Minnesota—125	South Dakota—124
Delaware—121	Mississippi—123	Tennessee—136
District of Columbia—141	Missouri—137	Utah—138
Georgia—136	Nevada—144	Vermont—141
Hawaii—136	New Hampshire—127	Virginia—147
Idaho—119	New Jersey—137	Washington—134
Indiana—136	North Carolina—*	West Virginia—133
Kansas—137	North Dakota—139	Wisconsin—135

Questions Commonly Asked About the Mathematics CK

Q. What is the Mathematics CK?

A. The Mathematics CK is a PRAXIS II Series subject assessment test. Currently, it is used by 36 states as part of their teacher certification/licensure requirements.

Q. Who administers the Mathematics CK?

A. The Mathematics CK is administered by the Educational Testing Service (ETS).

Q. When and where is the Mathematics CK given?

A. Currently, PRAXIS Series tests, including the Mathematics CK, are administered six times a year (usually in September, November, January, March, April, June, and August) at locations throughout the United States. You can find information on test dates, site locations, fees, registration procedures, and policies in the current *The Praxis Series Information and Registration Bulletin,* which you can download at http://www.ets.org/Media/Tests/PRAXIS/pdf/01361.pdf.

Q. How do I register to take to the test?

A. You can register online using a credit card at the PRAXIS Web site (www.ets.org/praxis) from 7 A.M. to 10 P.M. (Eastern Time), Monday through Friday; or you can register by mail by downloading the registration form available on the PRAXIS Web site and then mailing the completed form to ETS-The Praxis Series, Box 382065, Pittsburgh, PA 15251–8065.

Q. Are special testing arrangements available?

A. If you have a disabling condition (visual, physical, hearing, or so on), special testing arrangements and test materials can be made available for you. Complete the registration form and follow the instructions at www.ets.org/praxis/prxdsabl.html.

If you are unable to take the test on Saturdays because of your religious convictions or because of duties as a member of the U.S. armed forces, you can request a Monday testing day by following the instructions in the *Registration Bulletin.* A copy of your military duties or a letter from your clergy on the clergy's letterhead, verifying the religious basis for your request, must be included with your registration application.

If your primary language is not English, you can request extended testing time by following the instructions in the *Registration Bulletin.*

You should write your name, social security number, and phone number on all correspondence to ensure proper handling of your documentation. Don't forget to make copies of everything before you mail it.

Q. May I change my registration if I need to?

A. Yes, you may change tests, test sites, or transfer registration to a later test date by completing the appropriate forms, which you can download from the PRAXIS Web site (www.ets.org/praxis). For test and center changes, the form must be received by the late registration deadline. For test date changes, the form must be received within two weeks after your original test date. The current fee (in 2006) for this service is $40.

Q. What is the fee for the test?

A. The current fee (in 2006) for regular registration is $75. The fee for late registration is an additional $40 charge.

Q. What should I bring to the test site?

A. After you mail in your registration form, you should receive an admission ticket by one week before your scheduled test date. If you have not received your admission ticket by this time or if you have lost your admission ticket, call ETS at 1-800-772-9476. If you register online, you must print your admission ticket. Your admission ticket will include your name, the tests you are registered to take, the test date, the test site address, and the reporting time. Check the information on your admission ticket to make sure that it is correct. You will not be allowed to make changes at the test site.

The day of the test, you should bring your admission ticket, a valid form of photo and signature identification (for example, driver's license or military identification), your graphing calculator, several sharpened Number 2 soft lead pencils, a good eraser, a blue or black ink pen, and a watch to help pace yourself during the exam. Mechanical pencils cannot be used. No personal items such as handbags, cell phones, or study materials or other aids will be permitted in the testing room.

Q. Is the Mathematics CK divided into timed sections?

A. No, you have two hours to complete the 50 multiple-choice test items. You may work through the questions at your own pace as long as you stay within the two-hour timeframe.

Q. What is the passing score?

A. The passing score varies from state to state. Check with your preparation institution regarding the passing score in your state.

Q. When will I get my score report?

A. Your score report will be mailed approximately four weeks after the test administration date.

Q. How should I prepare?

A. Using this test prep book is your best preparation. This study guide gives you insights, reviews, and strategies for the question types. Some universities offer preparation programs to assist you in attaining a passing score. Check with them for further information.

Q. How do I get more information about the Mathematics CK?

A. Check the PRAXIS Web site (www.ets.org/praxis). If new information on the Mathematics CK becomes available, it will be posted on this site.

Q. What is the ETS Recognition of Excellence Award (ROE)?

A. This award is a way ETS recognizes test takers who demonstrate a high level of proficiency on any of 11 Praxis II tests. For the Mathematics CK, achieving a score of 165 or higher will earn you the ROE. You will receive a congratulatory letter and recognition certificate from ETS acknowledging your high score on the test. In addition, the award will be noted on your score report, and summary award data will be included on reports sent to institutions of higher education and state agencies.

How to Use This *CliffsTestPrep* Book

When you read through the list of content categories that are assessed on the Mathematics CK, you may feel overwhelmed by the task of preparing for the test. Here are some suggestions for developing an effective study program using this book.

1. To help you organize and budget your time, set up a specific schedule of study sessions. Try to set aside approximately two hours for each session. If you complete one session per day (including weekends), it should take you about three to four weeks to work your way through the review and practice material provided in this book.

   If your test date is coming up soon, you may need to lengthen your study time per day or skip sections that cover topics that you feel you already know fairly well. Nonetheless, be cautious about deciding to skip sections. You could find yourself struggling through material that would be easier to master if previous sections had been reviewed first. This caution is particularly important with regard to math topics, which are usually highly dependent on previously learned skills.

2. Choose a place for studying that is free of distractions and undue noise, so that you can concentrate. Make sure that you have adequate lighting and a room temperature that is comfortable—not too warm or too cold. Be sure that you have an ample supply of water to keep your brain hydrated, and you might also want to have some light snacks available. To improve mental alertness, choose snacks that are high in protein and low in carbohydrates (for example, nuts). Try to have all the necessary study aids (paper, pen, note cards, and so on) within easy reach, so that you don't have to interrupt your studying to go get something you need. Ask friends not to call you during your study time.

3. Take Practice Test 1 before you begin your study program to help you discover your strengths and weaknesses. Read the answer explanations for all the questions, not just the ones you missed, because you may have gotten some of your correct answers by guessing. Make a list of the content categories with which you had the most problems. Plan your study program so that you can concentrate first on content categories that your Practice Test 1 results indicate are weak areas for you. For instance, if you did very well in algebra and number theory, but poorly in geometry, then you should begin your Mathematics CK preparation with the geometry section.

4. Carefully study the review of the exam areas in Part II of this book to refresh your memory about the key ideas for each of the content categories, being sure to concentrate as you go through the material. Don't let yourself be diverted by extraneous thoughts or outside distractions. Monitor yourself by making a check mark on a separate sheet of paper when your concentration wanders. Work on reducing the number of check marks you record each study session. Take notes as you study, using your own words to express ideas.

5. Make flashcards to aid you in memorizing key ideas and keep them with you at all times. When you have spare moments of time, take out the flash cards and go over the information you've recorded on them.

6. Set aside certain days to review material you have already studied. This strategy will allow you to reinforce what you have learned and identify topics you may need to restudy.

7. Take several brief two- to three-minute breaks during your study sessions to give your mind time to absorb the review material you just read. According to brain research, you remember the first part and last part of something you've read more easily than you remember the middle part. Taking several breaks will allow you to create more beginnings and endings to maximize the amount of material you remember. It's best not to leave your study area during a break. Try stretching, closing your eyes for a few minutes, or getting a quick drink or snack.

8. When you complete your review, take Practice Test 2. Use a timer and take the test under the same conditions you expect for the actual test, being sure to adhere to the two-hour time limit for the test. When you finish taking the test, as you did for Practice Test 1, carefully study the answer explanations for *all* the questions. Then, go back and review again any topics in which you performed unsatisfactorily.

9. When you complete your second review, take Practice Test 3 under the same conditions you expect for the actual test, adhering to the two-hour time limit. When you finish taking the test, carefully study the answer explanations for *all* the questions and do additional study, if needed.

10. Organize a study group, if possible. A good way of learning and reinforcing the material is to discuss it with others. If possible, set up a regular time to study with one or more classmates or friends. Take turns explaining how to work the problems to each other. This strategy will help you to clarify your own understanding of the problems and, at the same time, help you discover new insights in how to approach various problems.

After completing your study program, you should find yourself prepared and confident to achieve a passing score on the Mathematics CK.

How to Prepare for the Day of the Test

There are several things you can do to prepare yourself for the day of the test.

1. Know where the test center is located and how to get there.

2. Make dependable arrangements to get to the test center in plenty of time and know where to park if you plan to go by car.

3. Keep all the materials you will need to bring to the test center—especially, your admission ticket and identification—in a secure place, so that you easily find them on the day of the test.

4. Go to bed in time to get a good night's rest. Avoid taking nonprescription drugs or alcohol as the use of these products may impair your mental faculties on test day.

5. On the day of the test, plan to get to the testing center early.

6. Dress in comfortable clothing and wear comfortable shoes. Even if it is warm outside, wear layers of clothing that can be removed or put on, depending on the temperature in the test center.

7. Eat a light meal. Select foods that you have found usually give you the most energy and stamina.

8. Drink plenty of water to make sure that your brain remains hydrated during the test for optimal thinking.

9. Be sure to put fresh batteries in your calculator just before you leave to go to the testing center.

10. Make a copy of this list and post it in a strategic location. Check over it before you leave for the testing center.

Test-Taking Strategies for the Mathematics CK

Here are some general test-taking strategies to help maximize your score on the test:

1. When you receive the test, take several deep, slow breaths, exhaling slowly while mentally visualizing yourself performing successfully on the test before you begin. Do not get upset if you feel nervous. Most of the people taking the test with you will be experiencing some measure of anxiety.

2. During the test, follow all the directions, including the oral directions of the test administrator and the written directions in the test booklet. If you do not understand something in the directions, ask the test administrator for clarification.

3. Move through the test at a steady pace. The test consists of 50 multiple-choice items. As you begin the test, skim through the booklet to find question 25, mark this question as an approximate halfway point. When you get to question 25, check your watch to see how much time has passed. If more than one hour has gone by, you will need to pick up the pace. Otherwise, continue to work as rapidly as you can without being careless, *but do not rush.*

4. Try to answer the questions in order. Skipping around can waste time and might cause mistakes on your answer sheet. However, if a question is taking too much of your time, place a large check mark next to it in the test booklet (*not* on the answer booklet), mark your best guess in the answer booklet, and move on.

5. Read each question entirely. Skimming to save time can cause you to misread a question or miss important information.

6. Write in the test booklet. Mark on diagrams, draw figures, underline or circle key words or phrases, and do scratch work in the test booklet. Remember, however, to mark your answer choice in the separate answer booklet. Answers marked only in the test booklet are not scored.

7. Don't read too much into a question. For instance, don't presume a geometric figure is drawn accurately or to scale.

8. Refer to the notation, definitions, and formulas provided with the test as often as you need to. *Always* double-check every formula after you write it down.

9. Use your calculator, but use it wisely. Keep in mind that graphing calculators are powerful tools, but they can make errors. See the discussion about graphing calculators that follows this section.

10. Be sure you are answering the *right question*. Circle or underline what you are being asked to find to help you stay focused on it.

11. Read all the answer choices before you select an answer. You might find an answer that immediately strikes you as correct, but this determination might have occurred because you jumped to a false conclusion or made an incorrect assumption.

12. Eliminate as many wrong choices as you can. Estimate the answer to help you decide which answers are unreasonable.

13. Change an answer only if you have a good reason to do so. Be sure to completely erase the old answer choice before marking the new one.

14. If you are trying to recall information during the test, close your eyes and try to visualize yourself in your study place. This may trigger your memory.

15. Remain calm during the test. If you find yourself getting anxious, stop and take several deep, slow breaths and exhale slowly, while mentally visualizing yourself in a peaceful place, to help you relax. Do not be upset if the student next to you finishes, gets up, and leaves before you do. Keep your mind focused on the task at hand—completing your exam. Trust yourself. You should not expect to know the correct response to every question on the exam. Think only of doing your personal best.

16. Record your answers in the answer booklet carefully. The test is scored electronically, so it is critical that you mark your answer booklet accurately. As you go through the test questions, circle the letters of your answer choices in the test booklet. Then mark those answers in the answer booklet in bunches of 5 to 10 (until the last minutes of the time allotted, when you should start marking answers one by one).

17. Before turning in your answer booklet, be sure you have marked an answer for every test question. You are not penalized for a wrong answer (you merely score a zero for that test question), so even if you have no clue about the correct answer, make a guess. Also, erase any stray marks in the answer booklet and brush off any loose eraser dust.

18. As you work through the practice tests provided in this book, consciously use the strategies suggested in this section as preparation for the actual Mathematics CK. Try to reach the point that the strategies are automatic for you.

Graphing Calculators and the Mathematics CK

Since you are required to bring a graphing calculator to use when you take the Mathematics CK, you should have your calculator on hand and use it, when needed, to work problems in the review material and practice tests in this book. Select a calculator that you will feel comfortable using. Don't purchase a high-powered calculator that will require an investment of your time to learn while you are preparing for the test.

A word of caution: Graphing calculators are very powerful tools, but you should be aware that they can make errors!

One situation in which errors might occur is when the calculator is finding the roots or zeros of a high-degree polynomial (for example, a polynomial of degree eight). The algorithm that the calculator uses to find the roots of the polynomial forces the calculator to round numbers to a certain number of decimal places before the final result is obtained, thus yielding inaccurate answers.

Another situation in which errors commonly occur is when the calculator is drawing the graph of a function. Your choice of viewing window dimensions can give results that are visually very misleading. For instance, you can be led to believe that a function has only two zeros when, in fact, it has three zeros. Changing the dimensions for the viewing window can clear up the problem in most cases; however, not every time. Most notably, for most graphing calculators, the graph of $y = \sin(1/x)$ at values near $x = $ zero will never be correct no matter what window dimensions you select.

The point of this discussion is to make you aware that such mistakes can happen. Therefore, you should use your mathematical expertise to evaluate all your calculator's answers for reliability and accuracy.

You will benefit greatly from this *CliffsTestPrep* book. By using the recommendations in this chapter as you complete your study program, you will be prepared to walk into the testing room with confidence. Good luck on the test and on your new career as a mathematics teacher!

PART I

SUBJECT AREA REVIEWS

Review for the Praxis Mathematics: Content Knowledge (0061)

The review of the Mathematics CK in this *CliffsTestPrep* book is designed around the 10 content categories that are assessed on the test: Algebra and Number Theory, Measurement, Geometry, Trigonometry, Functions, Calculus, Data Analysis and Statistics, Probability, Matrix Algebra, and Discrete Mathematics. Each content category is defined by a list of specific knowledge and skills. The review for each content category will discuss the key ideas and formulas that are most important for you to know for the Mathematics CK. Mathematical notation, definitions, and formulas like those that will be provided for you when you take the official exam are included on the following three pages.

Notation, Definitions, and Formulas

NOTATION

(a, b)	$\{x: a < x < b\}$
$[a, b)$	$\{x: a \leq x < b\}$
$(a, b]$	$\{x: a < x \leq b\}$
$[a, b]$	$\{x: a \leq x \leq b\}$
$\gcd(m, n)$	<u>greatest common divisor</u> of two integers m and n
$\mathrm{lcm}(m, n)$	<u>least common multiple</u> of two integers m and n
$[x]$	<u>greatest integer</u> m such that $m \leq x$
$m \equiv k(\mathrm{mod}\ n)$	m and k are <u>congruent modulo n</u> (m and k have the same remainder when divided by n, or equivalently, $m - k$ is a multiple of n)
f^{-1}	<u>inverse</u> of an invertible function f; (<u>not</u> to be read as $\frac{1}{f}$)
$\lim\limits_{x \to a^+} f(x)$	<u>right-hand limit</u> of $f(x)$; limit (if it exists) of $f(x)$ as x approaches a from the right
$\lim\limits_{x \to a^-} f(x)$	<u>left-hand limit</u> of $f(x)$; limit (if it exists) of $f(x)$ as x approaches a from the left
$\varnothing$	the empty set
$x \in S$	x is an element of set S
$S \subset T$	set S is a proper subset of set T
$S \subseteq T$	either set S is a proper subset of set T or $S = T$
$S \cup T$	union of sets S and T
$S \cap T$	intersection of sets S and T

DEFINITIONS

DISCRETE MATHEMATICS

A relation $\Re$ on a set S is

> <u>reflexive</u> if $x \Re x$ for all $x \in S$
>
> <u>symmetric</u> if $x \Re y \Rightarrow y \Re x$ for all $x, y \in S$
>
> <u>transitive</u> if $(x \Re y$ and $y \Re z) \Rightarrow x \Re z$ for all $x, y, z \in S$
>
> <u>antisymmetric</u> if $(x \Re y$ and $y \Re x) \Rightarrow x = y$ for all $x, y \in S$

An <u>equivalence</u> relation is a reflexive, symmetric, and transitive relation.

FORMULAS

Addition

$$\sin(x \pm y) = \sin x \cos y \pm \cos x \sin y$$

$$\cos(x \pm y) = \cos x \cos y \mp \sin x \sin y$$

$$\tan(x \pm y) = \frac{\tan x \pm \tan y}{1 \mp \tan x \tan y}$$

Half-Angle (sign depends on the quadrant of $\frac{\theta}{2}$)

$$\sin \frac{\theta}{2} = \pm \sqrt{\frac{1 - \cos \theta}{2}}; \qquad \cos \frac{\theta}{2} = \pm \sqrt{\frac{1 + \cos \theta}{2}}$$

Range of Inverse Trigonometric Functions

$\sin^{-1} x \quad [-\pi/2, \pi/2]; \qquad \cos^{-1} x \quad [0, \pi]; \qquad \tan^{-1} x \quad (-\pi/2, \pi/2)$

Law of Sines

$$\frac{\sin A}{a} = \frac{\sin B}{b} = \frac{\sin C}{c}$$

Law of Cosines

$$c^2 = a^2 + b^2 - 2ab(\cos C)$$

De Moivre's Theorem

$$(\cos \theta + i \sin \theta)^k = \cos(k\theta) + i\sin(k\theta)$$

Coordinate Transformation

Rectangular (x, y) to polar (r, θ) $\quad r^2 = x^2 + y^2; \qquad \tan \theta = \frac{y}{x}$ if $x \neq 0$

Polar (r, θ) to rectangular (x, y) $\quad x = r \cos \theta; \qquad y = r \sin \theta$

Distance from point (x_1, y_1) to line $Ax + By + C = 0$ $\qquad d = \dfrac{\left| Ax_1 + By_1 + C \right|}{\sqrt{A^2 + B^2}}$

Volume

Sphere: radius r $\qquad\qquad\qquad\qquad\qquad\qquad\qquad V = \frac{4}{3}\pi r^3$

Right circular cone: height h, base of radius r $\qquad V = \frac{1}{3}\pi r^2 h$

Right circular cylinder: height h, base of radius r $\qquad V = \pi r^2 h$

Pyramid: height h, base of area B $\qquad\qquad\qquad V = \frac{1}{3}Bh$

Right Prism: height h, base of area B $\qquad\qquad\quad V = Bh$

Surface Area

Sphere: radius r $A = 4\pi r^2$

Right circular cone: lateral surface area with radius r, slant height s $A = \pi rs$

Differentiation

$$(f(x)g(x))' = f'(x)g(x) + f(x)g'(x) \qquad (f(g(x)))' = f'(g(x))\, g'(x)$$

$$\left(\frac{f(x)}{g(x)}\right)' = \frac{f'(x)g(x) - f(x)g'(x)}{\left(g(x)\right)^2} \text{ if } g(x) \neq 0$$

Integration by Parts $\int u\ dv = uv - \int v\ du$

While you are practicing for the Mathematics CK, make sure that you become very familiar with the information that is given to you on the Notation, Definitions, and Formulas pages that are included in this chapter and at the beginning of the Mathematics CK test booklet. You will need to know other common mathematical formulas that are not listed on the Notation, Definitions, and Formulas pages, such as the three formulas given here.

Simple Interest Formula $I = Prt$, where I = simple interest earned, P = principal invested or present value of investment, r = annual simple interest rate, and t = time in years.

Compound Interest Formula $P = P_0(1 + \frac{r}{n})^{nt}$, where P is the total value of an initial investment of P_0 for t years at an annual rate r, compounded n times per year.

Distance Formula $d = rt$, where d = distance traveled, r = (uniform) rate of speed, and t = time.

In addition, you will need to know other familiar formulas relevant to the content categories, such as the formulas for the area and perimeter of common geometric shapes. Those formulas that are most important for you to know are given in the reviews for the content categories.

Since the test administrator will not clear the memory of your calculator before the test starts, if a common formula is particularly difficult for you to remember correctly, you should program the formula into your graphing calculator. This strategy is a good one because then you know the formula is correct, and, also, you will save time when evaluating the formula for specific values.

Algebra and Number Theory

According to the *Mathematics: Content Knowledge (0061) Test at a Glance* (www.ets.org/Media/Tests/PRAXIS/ pdf/0061.pdf), the Algebra and Number Theory content category of the Mathematics CK tests your knowledge and skills in nine topic areas:

- The real and complex number systems
- Properties of number systems
- Properties of the counting numbers
- Ratio, proportion, percent, and average
- Algebraic expressions, formulas, and equations
- Systems of equations and inequalities
- Geometric interpretations of algebraic principles
- Algebraic representations of lines, planes, conic sections, and spheres
- Formulas used in two- and three-dimensional coordinate systems

This review discusses the key ideas and formulas in each topic area that are most important for you to know for the Mathematics CK.

The Real and Complex Number Systems

For this topic, you must demonstrate an understanding of the structure of the natural, integer, rational, real, and complex number systems and the ability to perform the basic operations ($+$, $-$, $\times$, and $\div$) on numbers in these systems (*Mathematics: Content Knowledge (0061) Test at a Glance*, page 3).

Important sets of numbers in algebra follow:

natural numbers or counting numbers = $\{1, 2, 3, \ldots\}$

whole numbers = $\{0, 1, 2, 3, \ldots\}$

integers = $\{\ldots, -3, -2, -1, 0, 1, 2, 3, \ldots\}$

rational numbers = $\{\frac{p}{q}$, where p, q are integers with $q \neq 0\}$

irrational numbers $\{$nonterminating, nonrepeating decimals$\}$ = $\{$numbers that can*not* be written in the form $\frac{p}{q}$, where $q \neq 0\}$

real numbers = rational numbers $\cup$ irrational numbers. The natural numbers, whole numbers, integers, rational numbers, and irrational numbers are subsets of the real numbers. The real numbers can be represented on a number line. Every point on the number line corresponds to a real number.

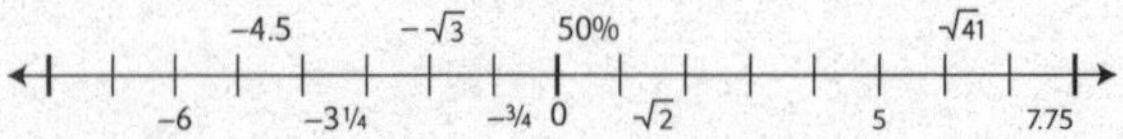

complex numbers = $\{x + yi$, where x and y are real numbers and $i^2 = -1\}$. For the complex number $z = x + yi$, the coefficients x and y are called the **real part** and **imaginary part,** respectively. When x is zero, the resulting set of numbers consists of **pure imaginary** numbers. When y is zero, the resulting set of numbers consists of the **real numbers.** Thus, the real numbers are a subset of the complex numbers. The complex numbers can be represented on the **complex plane,** where the horizontal axis is called the **real axis** and the vertical axis is called the **imaginary axis.** The complex numbers $z_1 = 2 + i$, $z_2 = 3 - 2i$, $z_3 = -3 + 2i$, and $z_4 = -2 - 4i$ are shown on the complex plane in the following figure.

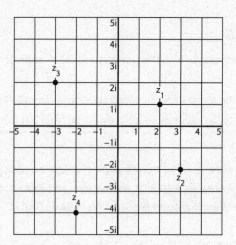

Computations using real numbers are performed by using the absolute values, which are always positive or zero, of the numbers. The **absolute value** of a real number is its distance from zero on the real number line. The absolute value of a real number x is either x or $-x$, whichever of these is **nonnegative.**

Rules to Compute By

For sums and differences of real numbers, use the following rules.

> **Rule 1.** To find the sum of two real numbers that have the same sign: add their absolute values and attach the common sign to the sum.
>
> **Rule 2.** To find the sum of two real numbers that have opposite signs: subtract the smaller absolute value from the larger absolute value and indicate the result has the same sign as the number with the larger absolute value; if both numbers have the same absolute value, the sum is 0.
>
> **Rule 3.** To find the difference of two real numbers: first, change the sign of the number following the minus symbol; next, change the minus symbol to a plus symbol; and then add using Rule 1 or Rule 2, whichever applies.

For products and quotients of real numbers, use the following rules.

> **Rule 4.** To find the product of two nonzero real numbers that have the same sign: multiply their absolute values and indicate the product is positive (no sign is necessary).
>
> **Rule 5.** To find the product of two nonzero real numbers that have opposite signs: multiply their absolute values and indicate the product is negative.
>
> **Rule 6.** When *zero* is one of the factors, the product is *always* zero; otherwise, products involving an *even* number of negative factors are positive, whereas those involving an *odd* number of negative factors are negative.
>
> **Rule 7.** To find the quotient of two nonzero real numbers that have the same sign: divide their absolute values and indicate that the product is positive (no sign is necessary).
>
> **Rule 8.** To find the quotient of two nonzero real numbers that have opposite signs: divide their absolute values and indicate that the product is negative.
>
> **Rule 9.** The quotient is *zero* when the dividend is zero and the divisor is a nonzero number. (For example: $\frac{0}{10} = 0$; $\frac{0}{-10} = 0$.)
>
> **Rule 10.** A quotient is *undefined* when the divisor is zero. (For example: $\frac{35}{0}$ = undefined; $\frac{0}{0}$ = undefined.)

When more than one operation is involved in a numerical expression, you must follow the **order of operations** to **evaluate** the expression. A commonly used mnemonic is the sentence, "Please Excuse My Dear Aunt Sally"—abbreviated as **PE(MD)(AS).** The first letters of the words remind you of the following:

Order of Operations

First, operations enclosed in <u>P</u>arentheses (or other grouping symbol, if present)

Next, <u>E</u>xponentiation

Then, <u>M</u>ultiplication and <u>D</u>ivision in the order in which they occur from left to right

Last, <u>A</u>ddition and <u>S</u>ubtraction in the order in which they occur from left to right

Tip: Note that multiplication does not have to be done before division, or addition before subtraction. You multiply and divide in the order they occur in the problem. Similarly, you add and subtract in the order they occur in the problem. That's why there are parentheses around MD and AS in PE(MD)(AS).

The rules for performing operations with complex numbers follow. Keep in mind that since the coefficients x and y in a complex number $x + yi$ are real numbers, the computations involving the real number coefficients must adhere to Rules 1 through 10 given previously.

Rule 1. Addition of two complex numbers: $(x + yi) + (u + vi) = (x + u) + (y + v)i$

Tip: Add the real parts. Add the imaginary parts.

Rule 2. Subtraction of two complex numbers: $(x + yi) - (u + vi) = (x - u) + (y - v)i$

Tip: Subtract the real parts. Subtract the imaginary parts.

When multiplying complex numbers, it is important to remember that $i^2 = -1$.

Rule 3. Multiplication of two complex numbers: $(x + yi)(u + vi) = (xu - yv) + (xv + yu)i$

Tip: Use F.O.I.L. (first terms, outer terms, inner terms, and last terms) to perform the multiplication.

The complex numbers $x + yi$ and $x - yi$ are **complex conjugates** of each other. The product of a complex number and its conjugate is a real number. Specifically, $(x + yi)(x - yi) = x^2 + y^2$. This concept is used in the division of complex numbers.

Rule 4. Division of two complex numbers: $\dfrac{x+yi}{u+vi} = \dfrac{(x+yi)(u-vi)}{(u+vi)(u-vi)} = \dfrac{(xu+yv)(yu-xv)i}{u^2+v^2} = \dfrac{(xu+yv)}{u^2+v^2} + \dfrac{(yu-xv)}{u^2+v^2}i$

Tip: Multiply the numerator and denominator by the conjugate of the denominator.

Properties of Number Systems

For this topic, you must be able to compare and contrast properties (for example, closure, commutativity, associativity, distributivity) of number systems under various operations (*Mathematics: Content Knowledge (0061) Test at a Glance*, page 3).

The set of real numbers has the following **field properties** under addition and multiplication:

Closure Property: $a + b$ and ab are real numbers.

Commutative Property: $a + b = b + a$ and $ab = ba$.

Associative Property: $(a + b) + c = a + (b + c)$ and $(ab)c = a(bc)$.

Distributive Property: $a(b + c) = ab + ac$ and $(b + c)a = ba + ca$.

Additive Identity Property: There exists a real number, namely 0, such that $a + 0 = a$ and $0 + a = a$.

Multiplicative Identity Property: There exists a real number, namely 1, such that $a \cdot 1 = a$ and $1 \cdot a = a$.

Additive Inverse Property: For every real number a, there exists a real number, denoted $-a$, such that $a + (-a) = 0$ and $(-a) + a = 0$.

Multiplicative Inverse Property: For every nonzero real number a, there exists a real number, denoted a^{-1}, such that $a \cdot a^{-1} = 1$ and $a^{-1} \cdot a = 1$.

The field properties also apply to the set of complex numbers for the operations of addition and multiplication. For the real and complex number systems, subtraction and division are defined as follows.

Subtraction: $a - b = a + (-b)$.

Division: $a \div b = \dfrac{a}{b} = a \cdot b^{-1} = a \cdot \dfrac{1}{b}$.

In general, a system consisting of a set S and two binary operations defined on S is called a **field** if the field properties are satisfied for S under the two operations.

Properties of the Counting Numbers

For this topic, you must demonstrate an understanding of the properties of counting numbers (for example, prime, composite, prime factorization, even, odd, factors, multiples) (*Mathematics: Content Knowledge (0061) Test at a Glance*, page 3).

The counting numbers are the natural numbers. Counting numbers that are greater than 1 are either *prime* or *composite*. A **prime number** is a whole number greater than 1 that has exactly two distinct factors: itself and 1. Thus, the primes are 2, 3, 5, 7, 11, 13, . . .

The counting numbers greater than 1 that are *not* prime are called the **composite numbers.** They are 4, 6, 8, 9, 10, 12, . . .

The counting number 1 is neither prime nor composite.

Besides classifying a counting number as prime or composite, a counting number can be classified as either *even* or *odd*. Counting numbers that are divisible by 2 are called **even.** The **even counting numbers** are 2, 4, 6, 8, . . .

Counting numbers that are *not* divisible by 2 are called **odd.** The **odd counting numbers** are 1, 3, 5, 7, 9, . . .

The **principle of mathematical induction** states that any set of counting numbers that contains the number 1 and $k + 1$, whenever it contains the counting number k, contains all the counting numbers.

The **Fundamental Theorem of Arithmetic** states that every counting number ≥ 2 is either a prime or can be factored into a product of primes in one and only one way, except for the order in which the factors appear.

The **greatest common factor** of two or more counting numbers is the greatest product that will divide evenly into each of the counting numbers. It can be obtained by factoring each counting number and building a product consisting of each factor the *least* number of times it appears as a factor in any one of the counting numbers in the set.

The **greatest common divisor** of two counting numbers m and n, denoted $\gcd(m,n)$, is the greatest common factor of m and n.

The **least common multiple** of a set of counting numbers is the least product that is a multiple of each of the counting numbers. It can be obtained by factoring each counting number and building a product consisting of each factor the *most* number of times it appears as a factor in any one of the counting numbers in the set. The **least common multiple** of two counting numbers m and n is denoted $\text{lcm}(m,n)$.

Ratio, Proportion, Percent, and Average

For this topic, you must be able to solve ratio, proportion, percent, and average (including arithmetic mean and weighted average) problems (*Mathematics: Content Knowledge (0061) Test at a Glance*, page 3).

A ratio is the comparison of two quantities. You can express a ratio in three different forms: a to b, a:b, or $\frac{a}{b}$. The quantities a and b are called the **terms** of the ratio. A ratio is a pure number—it does not have any units. When you find the ratio of two quantities, you must make sure they have the same units so that when you write the ratio, the units will divide out. If the two quantities cannot be converted to like units, then you must keep the units and write the quotient as a **rate.**

A **proportion** is a mathematical statement that two ratios are equal. The **terms** of the proportion are the four numbers that make up the two ratios. For example, take the proportion $\frac{a}{b} = \frac{c}{d}$. This proportion has terms a, b, c, and d. In a proportion, cross products are equal. **Cross products** are the product of the numerator of the first ratio times the denominator of the second ratio and the product of the denominator of the first ratio times the numerator of the second ratio. That is,

$$\frac{a}{b} \diagdown\!\!\!\!\diagup \frac{c}{d} \Rightarrow ad = bc.$$

When you are given a proportion that has a missing term, you can use cross products to find the missing term. You can shorten the process by doing the following: find a cross product that you can calculate and then divide by the numerical term in the proportion that you did not use. Since you are allowed to use a calculator on the Mathematics CK, this is the quickest and most reliable way to solve a proportion on the test.

Percent means per hundred. When used in computations, percents are changed to fractions or decimals. Thus, $6\% = \frac{6}{100} = 0.06$. The key idea in percent problems is that a specified percent of an amount is that percent multiplied times the amount. The formula is $P = RB$, where

P is the **percentage,** the "part of the whole."

R is the **rate,** the number with "%" or the word "percent" attached.

B is the **base,** the "whole amount."

An effective strategy for solving percent problems is to first identify P, R, and B; and then do one of the following:

1. Write and solve an equation, written in the form $P = RB$, for the unknown quantity.

2. Write and solve a proportion that has the following form: $\frac{r}{100} = \frac{\text{part}}{\text{whole}}$.

Tip: In application problems, a percent without a base is usually meaningless. Make sure that you identify the base associated with each percent mentioned in a problem.

The **mean** of a set of numbers is another name for the arithmetic average of the numbers. To calculate the mean: first, sum the numbers; and then divide by how many numbers are in the set. Thus, you have the following formula:

$$\text{mean} = \frac{\text{the sum of the numbers}}{\text{how many numbers in the set}}.$$

To find the **weighted mean** of a set of n values $x_1, x_2, \ldots, x_n$ that are given weights $w_1, w_2, \ldots, w_n$, respectively, use the formula:

$$\text{weighted mean} = \frac{w_1 x_1 + w_2 x_2 + \ldots + w_n x_n}{w_1 + w_2 \ldots + w_n}.$$

Algebraic Expressions, Formulas, and Equations

For this topic, you must be able to work with algebraic expressions, formulas, and equations; add, subtract, multiply, and divide polynomials; add, subtract, multiply, and divide algebraic fractions; and perform standard algebraic operations involving complex numbers, radicals, and exponents, including fractional and negative exponents (*Mathematics: Content Knowledge (0061) Test at a Glance*, page 3).

An **algebraic expression** is any symbol or combination of symbols that represents a number. A **term** is a constant, variable, or any product of constants or variables. In a term, the **coefficient** of a factor is the product of all the other factors in the term. The numerical factor of a term is called the **numerical coefficient.** A **monomial** consists of one term. **Like monomials** differ only in their numerical coefficients. A **polynomial** is an algebraic expression in which monomials are combined using only addition and subtraction. A **binomial** is a polynomial consisting of two terms. A **trinomial** is a polynomial consisting of three terms. The **degree of a monomial** is the sum of the exponents of its variables. The **degree of a polynomial** is the highest degree of its monomial terms.

Like monomials are combined by adding or subtracting their numerical coefficients and using the result as the coefficient of the common variable factors.

> **Tip: Remove parentheses preceded by a minus sign by changing the sign of every term within the parentheses.**

Special Products

To **multiply** polynomials, multiply each term in the first polynomial by each term in the second polynomial. F.O.I.L. is useful for obtaining the product of two binomials. Some special products are the following:

$(x + y)^2 = (x + y)(x + y) = x^2 + 2xy + y^2$	Perfect Trinomial Square
$(x - y)^2 = (x - y)(x - y) = x^2 - 2xy + y^2$	Perfect Trinomial Square
$(x + y)(x - y) = x^2 - y^2$	The Difference between Two Squares
$(x + y)(x^2 - xy + y^2) = x^3 + y^3$	The Sum of Two Cubes
$(x - y)(x^2 + xy + y^2) = x^3 - y^3$	The Difference between Two Cubes
$(x + y)^3 = x^3 + 3x^2y + 3xy^2 + y^3$	Perfect Cube
$(x - y)^3 = x^3 - 3x^2y + 3xy^2 - y^3$	Perfect Cube

Simplifying Polynomials

To **simplify** a polynomial expression follow these steps:

1. Perform all operations within grouping symbols, starting with the innermost grouping symbol and working outward.
2. Perform all indicated multiplication, including exponentiation.
3. Combine like terms.

To **divide** a polynomial by a monomial, divide each term of the polynomial by the monomial.

Long division of polynomials is accomplished in a manner analogous to long division in arithmetic. The result is usually written as a mixed expression: quotient $+ \dfrac{\text{remainder}}{\text{divisor}}$.

Factoring Polynomials

Factoring a polynomial completely means writing it as a product of prime polynomials. The following summarizes factoring polynomials:

1. Look for a greatest common monomial factor.
2. If a factor is a binomial, check for

   difference of two squares: $x^2 - y^2 = (x + y)(x - y)$

   sum of two cubes: $x^3 + y^3 = (x + y)(x^2 - xy + y^2)$

   difference of two cubes: $x^3 - y^3 = (x - y)(x^2 + xy + y^2)$.
3. If a factor is a trinomial, check for

   general factorable quadratic: $x^2 + (a + b)x + ab = (x + a)(x + b)$

   $$acx^2 + (ad + bc)x + bd = (ax + b)(cx + d)$$

   perfect trinomial square: $a^2x^2 + 2abxy + b^2y^2 = (ax + by)^2$

   $$a^2x^2 - 2abxy + b^2y^2 = (ax - by)^2$$
4. If a factor has four terms, look for a grouping arrangement that will work for factoring by grouping.
5. Write the original polynomial as the product of all the factors obtained. Check to make sure that all polynomial factors except monomial factors are prime.
6. Check by multiplying the factors to obtain the original polynomial.

A **rational expression** is an algebraic fraction in which both the numerator and denominator are polynomials. Values for which the denominator is zero are **excluded.** The principles used in the study of arithmetic fractions are generalized in work with rational expressions.

To **multiply** rational expressions, factor completely, cancel (meaning "divide out") common factors, and then multiply the remaining numerator factors to obtain the numerator of the product and the remaining denominator factors to obtain the denominator of the product. Canceling is permitted for factors only—do not cancel terms! To **divide** rational expressions, multiply the dividend by the reciprocal of the divisor.

To **add** or **subtract** rational expressions, find a common denominator, express each term as an equivalent rational expression having the common denominator, and then add or subtract numerators, writing the result over the common denominator, and simplify.

A **complex fraction** is a fraction that contains fractions in its numerator or denominator or both. A complex fraction can be simplified by treating it as a division problem or by multiplying its numerator and denominator by the least common denominator of the fractions they contain.

Every positive number has two square roots that are equal in absolute value and opposite in sign. The *positive* square root is called the **principal square root** of the number. If $a^n = x$, a is called an ***n*th root** of x, where n is a natural number. A *positive* real number x has exactly one real positive nth root whether n is even or odd; and *every* real number x has exactly one real nth root when n is odd. Negative numbers do not have real nth roots when n is even. If n is a natural number, the nth root of zero is zero. The quantity $\sqrt[n]{}$ is called a **radical;** a is called the **radicand;** n is called the **index** and indicates which root is desired. If no index is written, it is understood to be 2, and the radical expression indicates the *principal* square root of the radicand.

We have the following rules for radicals when x, $y \in$ real numbers, m, $n \in$ positive integers, and the radical expression denotes a real number:

Rules for Radicals

$\sqrt[n]{x^n} = x$ if n is odd $\qquad\qquad$ $\sqrt[n]{x^n} = |x|$ if n is even

$\sqrt[n]{x^m} = \left(\sqrt[n]{x}\right)^m$ $\qquad\qquad\qquad$ $\left(\sqrt[n]{x}\right)\left(\sqrt[n]{y}\right) = \sqrt[n]{xy}$

$\dfrac{\sqrt[n]{x}}{\sqrt[n]{y}} = \sqrt[n]{\dfrac{x}{y}}, (y \neq 0)$ $\qquad\qquad$ $\sqrt[m]{\sqrt[n]{x}} = \sqrt[mn]{x}$

$\sqrt[pn]{x^{pm}} = \sqrt[n]{x^m}$ $\qquad\qquad\qquad$ $a\left(\sqrt[n]{x}\right) + b\left(\sqrt[n]{x}\right) = (a + b)\left(\sqrt[n]{x}\right)$

These rules form the basis for simplifying radical expressions. (See the appendix for a discussion on simplifying radicals.)

Rules for Exponents

Exponentiation is indicated by a small raised number, called the **exponent,** written to the upper right of a quantity. A **positive integer** exponent indicates repeated multiplication. Any number raised to the zero power is 1. A **negative integer** exponent indicates the reciprocal of the corresponding positive power. A **fractional** or **rational** exponent indicates a root. You write, $\sqrt[n]{a} = a^{\frac{1}{n}}$. The following **rules for exponents** hold:

$$x^1 = x \qquad\qquad x^0 = 1 \qquad\qquad 0^0 \text{ is undefined.}$$

$$x^{-n} = \frac{1}{x^n} \qquad\qquad \left(\frac{x}{y}\right)^{-1} = \frac{y}{x} \qquad\qquad \left(\frac{x}{y}\right)^{-n} = \left(\frac{y}{x}\right)^n$$

$$(x^n)^p = x^{np} \qquad\qquad \left(\frac{x}{y}\right)^p = \frac{x^p}{y^p} \qquad\qquad (xy)^p = x^p y^p$$

If $m = n$, then $x^m = x^n$.

An **equation** is a statement that two mathematical expressions are equal. An equation may be true, or it may be false. A **one-variable linear equation** is an equation that can be written in the form $ax + b = 0$, $a \neq 0$. A **solution,** or **root,** of an equation is a number that when substituted for the variable makes the equation true. The set consisting of all the solutions of an equation is called its **solution set.** To **solve an equation** means to find its solution set. If the solution set consists of all real numbers, the equation is called an **identity.** If the solution set is empty, the equation has no solution. Equations that have the same solution set are called **equivalent.**

An equation is **solved** when the variable has a coefficient of 1 and is by itself on one and only one side of the equation. Two main tools used in solving equations are

1. Addition or subtraction of the same quantity on both sides of the equation.
2. Multiplication or division by the same *nonzero* quantity on both sides of the equation.

Except for some special situations, if you *do the same thing to both sides* of an equation, the results will be an equivalent equation.

Steps for Solving One-Variable Linear Equations

To solve a one-variable linear equation, use the following steps:

1. Remove grouping symbols, if any.
2. Eliminate fractions, if any.
3. Undo indicated addition or subtraction to isolate the variable on one side.
4. If necessary, factor the side containing the variable so that one of the factors is the variable.
5. Divide both sides by the coefficient of the variable.
6. Check the solution in the original equation.

An equation that expresses the relationship between two or more variables is called a **formula.** The procedure for solving one-variable linear equations can be used to solve a formula for a specific variable when the value(s) of the other variable(s) are known. The procedure also can be used to solve a formula or **literal equation** (an equation with no numbers, only letters) for a specific variable in terms of the other variable(s). In general, isolate the specific variable and treat all other variable(s) as constants. This is called **changing the subject** of the formula or literal equation.

The procedure for solving one-variable linear equations can be used to solve a two-variable equation for one variable in terms of the other variable. Another common use for the procedure for solving one-variable linear equations is to transform equations into the form: $y = mx + b$, where m and b are constants.

One-variable absolute value equations can be solved using the procedure for solving one-variable linear equations and the following:

> $|ax + b| = 0 \Leftrightarrow ax + b = 0$; or
>
> If c is any positive number: $|ax + b| = c \Leftrightarrow$ either $ax + b = c$ or $ax + b = -c$.

An **inequality** is a mathematical statement that two expressions are not equal. Use the symbols > (greater than), < (less than), ≥ (greater than or equal to), and ≤ (less than or equal to) to write one-variable linear inequalities. The **graph** of the solution set of the inequality can be illustrated on a number line. When solving inequalities, treat them just like equations *except* for one difference: If you multiply or divide both sides of the inequality by a *negative* number, *reverse* the direction of the inequality. Sometimes two statements of inequality apply to a variable expression simultaneously and, thus, can be combined into a **double inequality.**

One-variable absolute value inequalities can be solved using the procedure for solving one-variable linear equations and the following:

> If c is any positive number:
>
> $|ax + b| < c \Leftrightarrow -c < ax + b < c$
>
> $|ax + b| > c \Leftrightarrow ax + b < -c$ or $ax + b > c$

A **one-variable quadratic equation** is an equation that can be written in the standard form $ax^2 + bx + c = 0$. The constants a, b, and c are called the **coefficients** of the quadratic equation. The solutions of a quadratic equation are also called its **roots.** A quadratic equation may have exactly *one* real root, *two* real unequal roots, or *no* real roots.

Three algebraic methods for solving quadratic equations are (1) by **factoring,** (2) by **completing the square,** and (3) by using the **quadratic formula.**

Steps for Solving a Quadratic Equation by Factoring

To solve a quadratic equation by factoring, use the following procedure.

1. Express the equation in standard form: $ax^2 + bx + c = 0$.
2. Factor the left side of the equation.
3. Set each factor containing the variable equal to zero.
4. Solve each of the resulting linear equations.
5. Check each root by substituting it into the original equation.

Step 3 in this procedure is based on the *property of zero products* for numbers: If the product of two quantities is zero, at least one of the quantities is zero.

Quadratic equations, which can be written in the form: $x^2 = C$, have the solution $x = \pm \sqrt{C}$. If the quantity C is *zero*, there is *one* real root that has the value zero; if *positive*, there are *two* unequal real roots; and if *negative*, there are *no* real roots.

Steps for Solving a Quadratic Equation by Completing the Square

To solve a quadratic equation by completing the square, use the following procedure:

1. Get all terms containing the variable on the left side, and all other terms on the right.
2. If the coefficient of the squared term is not 1, divide each term by it.
3. Add half the square of the coefficient of the middle term to both sides.
4. Factor the left side as the square of a binomial.
5. Find the square root of both sides.

6. Solve for the variable.

7. Check each root by substituting it into in the original equation.

Steps for Solving a Quadratic Equation by Using the Quadratic Formula

To solve a quadratic equation by using the quadratic formula, use the following procedure:

1. Express the equation in standard form: $ax^2 + bx + c = 0$.

2. Determine the values of the coefficients a, b, and c.

3. Substitute into the quadratic formula: $x = \dfrac{-b \pm \sqrt{b^2 - 4ac}}{2a}$.

4. Evaluate and simplify.

5. Check each root by substituting it into the original equation.

The quantity $b^2 - 4ac$ is called the **discriminant** of the quadratic equation. The quadratic equation $ax^2 + bx + c = 0$ has exactly *one* real root if $b^2 - 4ac = 0$, *two* real unequal roots if $b^2 - 4ac > 0$, and *no* real roots if $b^2 - 4ac < 0$.

Tip: When solving quadratic equations, *never* divide both sides of the equation by the variable or by an expression containing the variable because you run the risk of unknowingly dividing by zero.

You can also solve linear and quadratic equations that have real zeros by using the **Trace** feature of your graphing calculator. When the trace cursor moves along the function, the *y*-value is calculated from the *x*-value. Move the trace cursor to the point or points where the graph appears to cross the *x*-axis (that is, where $y = 0$). **Zoom in** to obtain better resolution and more accurate results. Most likely, you will have to approximate the zeros because you are limited by the pixel resolution of your viewing screen. Pixels are the small cells that light up when you graph.

Many equations involving fractions, in which a denominator expression contains the variable, can be transformed into linear or quadratic equations by multiplying both sides of the equation by the least common denominator of all the fractions. An *excluded value* for the variable *cannot* be in the solution set.

Many equations containing radicals or fractional exponents can be transformed into linear or quadratic equations by raising both sides to an appropriate power. Use caution when doing this because the solution set of the transformed equation may contain an **extraneous root**, a value which is *not* a solution of the original equation. Therefore, check all answers obtained in the *original* equation.

Equations that are not quadratic equations, but can be written in the form of a quadratic, can be solved using the methods for solving quadratic equations. It naturally follows that equations which can be written so that one side is a factorable higher degree polynomial and the other side contains only zero can be solved by factoring completely, then setting each factor equal to zero.

The solution sets for quadratic inequalities are based on the rules for multiplying signed numbers: If two factors have the same sign, their product is positive; if they have opposite signs, their product is negative. If $ax^2 + bx + c$ $(a > 0)$ has no real roots, it is always positive; if it has exactly one real root, it is zero at that root; and if it has two real roots, it is negative between them, positive to the left of the leftmost root, positive to the right of the rightmost root, and zero only at its roots.

Systems of Equations and Inequalities

For this topic, you must be able to solve and graph systems of equations and inequalities including those involving absolute value (*Mathematics: Content Knowledge (0061) Test at a Glance*, page 3).

A set of equations, each with the same set of variables, is called a **system** when all the equations in the set are considered simultaneously. The system possesses a **solution** when the equations in the system are all satisfied by at least one set of values of the variables. A system that has a solution is said to be **consistent.** A system that has no solution is said to be **inconsistent.**

A **system of two linear equations in two variables** consists of a pair of linear equations in the same two variables. To **solve a system of two equations** in two variables you must find all pairs of values for the two variables that make *both* equations true simultaneously. A pair of values—for example, an x-value paired with a corresponding y-value—is called an ordered pair and is written as (x, y). An ordered pair that makes an equation true is said to **satisfy** the equation. When an ordered pair makes both equations in the system true, the ordered pair **satisfies** the system.

Four methods commonly used to solve a system of linear equations are **substitution, elimination, transformation** of the augmented matrix (see the chapter titled **Matrix Algebra** for this method), and using the **Trace** feature of the graphing calculator.

Steps for Solving a System of Two Linear Equations by Substitution

To solve a system of linear equations by using **substitution,** use the following procedure:

1. Select the simpler equation and express one of the variables in terms of the other.
2. Substitute this expression into the other equation, simplify, and solve, if possible.
3. Check the solution in the original equations.

Steps for Solving a System of Two Linear Equations by Elimination (That Is, by Addition)

To solve a system of linear equations by using **elimination,** use the following procedure:

1. Write both equations in standard form: $Ax + By = C$.
2. If necessary, multiply one or both of the equations by a nonzero constant or constants to make the coefficients of one of the variables sum to zero.
3. Add the equations.
4. Check the solution in the original equations.

Steps for Solving a System of Two Linear Equations by Using the Trace Feature

To solve a system of linear equations by using the **Trace** feature of the graphing calculator, use the following procedure:

1. Write both equations in the form: $y = mx + b$.
2. Enter the two functions into the graphing editor.
3. Plot the functions simultaneously.
4. Move the trace cursor to the point where the two graphs appears to cross. Adjust the viewing window, if needed. Zoom in to obtain better resolution and more accurate results. Most likely, you will have to approximate the zeros because you are limited by the pixel resolution of your viewing screen.
5. Check the solution by substituting it into the original equations.

The solution to a **system of three equations with three or more variables** can be solved using substitution, elimination, or transformation of the augmented matrix. In general, it is most efficient to solve such systems by using the augmented matrix. This method will be discussed in the chapter titled **Matrix Algebra.**

The graph of a **two-variable linear inequality** is a **half-plane.**

Steps for Graphing a Two-Variable Linear Inequality

To graph two-variable inequalities, follow these steps:

1. Graph the linear equation that results when the inequality symbol is replaced with an equal sign. Use a dashed line for < or > inequalities and a solid line for ≤ or ≥ inequalities. This is the boundary line.

2. Select and shade the correct portion of the plane by testing a point that is *not* on the boundary line (the origin is usually a good choice unless the boundary passes through it). If the coordinates of the point satisfy the inequality, shade the portion of the plane containing the test point; if not, shade the portion of the plane that does *not* contain the test point.

Geometric Interpretations of Algebraic Principles

For this topic, you must be able to interpret algebraic principles geometrically (*Mathematics: Content Knowledge (0061) Test at a Glance*, page 3).

Many algebraic principles can be interpreted geometrically. For instance, in the previous discussion (see the section, "Systems of Equations and Inequalities") of systems of two-linear equations, the two-linear equations can be represented as lines in the plane. For the two lines, there are three possibilities that can occur. If the system is consistent and has *exactly one solution*, then the two lines **intersect in a unique point** in the plane. If the system is consistent and has *infinitely many solutions*, then the two lines are **coincident** (that is, have all points in common). If the system is inconsistent having *no solution*, then the two lines are **parallel** in the plane.

The distance between two points on a coordinate graph can be interpreted geometrically as the hypotenuse of a right triangle having legs of length $x_2 - x_1$ and $y_2 - y_1$. (See "Formulas Used in Two- and Three-Dimensional Coordinate Systems" for the formula: Distance between two points $= \sqrt{\left(x_2 - x_1\right)^2 + \left(y_2 - y_1\right)^2}$.)

Algebraic Representations of Lines, Planes, Conic Sections, and Spheres

For this topic, you must be able to recognize and use algebraic representations of lines, planes, conic sections, and spheres (*Mathematics: Content Knowledge (0061) Test at a Glance*, page 3).

If two copies of the real number line are placed perpendicular to each other; so that they intersect at the zero point on each line, the lines form the **axes** of a rectangular coordinate system called the **Cartesian coordinate plane.** The horizontal real line with positive direction to the right is called the **horizontal axis,** or the **x-axis,** and the vertical real line with positive direction upward is called the **vertical axis,** or the **y-axis.** Their point of intersection is called the **origin.**

Each point in the plane is associated with an **ordered pair** (x, y) of real numbers x and y, called its **coordinates.** In an ordered pair, the first element is called the **abscissa** and the second element, the **ordinate.**

Two ordered pairs are **equal** if and only if they have *exactly* the same coordinates. The plane in which the coordinate system lies is divided into four sections called **quadrants.** They are named with the Roman numerals **I, II, III,** and **IV.** The numbering process begins in the upper-right section and proceeds counterclockwise.

Algebraic Representation of a Line

The **equation of a line** can be determined using one of the following:

- The **slope-intercept form:** $y = mx + b$, where the line determined by the equation has slope* $= m$ and y-intercept $= b$

- The **standard form:** $Ax + By = C$, where the line determined by the equation has slope $= \frac{-A}{B}$ and y-intercept $= \frac{C}{B}$, $(B \neq 0)$

- The **point-slope form:** $y - y_1 = m(x - x_1)$, where m is the slope of the line and (x_1, y_1) is a point on the line.

*Note: See the section "Formulas Used in Two- and Three-Dimensional Coordinate Systems" for the formula for finding the slope of a line given two points on the line.

The four basic kinds of **conics** are the **parabola, circle, ellipse,** and **hyperbola.** The equation of a conic can be written as $Ax^2 + By^2 + Cx + Dy + F = 0,$ where A and B are not both zero.

Algebraic Representation of Conic Sections

This equation defines a relation that has different graphs depending on the values of the coefficients A, B, and C, according to the following:

The graph of the equation $Ax^2 + By^2 + Cx + Dy + F = 0$ ($A \neq 0$ and $B \neq 0$) is

- a **circle** if $A = B$ and has standard form: $(x - h)^2 + (y - k)^2 = r^2$ where (h, k) is the **center** and the **radius** is $|r|$ units.

- an **ellipse,** if $AB > 0$ and has standard form: $\frac{(x-h)^2}{a^2} + \frac{(y-k)^2}{b^2} = 1$ with **center** at (h, k). The ellipse has **vertices** $(h - a, k)$, $(h + a, k)$, $(h, k - b)$, and $(h, k + b)$. The line segment joining the vertices $(h - a, k)$ and $(h + a, k)$ is a **horizontal axis** of symmetry and the line segment joining the vertices $(h, k - b)$ and $(h, k + b)$ is a **vertical axis** of symmetry. The longer axis is called the **major axis** and the shorter axis is called the **minor axis.** The length of the two axes are $2|a|$ and $2|b|$.

- a **hyperbola** if $AB < 0$ and has standard forms:

Form (1) $\frac{(x-h)^2}{a^2} - \frac{(y-k)^2}{b^2} = 1$ with center at (h, k). It opens left and right along the line $y = k$, and it passes through the **vertices** $(h - a, k)$ and $(h + a, k)$. It has the intersecting lines $y = k + \frac{b}{a}(x - h)$ and $y = k - \frac{b}{a}(x - h)$ as (slanting) **asymptotes.** The asymptotes are the diagonals of a rectangle with dimensions $2|a|$ by $2|b|$ centered at (h, k).

Form (2) $\frac{(y-k)^2}{b^2} - \frac{(x-h)^2}{a^2} = 1$ with center at (h, k). It opens up and down along the line $x = h$, and it passes through the **vertices** $(h, k - b)$, and $(h, k + b)$. As in the preceding case, this form has the intersecting lines $y = k + (x - h)$ and $y = k - (x - h)$ as (slanting) **asymptotes.** The asymptotes are the diagonals of a rectangle with dimensions $2|a|$ by $2|b|$ centered at (h, k).

If the equation of a conic section is not in standard form, it can be put in standard form by completing the squares on the x and y terms.

The general equation for a **sphere** in a three-dimensional coordinate system is $(x - x_0)^2 + (y - y_0)^2 + (z - z_0)^2 = r^2$, with center (x_0, y_0, z_0) and radius $|r|$.

Formulas Used in Two- and Three-Dimensional Coordinate Systems

For this topic, you must be able to solve problems in two- and three-dimensions (for example, distance between two points, the coordinates of the midpoint of a line segment (*Mathematics: Content Knowledge (0061) Test at a Glance,* page 3).

If (x_1, y_1) and (x_2, y_2) are the coordinates of two points on a line, the formula for the **slope** of the line is $m = \frac{y_2 - y_1}{x_2 - x_1}$ $(x_1 \neq x_2)$. When a line slopes *upward* to the right, its slope is *positive* and when a line slopes *downward* to the right, its slope is *negative*. All **horizontal lines** have slope 0. **Vertical lines** have no slope. If two lines are **parallel** their slopes are equal; and if two lines are **perpendicular,** their slopes are negative reciprocals of each other.

To find the distance between two points on a coordinate graph, use the formula:

$$\text{Distance between two points} = \sqrt{\left(x_2 - x_1\right)^2 + \left(y_2 - y_1\right)^2}$$

To find the midpoint between two points on a coordinate graph, use the formula:

$$\text{Midpoint between two points} = \left(\frac{x_1 + x_2}{2}, \frac{y_1 + y_2}{2}\right)$$

Tip: Notice that you *add*, not subtract, the coordinates in the numerator.

To find the distance d from point (x_1, y_1) to line $Ax + By + C = 0$, use the formula:

$$d = \frac{\left|Ax_1 + By_1 + C\right|}{\sqrt{A^2 + B^2}}$$

Note: The formula to find the distance from a point to a line is given in the Notation, Definitions, and Formulas pages at the beginning of the Mathematics CK test booklet.

Tip: When substituting values into formulas, enclose in parentheses any substituted value that is negative to avoid making a sign error.

Measurement

According to the *Mathematics: Content Knowledge (0061) Test at a Glance* (www.ets.org/Media/Tests/PRAXIS/pdf/0061.pdf), the Measurement content category of the Mathematics CK tests your knowledge and skills in three topic areas:

- Unit analysis
- Precision, accuracy, and approximate error
- Informal approximation concepts

This review will discuss the key ideas and formulas in each topic area that are most important for you to know for the Mathematics CK.

Unit Analysis

For this topic, you must be able to make decisions about units and scales that are appropriate for problem situations involving measurement and use unit analysis (*Mathematics: Content Knowledge (0061) Test at a Glance*, page 3).

On the Mathematics CK, you will have to demonstrate your knowledge of measurement using the U.S. customary system and the metric system. Here are some common conversion facts you will be expected to know.

1 yard = 3 feet = 36 inches	1 cup = 8 fluid ounces
1 mile = 1760 yards = 5280 feet	1 pint = 2 cups
1 acre = 43,560 square feet	1 quart = 2 pints
1 hour = 60 minutes	1 gallon = 4 quarts
1 minute = 60 seconds	1 pound = 16 ounces
	1 ton = 2000 pounds

1 liter = 1000 milliliters = 1000 cubic centimeters
1 meter = 100 centimeters = 1000 millimeters
1 kilometer = 1000 meters
1 gram = 1000 milligrams
1 kilogram = 1000 grams

You can convert from one measurement unit to another by using an appropriate "conversion fraction." You make conversion fractions by using a conversion fact, such as 1 yard = 3 feet. For each conversion fact, you can write *two* conversion fractions. For example, for the conversion fact given, you have $\frac{1 \text{ yd}}{3 \text{ ft}}$ and $\frac{3 \text{ ft}}{1 \text{ yd}}$ as your two conversion fractions.

Every conversion fraction is equivalent to the number 1 because the numerator and denominator are different names for measures of the same quantity. Therefore, if you multiply a quantity by a conversion fraction, you will not change the value of the quantity. When you need to change one measurement unit to another unit, multiply by the conversion fraction whose **denominator is the same as the units of the quantity to be converted.** When you do the multiplication, the units you started out with will "cancel" (divide) out, and you will be left with the desired new units. If this doesn't happen, then you used the wrong conversion fraction, so do it over again with the other conversion fraction. Also, for some conversions you may need to make a "chain" of conversion fractions to obtain your desired units.

> **Tip:** It is a good idea to assess your final answer to see if it makes sense. When you are converting from a larger unit to a smaller unit, you should expect that it will take more of the smaller units to equal the same amount. When you are converting from a smaller unit to a larger unit, you should expect that it will take less of the larger units to equal the same amount.

Precision, Accuracy, and Approximate Error

For this topic, you must be able to analyze precision, accuracy, and approximate error in measurement situations (*Mathematics: Content Knowledge (0061) Test at a Glance*, page 3).

In the physical world, measurement of continuous quantities is always approximate. The precision and accuracy of the measurement relate to the worthiness of the approximation.

Precision refers to the degree to which a measurement is repeatable and reliable; that is, consistently getting the same data each time the measurement is taken. The precision of a measurement depends on the magnitude of the smallest measuring unit used to obtain the measurement (for example, to the nearest meter, to the nearest centimeter, to the nearest millimeter, and so on). In theory, the smaller the measurement unit used, the more precise the measurement.

Accuracy refers to the degree to which a measurement is true or correct. A measurement can be precise without being accurate. This can occur, for example, when a measuring instrument needs adjustment, so that the measurements obtained, no matter how precisely measured, are inaccurate.

The amount of error involved in a physical measurement is the **approximate error** of the measurement. The **maximum possible error** of a measurement is half the magnitude of the smallest measurement unit used to obtain the measurement. For example, if the smallest measurement unit is 1 inch, the maximum possible error is 0.5 inch.

The most accurate way of expressing a measurement is as an interval. For instance, a measurement of 10 inches, to the nearest inch, should be reported as 10 inches $\pm$ 0.5 inches. In other words, the true measurement lies between 9.5 inches and 10.5 inches. Closer approximations can be obtained by refining the measurement to a higher degree of precision (for example, by measuring to the nearest half-inch).

Results of calculations with approximate measurement should not be reported with a degree of precision that would be misleading, that is, suggesting a degree of accuracy greater than the actual accuracy that could be obtained using the approximate measurements. Generally, such calculations should be rounded to have the same precision as the measurement with least precision in the calculation.

Informal Approximation Concepts

For this topic, you must be able to apply informal concepts of successive approximation, upper and lower bounds, and limit in measurement situations (*Mathematics: Content Knowledge (0061) Test at a Glance*, page 3).

Methods of **successive approximation** can be used to approximate the area of plane regions. The area of the region is approximated using the sum of the areas of a sequence of rectangles. One technique is to partition the region in two different ways—so that one partitioning overestimates the area, yielding an **upper bound,** and the other partitioning underestimates the area, yielding a **lower bound.** Sequences of increasingly accurate approximations are obtained by refining the precision of the partitioning. The upper and lower bounds get increasingly close to each other, and their average approaches the true area of the plane region. The volume of a solid can be approximated in a similar manner using the sum of the volumes of a sequence of geometric solids.

Sigma notation is an abbreviated way to represent the sums of the areas of the rectangles or the sums of the volumes of the geometric solids. For instance, a Riemann sum for the area under the curve of a continuous function on the interval $[a, b]$, using n rectangles of equal length, $\triangle x_i$, has the form $\sum_{i-1}^{n} f(\varepsilon_i) \triangle x_i$, where $\triangle x_i = \dfrac{b-a}{n}$ and $\{\varepsilon_i \mid x_{i-1} \le \varepsilon_i < x_i, i = 1, 2, \ldots, n\}$ are an associated network of points such that the point ε_i can be any point in the subinterval $[x_{i-1}, x_i]$; but, for convenience, can consist of the left endpoints of each subinterval, or the right endpoints of each subinterval, or the midpoints of each subinterval, or so on.

Geometry

According to the *Mathematics: Content Knowledge (0061) Test at a Glance* (www.ets.org/Media/Tests/PRAXIS/pdf/0061. pdf), the Geometry content category of the Mathematics CK tests your knowledge and skills in seven topic areas:

- Relationships involving geometric figures
- Relationships among quadrilaterals
- Problems involving properties of plane figures
- Problems involving properties of circles
- The Pythagorean theorem
- Perimeter, area, and volume
- Geometric transformations

This review will discuss the key ideas and formulas in each topic area that are most important for you to know for the Mathematics CK.

Relationships Involving Geometric Figures

For this topic, you must be able to solve problems using relationships of parts of geometric figures (for example, medians of triangles, inscribed angles in circles) and among geometric figures (for example, congruence, similarity) in two and three dimensions (*Mathematics: Content Knowledge (0061) Test at a Glance*, page 3).

An **altitude** of a triangle is the line segment drawn from a vertex perpendicular to the side opposite the angle. Every triangle has three altitudes, one from each vertex. The lines containing the altitudes of a triangle are **concurrent,** meaning they intersect in a point (called the **orthocenter** of the triangle). The **height** of a triangle is the length of the line segment from a vertex perpendicular to the side, called the **base,** opposite the angle. **Note:** The term *altitude* is sometimes used to mean the *height* of the triangle, rather than the line segment that determines the height. On the Mathematics CK, you will be able to tell from the context of the problem which meaning is intended for the term altitude.

A **median** of a triangle is a line segment connecting the vertex of an angle to the midpoint of the side opposite the angle. The medians of a triangle are concurrent, and their point of concurrency, called the **centroid,** is two-thirds of the way along each median, from the vertex to the opposite side.

The **perpendicular bisectors** of a triangle are concurrent, and their point of concurrency is equidistant from the vertices of the triangle.

An **angle bisector** in a triangle is a line that cuts in half an angle of the triangle. The angle bisectors of a triangle are concurrent in a point that is equidistant from the three sides.

Congruent (symbolized by ≅) geometric figures have exactly the same size and same shape. They are superimposable, meaning that they will fit exactly on top of each other.

Similar (symbolized by ≈) geometric figures have the same shape, but not necessarily the same size. Their corresponding angles are congruent and their corresponding sides are proportional.

Symmetry describes the shape of a figure or object. A figure or object is **symmetric** if it can be folded exactly in half and the two parts are congruent. The line along the fold is the **line of symmetry.** Some shapes might have more than one line of symmetry.

Relationships among Quadrilaterals

For this topic, you must be able to describe relationships among sets of special quadrilaterals, such as the square, rectangle, parallelogram, rhombus, and trapezoid (*Mathematics: Content Knowledge (0061) Test at a Glance*, page 3).

A **quadrilateral** is a closed two-dimensional geometric figure that is made up of four straight line segments.

Quadrilaterals are subclassified as parallelograms or trapezoids.

A **parallelogram** is a quadrilateral that has two pairs of opposite parallel sides. Some useful properties of parallelograms are the following: Opposite sides are congruent; the sum of the four interior angles is 360°; opposite interior angles are congruent; consecutive interior angles are supplementary; the diagonals bisect each other; and each diagonal divides the parallelogram into two congruent triangles.

Some parallelograms have special names because of their special properties. A **rhombus** is a parallelogram that has four congruent sides. A **rectangle** is a parallelogram that has four right angles. A **square** is a parallelogram that has four right angles and four congruent sides. These three figures have all the general properties of parallelograms. In addition, in rectangles and squares, the diagonals are congruent. In rhombuses and squares, the diagonals intersect at right angles.

A **trapezoid** has two definitions, both of which are widely accepted. One definition is that a trapezoid is a quadrilateral that has *exactly* one pair of opposite sides that are parallel. This definition would exclude parallelograms as a special case. The other definition is that a trapezoid is a quadrilateral that has *at least* one pair of parallel sides. This definition would allow any parallelogram to be considered a special kind of trapezoid. This situation is one of the few times that mathematicians do not agree on the definition of a term. For purposes of this CliffsTestPrep book, we will have to assume that answers to problems involving trapezoid(s) on the Mathematics CK will not hinge on the definition for trapezoid you choose to use during the test.

Problems Involving Properties of Plane Figures

For this topic, you must be able solve problems using the properties of triangles, quadrilaterals, polygons, circles, and parallel and perpendicular lines (*Mathematics: Content Knowledge (0061) Test at a Glance*, page 3).

A **ray** is a line extending from a point. When two rays meet at a common point, they form an **angle.** The point where the rays meet is called the **vertex** of the angle.

You can classify angles by the number of degrees in their measurement. An **acute angle** measures between 0° and 90°. A **right angle** measures exactly 90°. An **obtuse angle** measures between 90° and 180°. A **straight angle** measures exactly 180°. Two angles whose sum is 90° are **complementary angles.** Two angles whose sum is 180° are **supplementary angles.** Two angles with the same measure are **congruent. Adjacent angles** are angles that have a common vertex and a common side.

A **plane** is a set of points that form a flat surface. Lines in a plane can be parallel or intersecting.

Intersecting lines in a plane cross at a point. Two nonadjacent angles formed by intersecting lines are called **vertical angles.** Vertical angles formed by two intersecting lines are congruent.

Parallel lines in a plane never meet. The distance between them is always the same. A shorthand way to indicate that a line *AB* is parallel to a line *CD* is to write *AB*||*CD*.

A **transversal** is a straight line that intersects two or more given lines. When two parallel lines are cut by a transversal, eight angles are formed as shown in the following figure.

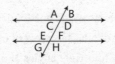

The **interior angles** are $\angle$ C, $\angle$ D, $\angle$ E, and $\angle$ F. The **exterior angles** are $\angle$ A, $\angle$ B, $\angle$ G, and $\angle$ H. The **corresponding angles** are the pair of angles $\angle$ A and $\angle$ E, the pair of angles $\angle$ B and $\angle$ F, the pair of angles $\angle$ C and $\angle$ G, and the pair of angles $\angle$ D and $\angle$ H. The **alternate exterior angles** are the pair of angles $\angle$ A and $\angle$ H and the pair of angles $\angle$ B and $\angle$ G. The **alternate interior angles** are the pair of angles $\angle$ C and $\angle$ F and the pair of angles $\angle$ D and $\angle$ E.

If two parallel lines are cut by a transversal, then any pair of corresponding angles, alternate exterior angles, or alternate interior angles are congruent.

Perpendicular lines intersect at right angles. A shorthand way to indicate that a line *AB* is perpendicular to a line *CD* is to write $AB \perp CD$.

The **perpendicular bisector** of a line segment is the set of all points in the plane of the line segment that are equidistant from the endpoints of the line segment.

The shortest distance from a point to a line is the measure of the perpendicular line segment from the point to the line.

A **polygon** is a closed plane figure, whose **sides** are straight line segments. The point at which the two sides of a polygon intersect is called a **vertex.** A **regular polygon** has all sides congruent. Polygons are classified by the number of sides they have. A **triangle** is a three-sided polygon. A **quadrilateral** is a four-sided polygon. A **pentagon** is a five-sided polygon. A **hexagon** is a six-sided polygon. A **heptagon** is a seven-sided polygon. An **octagon** is an eight-sided polygon. A **nonagon** is a nine-sided polygon. A **decagon** is a ten-sided polygon. In general, an ***n*-gon** is an *n*-sided polygon. The sum of the interior angle of a polygon equals $(n-2)180°$.

A line segment that connects two nonconsecutive vertices of a polygon is called a **diagonal.** If all the diagonals of a polygon lie within the interior of the polygon, the polygon is **convex;** otherwise, the polygon is **concave.** The number of diagonals of an *n*-sided polygon is given by the formula: $\dfrac{n(n-3)}{2}$.

Triangles can be classified in two different ways. You can classify triangles according to their sides as equilateral, isosceles, or scalene. An **equilateral** triangle has three congruent sides. An **isosceles** triangle has at least two congruent sides. A **scalene** triangle has no congruent sides. Another way to classify triangles is according to their interior angles. An **acute** triangle has three acute angles. A **right** triangle has exactly one right angle. An **obtuse** triangle has exactly one obtuse angle. The sum of the angles of a triangle is 180°.

The **triangle inequality theorem** states that the sum of the measures of any two sides of a triangle must be greater than the measure of the third side.

If two sides of a triangle are congruent, then the angles opposite those sides are congruent, and conversely.

The segment between the midpoints of two sides of a triangle is parallel to the third side and half as long.

Congruent triangles are triangles for which corresponding sides and corresponding angles are congruent. If three sides of one triangle are congruent, respectively, to three sides of another triangle, then the two triangles are congruent (**SSS**). If two sides and the included angle of one triangle are congruent, respectively, to two sides and the included angle of another triangle, then the two triangles are congruent (**SAS**). If two angles and the included side of one triangle are congruent, respectively, to two angles and the included side of another triangle, then the two triangles are congruent (**ASA**). If two angles and the nonincluded side of one triangle are congruent, respectively, to two angles and the nonincluded side of another triangle, then the two triangles are congruent (**AAS**).

Similar triangles are triangles for which corresponding sides are proportional and corresponding angles are congruent. If two angles of one triangle are congruent to two corresponding angles of another triangle, then the two triangles are similar.

Certain properties of quadrilaterals can be used to identify a quadrilateral. Following are some geometric theorems that illustrate this idea.

- If the diagonals of a quadrilateral bisect each other, the quadrilateral is a parallelogram.
- If the diagonals of a quadrilateral are perpendicular bisectors of each other, the quadrilateral is a rhombus.
- If a parallelogram has one right angle, it has four right angles and is a rectangle.

Problems Involving Properties of Circles

For this topic, you must be able to solve problems using the properties of circles, including those involving inscribed angles, central angles, chords, radii, tangents, secants, arcs, and sectors (*Mathematics: Content Knowledge (0061) Test at a Glance*, page 3).

A **circle** is a closed plane figure for which all points are the same distance from a point within, called the **center.** A **radius** of a circle is a line segment joining the center of the circle to any point on the circle. A **diameter** is a line segment through the center of the circle with endpoints on the circle. The diameter of a circle is twice the radius. Conversely, the radius of a circle is half the diameter.

Concentric circles are circles that have the same center.

An **arc** is part of a circle; it is the set of points between and including two points on the circle.

A **semicircle** is an arc whose endpoints are the endpoints of a diameter of the circle.

A **chord** of a circle is a line segment with both endpoints on the circle.

A chord that passes through the center of the circle is a diameter.

A **secant** to a circle is a line that contains a chord.

A **tangent** to a circle is a line in the plane of the circle that intersects the circle in only one point. The point of contact is called the **point of tangency.**

If a straight line is tangent to a circle, then the radius drawn to the point of tangency will be perpendicular to the tangent.

A **central angle** of a circle is an angle that has its vertex at the center of the circle. A central angle determines two arcs on the circle. If the two arcs are of unequal measure, the arc with the smaller measure is called the **minor arc** and the arc with the greater measure is called the **major arc.** Arcs are measured in degrees. The measure of a minor arc is equal to the measure of its central angle. The measure of a major arc equals 360° minus the measure of its central angle.

The degree measure of a semicircle is 180°.

An **inscribed angle** is an angle whose vertex is on a circle and whose sides contain chords of the circle. The arc of the circle that is in the interior of the inscribed angle and whose endpoints are on the sides of the angle is its **intercepted arc.** The measure of an inscribed angle is half the measure of its intercepted arc.

An angle inscribed in a semicircle is a right angle.

The measure of an angle formed by two secants intersecting in the interior of a circle equals one-half the sum of the measures of the arc opposite the angle and the arc opposite the angle's congruent vertical angle.

The measure of an angle formed by two secants intersecting exterior to a circle equals one-half the difference of the measures of the two arcs whose endpoints lie on the sides of the angles and whose other points lie within the angle.

If an arc has measure θ in radians and radius r, then its length s is $r\theta$.

A **sector** of a circle is a region bounded by two radii and an arc of the circle.

A polygon is **inscribed** in a circle if each of its vertices lies on the circle.

A polygon is **circumscribed** about a circle if each of its sides is tangent to the circle.

The Pythagorean Theorem

For this topic, you must demonstrate an understanding of the Pythagorean theorem and its converse (*Mathematics: Content Knowledge (0061) Test at a Glance*, page 3).

A **right triangle** is a triangle that has exactly one right angle. The side opposite the right angle is called the **hypotenuse** of the triangle. The hypotenuse is *always* the longest side of the right triangle. The other two sides are called the **legs** of the triangle. Commonly, the letter c is used to represent the hypotenuse of a right triangle and the letters a and b to represent the legs. A special relationship, named after the famous Greek mathematician Pythagoras, exists between the sides of a right triangle. This special relationship is the **Pythagorean theorem,** which states that $c^2 = a^2 + b^2$.

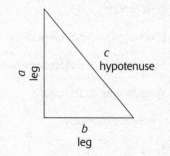

The Pythagorean relationship applies only to right triangles. If you know any two sides of a right triangle, you can find the third side by using the formula $c^2 = a^2 + b^2$. Moreover, if the measures of the three sides of a triangle satisfy the Pythagorean relationship, the triangle is a right triangle.

Perimeter, Area, and Volume

For this topic, you must be able to compute and reason about perimeter, area/surface area, or volume of two- or three-dimensional figures or of regions or solids that are combinations of these figures (*Mathematics: Content Knowledge (0061) Test at a Glance*, page 3).

Here are the most important formulas for perimeter, area/surface area, and volume that you need to know for the Mathematics CK.

Triangle: height h, base b area $= \frac{1}{2}bh$ **Triangle:** sides a, b, and c perimeter $= a + b + c$	**Square:** side s area $= s^2$ perimeter $= 4s$	**Rectangle:** length l, width w area $= lw$ perimeter $= 2l + 2w$	**Parallelogram:** height h, base b area $= bh$ perimeter $= 2b + 2a$

(continued)

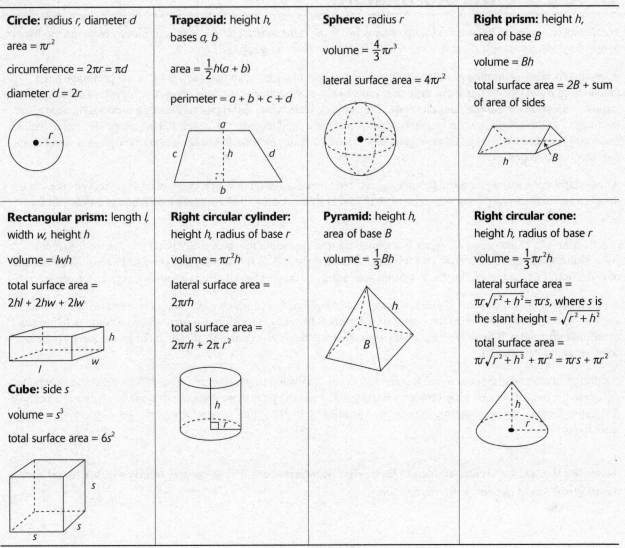

Circle: radius r, diameter d

area = πr^2

circumference = $2\pi r = \pi d$

diameter $d = 2r$

Trapezoid: height h, bases a, b

area = $\frac{1}{2}h(a + b)$

perimeter = $a + b + c + d$

Sphere: radius r

volume = $\frac{4}{3}\pi r^3$

lateral surface area = $4\pi r^2$

Right prism: height h, area of base B

volume = Bh

total surface area = $2B$ + sum of area of sides

Rectangular prism: length l, width w, height h

volume = lwh

total surface area = $2hl + 2hw + 2lw$

Cube: side s

volume = s^3

total surface area = $6s^2$

Right circular cylinder: height h, radius of base r

volume = $\pi r^2 h$

lateral surface area = $2\pi rh$

total surface area = $2\pi rh + 2\pi r^2$

Pyramid: height h, area of base B

volume = $\frac{1}{3}Bh$

Right circular cone: height h, radius of base r

volume = $\frac{1}{3}\pi r^2 h$

lateral surface area = $\pi r\sqrt{r^2 + h^2} = \pi rs$, where s is the slant height = $\sqrt{r^2 + h^2}$

total surface area = $\pi r\sqrt{r^2 + h^2} + \pi r^2 = \pi rs + \pi r^2$

Here are additional formulas that you might need to know for the Mathematics CK.

Triangle: sides a, b, and c

area = $\sqrt{s(s-a)(s-b)(s-c)}$

where s (the semiperimeter) $= \frac{a+b+c}{2}$

perimeter = $a + b + c$

Equilateral triangle: side s

area = $\frac{\sqrt{3}}{4}s^2$

Perimeter = $3s$

Isosceles triangle: sides a, a, and b

area = $\frac{1}{2}b\sqrt{a^2 - \frac{b^2}{4}}$

Perimeter = $2a + b$

Sector of circle: radius r, θ measure of subtended central angle in radians

area = $\frac{\theta r^2}{2}$

arc length = $s = r\theta$

Geometric Transformations

For this topic, you must be able to solve problems involving reflections, rotations, and translations of geometric figures in the plane (*Mathematics: Content Knowledge (0061) Test at a Glance*, page 3).

A **geometric transformation** is a mapping between two sets of points such that each point in the **preimage** has a unique **image** and that each point in the image has exactly one preimage. The four geometric transformations are **translations, reflections, rotations,** and **dilations.** Translations, reflections, and rotations are **rigid motions,** meaning that the image and the preimage are congruent. A dilation is not a rigid motion; the image and preimage are similar, but not necessarily congruent. You can think of geometric transformations as ways to change geometric figures without changing their basic properties.

A **translation** of a plane geometric figure is a geometric transformation in which every point P is "moved" the same distance and in the same direction along a straight line to a new point P'. Informally, a translation is a **slide** in a horizontal or vertical direction.

A **reflection** of a plane geometric figure is a geometric transformation in which every point P is "moved" to a new point P' that is the same distance from a fixed line, but on the opposite side of the line. The fixed line is called the **line of reflection.** Informally, a reflection is a **flip** across a line, so that the new figure is a mirror image of the original.

A **rotation** of a plane geometric figure is a geometric transformation in which every point P is "rotated" through an angle around a fixed point, called the **center of rotation.** Informally, a rotation is a **turn** around a point. A figure has **rotational symmetry** if there is a rotation through an angle that is less than 360° in which the image and its preimage coincide under the rotation.

A **dilation** of a plane geometric figure is a geometric transformation in which every point P is mapped to a new point P', where the point P' lies on a ray through a fixed point O and the point P, so that the $\overline{OP}' = r\overline{OP}$, where r is a positive real number, called the **scale factor.** Informally, a **dilation** is an expanding or contracting of a geometric shape using a scale factor.

> **Note:** See the section "Representation of Geometric Transformations" in the chapter Matrix Algebra for an additional discussion of geometric transformation.

Trigonometry

According to the *Mathematics: Content Knowledge (0061) Test at a Glance* (www.ets.org/Media/Tests/PRAXIS/pdf/0061.pdf), the Trigonometry content category of the Mathematics CK tests your knowledge and skills in five topic areas:

- The six basic trigonometric functions
- The law of sines and the law of cosines
- Special angle formulas and identities
- Trigonometric equations and inequalities
- Rectangular and polar coordinate systems

This review discusses the key ideas and formulas in each topic area that are most important for you to know for the Mathematics CK.

The Six Basic Trigonometric Functions

For this topic, you must be able to define and use the six basic trigonometric functions using the degree or radian measure of angles and know their graphs and be able to identify their periods, amplitudes, phase displacements or shifts, and asymptotes (*Mathematics: Content Knowledge (0061) Test at a Glance*, page 4).

To define the six basic trigonometric ratios, begin with a right triangle *ABC* and label its parts as follows:

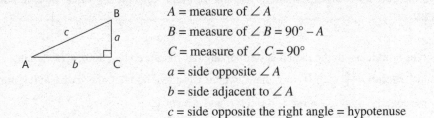

A = measure of $\angle A$

B = measure of $\angle B$ = $90° - A$

C = measure of $\angle C$ = $90°$

a = side opposite $\angle A$

b = side adjacent to $\angle A$

c = side opposite the right angle = hypotenuse

The basic formulas relative to angle *A* in right triangle *ABC* are as follows:

$$\text{sine of } \angle A = \sin A = \frac{\text{side opposite}}{\text{hypotenuse}} = \frac{a}{c} \qquad \text{cosecant of } \angle A = \csc A = \frac{\text{hypotenuse}}{\text{side opposite}} = \frac{c}{a}$$

$$\text{cosine of } \angle A = \cos A = \frac{\text{side adjacent}}{\text{hypotenuse}} = \frac{b}{c} \qquad \text{secant of } \angle A = \sec A = \frac{\text{hypotenuse}}{\text{side adjacent}} = \frac{c}{b}$$

$$\text{tangent of } \angle A = \tan A = \frac{\text{side opposite}}{\text{side adjacent}} = \frac{a}{b} \qquad \text{cotangent of } \angle A = \cot A = \frac{\text{side adjacent}}{\text{side opposite}} = \frac{b}{a}$$

From the preceding formulas, you can see that sine and cosine are reciprocals of each other, that cosine and secant are reciprocals of each other, and that tangent and cotangent are reciprocals of each other. Therefore, it is necessary to remember only the sine, cosine, and tangent ratios because the other ratios can be determined by using the reciprocal relationships.

> **Tip: The mnemonic SOH-CAH-TOA (pronounced "soh-kuh-toh-uh") can help you remember that S (s̲ine) is O (o̲pposite) over H (h̲ypotenuse), that C (c̲osine) is A (a̲djacent) over H (h̲ypotenuse), and T (t̲angent) is O (o̲pposite) over A (a̲djacent).**

Typically, when working with right triangles on the Mathematics CK, you need to find a missing angle or a missing side of a right triangle. If you are given two sides of the right triangle, you should use the Pythagorean theorem to find the missing side. (See the chapter titled "Geometry" for a discussion of the Pythagorean theorem.) If you are given a side and one of the acute angles, label the sides as follows: **opposite** side (the side across from the given angle), the **hypotenuse** (across from the right angle), and the **adjacent** side (the leftover side). Then select the trigonometric ratio that best fits the information you are given.

> **Tip:** When solving a right triangle in which the angles are given in degrees, be sure to set the mode of your calculator to degree mode.

The **unit circle** is the circle with equation $x^2 + y^2 = 1$, centered at the origin with radius 1. An angle θ is in **standard position** if its initial side intersects the unit circle at the point $(1, 0)$, and its terminal side intersects the unit circle at some point (a, b). The following relationships hold: $b = \sin \theta$, $a = \cos \theta$, and $\frac{b}{a} = \tan \theta$, $(a \neq 0)$.

As the terminal side of θ moves around the unit circle passing through the four quadrants of the coordinate plane, the value of the trigonometric functions, $y = \sin \theta$, $y = \cos \theta$, $y = \tan \theta$, $y = \csc \theta$, $y = \sec \theta$, and $y = \cot \theta$, can be determined by using the appropriate reference angle. The **reference angle** is the acute angle formed by the terminal side of θ and the x-axis. Also, the sign of a trigonometric function may be positive or negative depending in which quadrant the terminal side of θ is located. For the Mathematics CK, it is necessary to remember only in which quadrants the sine, cosine, and tangent are positive because they will be negative in the other quadrants. Moreover, their reciprocals will have the same signs as the functions themselves do. The sine function is positive in QI and QII; the cosine function is positive in QI and QIV; and the tangent function is positive in QI and QIII.

> **Tip:** The mnemonic "**A**ll **S**tudents **T**ake **C**alculus" might help you remember the correct sign of a function as you move in a counterclockwise direction from QI to QIV. The initial letters A-S-T-C in the mnemonic remind you that: **A**ll the functions are positive in QI; the **S**ine function is positive in QII; the **T**angent function is positive in QIII; and the **C**osine function is positive in QIV.

The angle θ can be expressed in degrees or radians. In the radian system of angular measurement, $360° = 2\pi$ radians. Thus, you have: $1° = \frac{\pi}{180}$ radians and 1 **radian** $= \frac{180}{\pi}°$. If $\theta = x$ radians, where x is a real number, the six basic **trigonometric functions** of x are $y = \sin x$, $y = \cos x$, $y = \tan x$, $y = \csc x$, $y = \sec x$, and $y = \cot x$.

The following table summarizes the domain, range, and asymptotes for the trigonometric functions.

Trigonometric Function	Domain	Range	Asymptotes
	Let k be any integer		*Let k be any integer*
$y = \sin x$	all reals	$-1 \leq y \leq 1$	none
$y = \cos x$	all reals	$-1 \leq y \leq 1$	none
$y = \tan x$	$\{x \in \text{reals}, x \neq \frac{\pi}{2} + k\pi\}$	all reals	$x = \frac{\pi}{2} + k\pi$
$y = \csc x$	$\{x \in \text{reals}, x \neq k\pi\}$	$[-\infty, -1] \cup [1, \infty]$	$x = k\pi$
$y = \sec x$	$\{x \in \text{reals}, x \neq \frac{\pi}{2} + k\pi\}$	$[-\infty, -1] \cup [1, \infty]$	$x = \frac{\pi}{2} + k\pi$
$y = \cot x$	$\{x \in \text{reals}, x \neq k\pi\}$	all reals	$x = k\pi$

> **Tip:** Switch to radian mode when the argument of the trigonometric function is a real number.

The following table summarizes the value of the trigonometric functions for some special angles.

angle (°)	angle (radians)	sine	cosine	tangent	cotangent	secant	cosecant
0	0	0	1	0	undefined	1	undefined
30°	$\frac{\pi}{6}$	$\frac{1}{2}$	$\frac{\sqrt{3}}{2}$	$\frac{1}{\sqrt{3}}$	$\sqrt{3}$	$\frac{2}{\sqrt{3}}$	2
45°	$\frac{\pi}{4}$	$\frac{1}{\sqrt{2}}$	$\frac{1}{\sqrt{2}}$	1	1	$\sqrt{2}$	$\sqrt{2}$
60°	$\frac{\pi}{3}$	$\frac{\sqrt{3}}{2}$	$\frac{1}{2}$	$\sqrt{3}$	$\frac{1}{\sqrt{3}}$	2	$\frac{2}{\sqrt{3}}$
90°	$\frac{\pi}{2}$	1	0	undefined	0	undefined	1

The graphs of $y = \sin x$, $y = \cos x$, and $y = \tan x$, the three main trigonometric functions, are shown in the following figures.

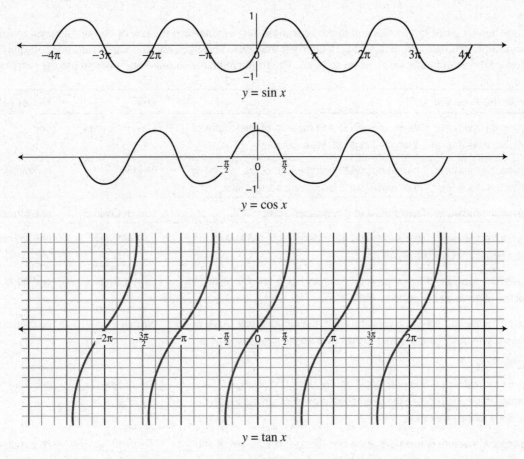

$$y = \sin x$$

$$y = \cos x$$

$$y = \tan x$$

The general forms for the sine and cosine functions, $y = a\sin (bx - c) + k$ and $y = a\cos (bx - c) + k$, have graphs with **amplitude** = $|a|$, **period** = $\frac{2\pi}{b}$, a horizontal or **phase shift** of $|\frac{c}{b}|$ units (to the right of the origin if $\frac{c}{b}$ is positive; to the left of the origin if $\frac{c}{b}$ is negative), and a **vertical shift** of $|k|$ units (up from the origin if k is positive; down from the origin if k is negative). Graphically, the coefficient a causes the function to be "stretched" or "shrunk" in the vertical direction by the multiple $|a|$. For the sine and cosine function the maximum height of the graph is $|a|$, and the minimum height is $-|a|$.

The general form for the tangent function, $y = a\tan (bx - c) + k$, has a graph with period = $\frac{\pi}{b}$, a horizontal or phase shift of $|\frac{c}{b}|$ units (to the right of the origin if $\frac{c}{b}$ is positive; to the left of the origin if $\frac{c}{b}$ is negative), and a vertical shift of $|k|$ units (up from the origin if k is positive; down from the origin if k is negative). Graphically, the coefficient a causes the function to be "stretched" or "shrunk" in the vertical direction by the multiple $|a|$; however, unlike the sine and cosine functions, the tangent function has neither a maximum nor a minimum value.

The Law of Sines and the Law of Cosines

For this topic, you must be able to apply the law of sines and the law of cosines (*Mathematics: Content Knowledge (0061) Test at a Glance*, page 4).

The formulas for the law of sines and the law of cosines are on the Notation, Definitions, and Formulas pages that are given at the beginning of the Mathematics CK test booklet.

Law of Sines: $\dfrac{\sin A}{a} = \dfrac{\sin B}{b} = \dfrac{\sin C}{c}$

Law of Cosines: $c^2 = a^2 + b^2 - 2ab(\cos C)$

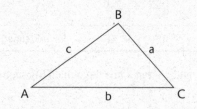

Every triangle has six parts: three sides and three angles. The law of sines and the law of cosines are used to find missing parts of **oblique triangles,** triangles that are not right triangles. Three possibilities can result: one solution, two solutions (called the **ambiguous case**), or no solution. The following table summarizes when to use the two laws.

Situation in the Problem	Use	No. of solutions
You are given the measures of three sides (SSS), and the sum of the lengths of the two smaller sides is greater than the length of the larger side.	Law of Cosines	one
You are given the measures of three sides (SSS), and the sum of the lengths of the two smaller sides is less than or equal to the length of the larger side.	Neither	no solution
You are given the measures of two sides and the included angle (SAS).	Law of Cosines	one solution
You are given the measure of two angles and the included side (ASA), and the sum of the given angles is less than 180°.	Law of Sines	one solution
You are given the measure of two angles and a non-included side (AAS), and the sum of the given angles is less than 180°.	Law of Sines	one solution
You are given the measure of two angles and either the included side (ASA) or a non-included side (AAS), and the sum of the given angles is greater than or equal to 180°.	Neither	no solution
You are given the measure of two sides and a non-included obtuse angle (SSA), and the length of the side opposite the given angle is greater than the length of the side adjacent to the given angle.	Law of Sines	one solution
You are given the measure of two sides and a non-included obtuse angle, and the length of the side opposite the given angle is less than or equal to the length of the side adjacent to the given angle.	Neither	no solution
You are given the measure of two sides and a non-included acute angle (SSA), and the length of the side opposite the given angle is greater than or equal to the length of the side adjacent to the given angle.	Law of Sines	one solution
You are given the measure of two sides and a non-included acute angle (SSA), and the length of one side falls between the length of the altitude from the vertex where the two given sides meet and the length of the other side.	Law of Sines	two solutions

Situation in the Problem	Use	No. of solutions
You are given the measure of two sides and a non-included acute angle (SSA), and the length of the altitude from the vertex where the two given sides meet falls between the lengths of the two given sides.	Neither	no solution
You are given the measure of three angles (AAA).	Neither	no unique solution

Tip: When solving an oblique triangle, be sure to set the mode of your calculator to degree mode if the angle measurements are in degrees and to radian mode if the angle measurements are given in radians.

Special Angle Formulas and Identities

For this topic, you must be able to apply the formulas for the trigonometric functions of $\frac{x}{2}$, $2x$, $x + y$, and $x - y$ and prove trigonometric identities (*Mathematics: Content Knowledge (0061) Test at a Glance*, page 4).

For the Mathematics CK you need to know certain fundamental identities and formulas that can be used to simplify or change trigonometric expressions. Following is a list of the most important identities to commit to memory before the test.

Reciprocal Identities: $\sec \theta = \frac{1}{\cos \theta}$, $\csc \theta = \frac{1}{\sin \theta}$, and $\cot \theta = \frac{1}{\tan \theta}$

Ratio Identities: $\tan \theta = \frac{\sin \theta}{\cos \theta}$, $\cot \theta = \frac{\cos \theta}{\tan \theta}$

Pythagorean Identities: $\sin^2 \theta + \cos^2 \theta = 1$, $1 + \tan^2 \theta = \sec^2 \theta$, and $\cot^2 \theta + 1 = \sec^2 \theta$

Cofunction Identities: $\cos \theta = \sin (90° - \theta)$, $\csc \theta = \sec (90° - \theta)$, and $\cot \theta = \tan (90° - \theta)$

The following formulas are given on the formula sheet that will be provided:

Addition Formulas: $\sin(x \pm y) = \sin x \cos y \pm \cos x \sin y$, $\cos(x \pm y) = \cos x \cos y \mp \sin x \sin y$, and $\tan(x \pm y) = \frac{\tan x \pm \tan y}{1 \mp \tan x \tan y}$

Half-Angle Formulas: $\sin \frac{\theta}{2} = \pm \sqrt{\frac{1 - \cos \theta}{2}}$ and $\cos \frac{\theta}{2} = \pm \sqrt{\frac{1 + \cos \theta}{2}}$ (sign depends on the quadrant of $\frac{\theta}{2}$)

Even though you can derive the following formulas from the addition formulas, it is a good idea to be familiar with them.

Double Angle Formulas: $\sin (2\theta) = 2\sin \theta \cos \theta$, $\cos(2\theta) = \cos^2 \theta - \sin^2 \theta = 2 \cos^2 \theta - 1 = 1 - 2\sin^2 \theta$, and $\tan 2\theta = \frac{2 \tan \theta}{1 - \tan^2 \theta}$

Since the Mathematics CK is a multiple-choice test, you will not have to prove identities *per se* on the test; however, you likely will have to select which trigonometric expression is an identity for a given trigonometric expression. Here are some strategies you might find helpful.

- Change all the trigonometric functions in the given expression to sines and cosines and simplify.
- Combine fractions and simplify.
- If the numerator or denominator of a fraction has the form $f(x) + 1$, multiply the numerator and denominator by $f(x) - 1$ to obtain the difference of two squares, and then look for a Pythagorean identity; for $f(x) - 1$ multiply by $f(x) + 1$.
- Evaluate the given trigonometric expression for a convenient value of the angle, and then evaluate each of the answer choices for the same value of the angle to find one that evaluates to be the same value as you obtained for the given trigonometric expression.

Trigonometric Equations and Inequalities

For this topic, you must be able to solve trigonometric equations and inequalities (*Mathematics: Content Knowledge (0061) Test at a Glance*, page 4).

Trigonometric equations and inequalities are solved in a manner similar to the way that algebraic equations and inequalities are solved. (See the chapter "Algebra and Number Theory" for a discussion on solving algebraic equations.) The main difference is that due to the periodic nature of the trigonometric functions, there might be multiple solutions to the equation, depending on the specifications given in the problem. For instance, to solve $\cos \theta = \frac{1}{2}$, you must find all values for θ that make the equation true. For simplicity, suppose that you want to express the answer in radians. Since this is the cosine of a special angle (see "The Six Basic Trigonometric Functions" earlier in this chapter for a summary of special angles), you know that θ equal to $\frac{\pi}{3}$ is a solution. However, the cosine function is also positive in QIV. Therefore, the angle $\frac{5\pi}{3}$, which is the angle in QIV with reference angle $\frac{\pi}{3}$ is also a solution. Since you know that the cosine function is periodic with period 2π, you need to add multiples of 2π to each of the values to obtain the full solution set: $\theta = \frac{\pi}{3} + 2\pi k$ and $\theta = \frac{5\pi}{3} + 2\pi k$, where k is any integer. If the problem specifies that you are to find only values in a particular interval, then you omit any values outside the given interval.

You can use your graphing calculator to solve trigonometric equations by using the keys for the inverse trigonometric functions, $y = \sin^{-1}x$, $y = \cos^{-1}x$, and $y = \tan^{-1}x$. The range for an inverse trigonometric function is restricted, so that the inverse will be a function. (See the chapter "Functions" for a discussion on inverses of functions.) The following applies:

Range of Inverse Trigonometric Functions: $\sin^{-1}x$ $[-\pi/2, \pi/2]$; $\cos^{-1}x$ $[0, \pi]$; $\tan^{-1}x$ $(-\pi/2, \pi/2)$

When you use the keys for the inverse functions, the values returned will be in the restricted ranges. You will have to use your knowledge of reference angles and the periodicity of the functions to determine other values in the solution set if needed.

> **Tip:** If the answer choices are given as radians expressed in terms of π, you might set your calculator to degree mode when obtaining the value of the angle, then convert the angle into radians using the relationship that $1° = \frac{\pi}{180}$ radians. If you set your calculator to radian mode, the value of the solution will be displayed as a real number. You will have to convert the answer choices to real numbers to decide which answer is the same as your solution.

Rectangular and Polar Coordinate Systems

For this topic, you must be able to convert between rectangular and polar coordinate systems (*Mathematics: Content Knowledge (0061) Test at a Glance*, page 4).

In a **polar coordinate system,** a point P is represented by an ordered pair of coordinates (r, π). The number r is the distance of the point from the origin at point **O,** and π is the smallest nonnegative angle (measured in a counterclockwise direction) that **OP** makes with the positive horizontal axis.

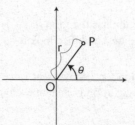

To change from rectangular (x, y) to polar (r, π): $r^2 = x^2 + y^2$; $\tan \theta = \frac{y}{x}$ if $x \neq 0$.

To change from polar (r, θ) to rectangular (x, y): $x = r \cos \theta$; $y = r \sin \theta$.

Note: These formulas are given on the Notation, Definitions, and Formulas pages that are given at the beginning of the Mathematics CK test booklet. The trigonometric form of a complex number $z = x + yi$ is $r \cos \theta + r \sin \theta i = r(\cos \theta + i\sin \theta)$, where $r = \sqrt{x^2 + y^2}$ and $\tan \theta = \frac{y}{x}$ if $x \neq 0$. Since z can also be represented by the ordered pair (x, y), the similarity to formulas for polar coordinates is logical.

De Moivre's Theorem is stated as follows: $(\cos \theta + i\sin \theta)^k = \cos(k\theta) + i\sin(k\theta)$. It is useful for finding powers and roots of complex numbers.

Note: The formula is given on the Notation, Definitions, and Formulas pages that are given at the beginning of the Mathematics CK test booklet.

According to the *Mathematics: Content Knowledge Test (0061) at a Glance* (www.ets.org/Media/Tests/PRAXIS/pdf/0061.pdf), the Functions content category of the Mathematics CK tests your knowledge and skills in six topic areas:

- Representation of functions
- Modeling with functions
- Properties of functions
- Solving problems involving functions
- Composition and inverses of functions
- Functions of two variables

This review discusses the key ideas and formulas in each topic area that are most important for you to know for the Mathematics CK.

Representation of Functions

For this topic, you must demonstrate an understanding of and ability to work with functions in various representations (for example, graphs, tables, symbolic expressions, and verbal narratives) and to convert flexibly among them (*Mathematics: Content Knowledge (0061) Test at a Glance*, page 4).

The **Cartesian product** of two sets A and B, denoted $A \times B$, is the set of all ordered pairs (x, y) such that $x \in A$ and $y \in B$. The set of all possible ordered pairs of real numbers is denoted $R \times R$, or simply R^2. The set R^2 is represented by the Cartesian coordinate plane. Any subset of R^2 is a **relation** in R^2. The set of all first components in the ordered pairs in a relation is called the **domain** of the relation, and the set of all second components is called the **range** of the relation.

A **function** is a relation in which each first component is paired with *one and only one* second component. All functions are relations, but not all relations are functions. A function is a relation in which no two different ordered pairs have the same first component, that is, if (a, b) and (a, c) are elements in the function, then $b = c$.

Since a function is a set of ordered pairs, its graph can be determined in a coordinate plane. Each ordered pair is represented by a point in the plane. By definition, each element in the domain of the function is paired with exactly one element in the range; thus, any vertical line in the plane will intersect the graph of the function no more than once. This is known as the **vertical line test:** If any vertical line can be drawn so that it cuts the graph of a relation in more than one point, the relation is *not* a function.

Functions are usually (but not necessarily always) denoted by lowercase letters such as *f, g, h,* and so on. A function that contains a *finite* number of ordered pairs may be defined by listing its **ordered pairs,** a **table,** an **arrow diagram,** using two **number lines,** a **rule,** an **equation,** or a **graph.** When the number of ordered pairs is *infinite*, the function is usually defined by either an **equation** or a **graph.**

Modeling with Functions

For this topic, you must be able to find an appropriate family of functions to model particular phenomena (for example, population growth, cooling, simple harmonic motion) (*Mathematics: Content Knowledge (0061) Test at a Glance*, page 4).

Some common families of functions that are used to model phenomena in the real world are the families of linear functions, quadratic functions, exponential functions, and trigonometric functions.

Linear functions model processes in which the rate of change is constant. For instance, a linear function can be used to describe the distance a moving object travels at a constant rate of speed.

Quadratic functions are used to model processes that involve a maximum or a minimum value. For instance, in business a quadratic function can be used to model the profit or revenue of a company, which depends on the number of units sold.

Exponential functions are used to model physical phenomena such as population growth and population decay. This family of functions is also used in business for determining the growth of money when interest is compounded.

Trigonometric functions are used to model periodic processes. For example, physical phenomena such as light waves, sound waves, the movement of a pendulum, or a weight attached to a coiled spring can be modeled using the trigonometric sine or cosine function.

Properties of a Function

For this topic, you must be able to find properties of a function such as domain, range, intercepts, symmetries, intervals of increase or decrease, discontinuities, and asymptotes (*Mathematics: Content Knowledge (0061) Test at a Glance*, page 4).

For the function f defined by $y = f(x)$, y is the **dependent variable** and x is the **independent variable.** The notation $f(x)$ is read "f of x" and indicates you must substitute a value of x, called an **argument** of f, into the equation defining the function to find y, the **value** of f at x, or the **image** of x under f. The notation D_f is used to indicate the **domain,** and the notation R_f is used to indicate the **range** of a function f. You can think of a function as a process f which takes a number $x \in D_f$ in the domain of f and produces from it the number $f(x) \in R_f$ in the range of f. The ordered pairs of the function are written in the form (x, y) or $(x, f(x))$. For the Mathematics CK test, unless the problem clearly indicates otherwise, the functions you will work with are "real-valued" functions. This means both D_f and R_f consist of real numbers.

If a function f is defined by an equation and no domain is specified, the largest possible subset of the real numbers for which each first component causes the corresponding function value to be a *real* number is its **domain of definition.** When a function is discussed, it is customary to consider its domain of definition to be the domain of the function. In determining the domain of a function defined by an equation, start with the set of real numbers and eliminate any numbers that would make the equation undefined. If a rational expression is involved, exclude any numbers that would make a denominator zero. If a radical with an *even* index is involved, omit all values for which the expression under the radical is negative.

The **graph** of a function f in a coordinate plane is the set of all ordered pairs (x, y) for which $x \in D_f$ and $y = f(x)$. The points (or point) at which the graph of the function intersects the x-axis are called the real **zeros** of the function and are determined by finding all points x for which $f(x) = 0$. A real **zero** of a function can also be described as one of the following: an **x-value** for which $f(x) = 0$, a real **root** of the equation $f(x) = 0$, or an **x-intercept** for the graph of $y = f(x)$.

If zero is in the domain of f, then $f(0)$ is the **y-intercept** of the graph. Since each x in the domain of a function corresponds to one and only one $f(x)$ in the range, a function cannot have more than one y-intercept. A way to determine the range of a function is to look at its graph. A graphing calculator is very useful for this purpose.

Adding or subtracting a positive constant k to $f(x)$ is called a **vertical shift.** Adding or subtracting a positive constant h to x is a called a **horizontal shift.** Vertical and horizontal shifts are summarized in the following table:

Vertical and Horizontal Shifts	
Type of change	*Effect on y = f(x)*
$y = f(x) + k$	vertical shift: k units up
$y = f(x) - k$	vertical shift: k units down
$y = f(x + h)$	horizontal shift: h units to left
$y = f(x - h)$	horizontal shift: h units to right

Multiplying $f(x)$ by $c > 1$ enlarges or **stretches** the graph of f. Multiplying $f(x)$ by $0 < c < 1$ reduces or **shrinks** the graph of f.

The graph of $y = -f(x)$ is a **reflection** of $y = f(x)$ in the x-axis.

A line $x = k$ is a **vertical asymptote** if the function approaches $-\infty$ or ∞ as x approaches k from the left or right. A line $y = h$ is a **horizontal asymptote** if the function approaches h as x increases or decreases without bound. A function $y = g(x)$ is an **oblique asymptote** or **slant asymptote** if the function approaches $g(x)$ as x increases or decreases without bound.

A function f is **one-to-one** if and only if $f(a) = f(b)$ implies that $a = b$; that is, if $(a, c) \in f$ and $(b, c) \in f$, then $a = b$. In a one-to-one function each first component is paired with *exactly one* second component *and* each second component is paired with *exactly one* first component. The **horizontal line test** for one-to-one states that if any horizontal line can be drawn so that it cuts the graph of a function in more than one point, the function is *not* a one-to-one function.

If in an interval whenever $x_1 < x_2, f(x_1) < f(x_2)$, the function f is *increasing* in the interval; if $f(x_1) > f(x_2)$, the function is *decreasing* in the interval; if $f(x_1) = f(x_2)$, the function is *constant* in the interval. A function is **monotone** if, on its entire domain, the function is either only increasing or only decreasing. A monotone increasing or decreasing function is one-to-one.

A function is **even** if for every x in the domain of f, $-x$ is in the domain of f and $f(-x) = f(x)$. A function is **odd** if for every x in the domain of f, $-x$ is in the domain of f and $f(-x) = -f(x)$. The graph of an even function is **symmetric** with respect to the **y-axis.** The graph of an odd function is **symmetric** with respect to the **origin.**

In an informal sense, a function has **discontinuities** if the graph of the function has vertical asymptotes, holes, or jumps that make it impossible to sketch the graph of the function without lifting the pencil. See the chapter "Calculus" for a mathematically rigorous discussion of continuity and discontinuity.

Problems Involving Functions

For this topic, you must be able to use the properties of trigonometric, exponential, logarithmic, polynomial, and rational functions to solve problems (*Mathematics: Content Knowledge (0061) Test at a Glance*, page 4).

A **linear function** is defined by $y = f(x) = mx + b$ ($m \neq 0$). The domain and range are both equal to the set of real numbers. The zeros are found by solving the equation $mx + b = 0$. Thus, $x = \frac{-b}{m}$ is the only zero of the function. The graph crosses the x-axis at the point $(\frac{-b}{m}, 0)$. The graph of $y = mx + b$ is a **straight line** with **slope m** and **y-intercept b.** This is called the **slope-intercept** form of a line. Every **linear equation** $Ax + By = C$ with $B \neq 0$ determines a linear function. The following table summarizes linear equations.

Linear Equations	
Slope-intercept form (functional form)	$y = mx + b$
Point-slope form	$y - y_1 = m(x - x_1)$
Standard form	$Ax + By = C$
Horizontal line	$y = k$ for any constant k
Vertical line (not a function)	$x = h$ for any constant h

A **constant function** is defined by $y = f(x) = b$. The domain is the set of real numbers and the range is the set $\{b\}$ consisting of the single element b. If $b \neq 0$, the constant function $f(x) = b$ has no zeros; if $b = 0$, every value of x is a zero of the function. The graph of a constant function is a horizontal line (has slope zero) which is $|b|$ units above or below the x-axis.

An **identity function** is defined by $y = x$. It is called the identity function because the value of y is identical with that of x. The domain is the set of real numbers and the range is the set of real numbers. The identity function passes through the origin, where it has a zero.

A **quadratic function** is defined by $y = f(x) = ax^2 + bx + c, (a \neq 0)$. The domain is the set of all real numbers and the range is a subset of the real numbers. The zeros are determined by finding the roots of the quadratic equation $ax^2 + bx + c = 0$. If $b^2 - 4ac > 0$, there are two real unequal zeros. If $b^2 - 4ac = 0$, there is one real zero (double root). If $b^2 - 4ac < 0$, there are no real zeros for the function.

The graph of a quadratic function defined by $f(x) = ax^2 + bx + c$ is always a **parabola.** If $a > 0$, the parabola opens **upward** and has a **minimum.** If $a < 0$, the parabola opens **downward** and has a **maximum.** The parabola is **symmetric** about a vertical line through its vertex. This line is called its **axis of symmetry.** The graph of the function might or might not intersect the x-axis (the real axis), depending on the solution set of $ax^2 + bx + c = 0$. The following guidelines hold:

a. No real roots: the parabola will *not* intersect the x-axis.
b. Exactly *one* real root: the parabola will intersect the x-axis at only that *one* point.
c. *Two* real unequal roots: the parabola will intersect the x-axis at those *two* points.

The graph of the equation $f(x) = a(x - h)^2 + k \ (a \neq 0)$ is a parabola with vertex (h, k). The parabola opens upward if $a > 0$ and downward if $a < 0$. This is the **standard form** for the equation of a parabola. By **completing the square,** any quadratic function can be put in standard form.

A **polynomial function** is defined by $y = P(x) = a_n x^n + a_{n-1} x^{n-1} + a_{n-2} x^{n-2} + \ldots + a_1 x^1 + a_0$, where n is a nonnegative integer and $a_n \neq 0$. The domain is the set of real numbers. If the polynomial has odd degree, the range is also the set of real numbers. If the polynomial has even degree, the range is a subset of the real numbers. Linear, constant, and quadratic functions are special types of polynomial functions. The zeros are the solutions of the equation $P(x) = 0$. A number r is a **zero,** or **root,** of a polynomial $P(x)$ if $P(r) = 0$. If r is a real number, the graph of $P(x)$ intersects the x-axis at r.

Allowing complex roots, the **Fundamental Theorem of Algebra** assures us that $P(x) = 0$ has a solution. It states that every polynomial of degree one or greater has at least one root.

The **Remainder Theorem** states that if a polynomial $P(x)$ is divided by $x - a$, the remainder is $P(a)$.

A root r of $P(x)$ has **multiplicity** k if $(x - r)^k$ is a factor of $P(x)$. Allowing complex roots and counting multiplicities, we have: **every polynomial of degree n has exactly n roots.** If you allow complex roots and count a root again each time it occurs more than once, every first degree (linear) equation in x has exactly one root; every second degree (quadratic) equation in x has exactly two roots; every third degree (cubic) equation in x has exactly three roots; and so on.

The **Factor Theorem** states: $P(r) = 0$ if and only if $x - r$ is a factor of $P(x)$.

The **Rational Root Theorem** states: If $P(x) = a_n x^n + a_{n-1} x^{n-1} + a_{n-2} x^{n-2} + \ldots + a_1 x^1 + a_0$ is a polynomial function with integral coefficients and $\frac{p}{q}$ is a **rational root** of $P(x)$ in lowest terms, then p is a factor of a_0 and q is a factor of a_n.

Let $P(x)$ be a polynomial function with real coefficients. If $a + bi$ is a complex root of $P(x)$, then its **conjugate** $a - bi$ is also a root of $P(x)$.

Let $P(x)$ be a polynomial function with real coefficients. If a and b are real numbers such that $P(a)$ and $P(b)$ have opposite signs, then $P(x)$ has at least one zero between a and b.

A **rational function** is defined by $y = f(x) = \frac{p(x)}{q(x)}$, where $p(x)$ and $q(x)$ are polynomials $(q(x) \neq 0)$. The domain excludes any real number for which $q(x) = 0$. The range will be a subset of the real numbers. The zeros, if any, are the values of x for which $f(x) = 0$. To graph rational functions, you will usually need to look for **asymptotes** associated with the function. The vertical asymptotes, if any, will be the values for x, if any, for which $q(x)$ equals zero. If the degree of $p(x)$ is less than the degree of $q(x)$, then the x-axis is a horizontal asymptote of $y = \frac{p(x)}{q(x)}$. If the degree of $p(x)$ equals the degree of $q(x)$, then

$y = \dfrac{p(x)}{q(x)}$ will have a horizontal asymptote that is not the x-axis. If the degree of $p(x)$ exceeds the degree of $q(x)$ by exactly 1, then $y = \dfrac{p(x)}{q(x)}$ will have an oblique asymptote.

A **square root function** is defined by $y = f(x) = \sqrt{ax + b}$. The domain is the set of all real numbers such that $ax + b \geq 0$. The range is the set of nonnegative real numbers $(0, \infty)$. The function has a zero at $x = -\dfrac{b}{a}$. The graph of the function is to the right of $x = -\dfrac{b}{a}$ and above the x-axis.

An **absolute value function** is defined by $y = f(x) = |ax + b|$. The domain is the set of all real numbers and the range is restricted to nonnegative values. The function has a zero at $x = -\dfrac{b}{a}$. The absolute value function $f(x) = |ax + b|$ can be written as follows:

$$f(x) = \begin{cases} ax + b & if \ ax + b \geq 0 \\ -(ax + b) & if \ ax + b < 0 \end{cases}$$

Since the absolute value function is defined in two parts, we say it is a **piecewise function.**

A **greatest integer function** (also called a **floor function**) is defined by $y = f(x) = [x] = $ the greatest integer less than or equal to x. The domain is the set of all real numbers and the range is the set of integers. The zeros of the function lie in the interval $[0, 1)$.

A **ceiling function** is defined by $y = f(x) = $ the smallest integer greater than or equal to x. The domain is the set of all real numbers and the range is the set of integers. The zeros of the function lie in the interval $(-1, 0]$.

An **exponential function** is defined by $y = f(x) = b^x$ $(b \neq 1, b > 0)$, where b is called the **base** of the exponential function. The domain is the set of real numbers and the range is the set of positive real numbers; that is, $b^x > 0$ for all real numbers x. The function has no zeros.

The graph of $y = f(x) = b^x$ passes through the points $(0, 1)$ and $(1, b)$ and is asymptotic to the x-axis. The exponential function is an increasing function if $b > 1$ and is a decreasing function if $0 < b < 1$. The graph is located in the first and second quadrants only.

Two exponential functions that are of particular importance are the following:

- $y = f(x) = 10^x$ that has base 10
- $y = f(x) = e^x$, the **natural exponential function,** which has base e, the irrational number whose rational decimal approximation to nine digits is 2.718281828.

A **logarithmic function** is defined by $y = f(x) = \log_b x \Leftrightarrow b^y = x$ $(x > 0)$, where b is called the **base** of the logarithmic function, $(b \neq 1, b > 0)$. The domain is the set of positive real numbers and the range is the set of real numbers. The function has a zero at $x = 1$. Logarithms are **exponents.** If $y = \log_b x$, then y is the *exponent* that is used on b to get x; that is, $b^y = x$. The logarithmic function for a given base is the **inverse** of the exponential function with the same base and, reciprocally. (See the section in this chapter titled "Composition and Inverses of Functions" for a discussion of inverses of function.) We have the following **properties** for logarithmic functions:

Properties for Logarithmic Functions

For real numbers b $(b \neq 1, b > 0)$, u, v, w, and p:

$\log_b b^x = x$	$b^{\log_b x} = x$	$\log_b b = 1$ (because $b^1 = b$)	$\log_b 1 = 0$ (because $b^0 = 1$)
If $\log_b u = \log_b v$, then $u = v$	$\log_b \dfrac{1}{u} = -\log_b u$	$\log_b uv = \log_b u + \log_b v$	
$\log_b \dfrac{u}{v} = \log_b u - \log_b v$	$\log_b u^p = p \log_b u$		

For real numbers b ($b \neq 1$, $b > 0$), x, and y, the graph of $y = f(x) = b^x$ passes through $(1, 0)$ and $(b, 1)$ and is asymptotic to the y-axis. The logarithmic function is an increasing function if $b > 1$ and is a decreasing function if $0 < b < 1$. The graph of the function is located in the first and fourth quadrants only.

The logarithm function $y = f(x) = \log_{10} x$ (**common logarithmic function**) is the inverse of the exponential function $y = f(x) = 10^x$. The logarithm function $y = f(x) = \ln x$ (**natural logarithmic function**) is the inverse of the exponential function $y = f(x) = e^x$.

A variable y is said to **vary directly** (or **proportionately**) as the *nth* power of the variable x if $y = f(x) = kx^n$, where k is a positive constant and $n > 0$. The variable y is said to **vary inversely** (or **indirectly**) as the *nth* power of the variable x if $y = f(x) = \dfrac{k}{x^n}$, where k is a positive constant. The constant k is called the **constant of variation.**

The six **trigonometric functions** are called **sine, cosine, tangent, cosecant, secant,** and **cotangent.** The following table summarizes the domain, range, and asymptotes for the trigonometric functions $y = \sin x$, $y = \cos x$, $y = \tan x$, $y = \csc x$, $y = \sec x$, and $y = \cot x$.

Trigonometric Function	Domain	Range	Asymptotes
	Let k be any integer		**Let k be any integer**
$y = \sin x$	all reals	$-1 \leq y \leq 1$	none
$y = \cos x$	all reals	$-1 \leq y \leq 1$	none
$y = \tan x$	$\{x \in \text{reals}, x \neq \frac{\pi}{2} + k\pi\}$	all reals	$x = \frac{\pi}{2} + k\pi$
$y = \csc x$	$\{x \in \text{reals}, x \neq k\pi\}$	$(-\infty, -1] \cup [1, \infty)$	$x = k\pi$
$y = \sec x$	$\{x \in \text{reals}, x \neq \frac{\pi}{2} + k\pi\}$	$(-\infty, -1] \cup [1, \infty)$	$x = \frac{\pi}{2} + k\pi$
$y = \cot x$	$\{x \in \text{reals}, x \neq k\pi\}$	all reals	$x = k\pi$

Note: *See the chapter titled "Trigonometry" for a fuller discussion of the trigonometric functions.*

An **algebraic function** is a function that is defined in terms of polynomials and/or roots of polynomials. Examples of algebraic functions are polynomial functions, rational functions, square root functions, or combinations of these functions under addition, subtraction, multiplication, or division. Examples of nonalgebraic functions are the exponential function, the logarithmic function, and the trigonometric functions. These functions are examples of **transcendental functions.**

Composition and Inverses of Functions

For this topic, you must be able to determine the composition of two functions, find the inverse of a one-to-one function in simple cases, and know why only one-to-one functions have inverses (*Mathematics: Content Knowledge (0061) Test at a Glance*, page 4).

Two functions f and g are **equal,** written $f = g$, if and only if their domains are equal and $f(x) = g(x)$ for all x in their common domain.

The following definitions for the arithmetic of functions hold for all real numbers x in the domain of *both* f and g:

If the ranges of f and g are real numbers,

The **sum** of f and g, denoted $f + g$, is defined by $(f + g)(x) = f(x) + g(x)$.

The **difference** of f and g, denoted $f - g$, is defined by $(f - g)(x) = f(x) - g(x)$.

The **product** of f and g, denoted $f \cdot g$, is defined by $(f \cdot g)(x) = f(x) \cdot g(x)$.

The **quotient** of f and g, denoted $f(x)/g(x)$, is defined by $(f/g)(x) = \dfrac{f(x)}{g(x)}$, $g(x) \neq 0$.

The **composite** of f and g, denoted $f \circ g$ is the function defined by $(f \circ g)(x) = f(g(x))$ where $R_g \subseteq D_f$. Composition of functions is *not* a commutative process; that is, in general, $(f \circ g)(x) \neq (g \circ f)(x)$.

Two functions f and g are called **inverses** of each other, if and only if $(f \circ g)(x) = (g \circ f)(x) = x$, where $R_g \subseteq D_f$ and $R_f \subseteq D_g$. The inverse of a function f is usually denoted f^{-1} (read "f inverse"). If a function is one-to-one, then f^{-1} may be found by interchanging the first and second components in the ordered pairs of f. If f is a one-to-one function, f^{-1} is the set of ordered pairs obtained from f by interchanging the first and second components of each of its ordered pairs. The graphs of f and f^{-1} are **reflections** of one another about the line $y = x$. Two common methods for determining the equation that defines the inverse of a function are the following:

Method 1. Set $(f \circ f^{-1})(x) = x$ and solve for $f^{-1}(x)$.

Method 2. First, interchange x and y in $y = f(x)$, then solve $x = f(y)$, for y.

If a function is not one-to-one, we can restrict the domain so that the function is one-to-one in the **restricted domain.** The inverse of the function will be defined in the restricted domain of the function.

Functions of Two Variables

For this topic, you must be able to interpret representations of functions of two variables, such as three-dimensional graphs, level curves, and tables (*Mathematics: Content Knowledge (0061) Test at a Glance*, page 4).

A **real-valued function of two variables** is a function f that associates with each pair (x, y) of real numbers of a set $D_f \subseteq R^2$ one and only one real number with $z = f(x, y)$. The set D_f is called the **domain** of f, and the set of all real numbers $z = f(x, y)$ is the **range** of f, D_f.

As with functions of one variable, functions of two variables can be represented numerically (using a table of values), algebraically (using a formula), and sometimes graphically (using a graph).

The **graph of the function f of two variables** is the set of all points $(x, y, f(x, y))$ defining a region or curved surface in three-dimensional space, where we restrict the values of (x, y) to lie in the domain of f. In other words, the graph is the set of all points (x, y, z) with $z = f(x, y)$.

Calculus

According to the *Mathematics: Content Knowledge Test (0061) at a Glance* (www.ets.org/Media/Tests/PRAXIS/pdf/0061.pdf), the Calculus content category of the Mathematics CK tests your knowledge and skills in nine topic areas:

- Limits
- Derivatives
- Continuity
- Analyzing the behavior of a function
- The Mean Value Theorem and the Fundamental Theorem of Calculus
- Integration as a limiting sum
- Differentiation and integration techniques
- Numerical approximation of derivatives and integrals
- Limits of sequences and series

This review will discuss the key ideas and formulas in each topic area that are most important for you to know for the Mathematics CK.

Limits

For this topic, you must demonstrate an understanding of what it means for a function to have a limit at a point; calculate limits of functions or determine that the limit does not exist; and solve problems using the properties of limits (*Mathematics: Content Knowledge (0061) Test at a Glance*, page 4).

The study of calculus begins with the study of limits. For the Mathematics CK, the following definitions and properties of limits are essential to know.

Let f be a function defined at every number in an open interval containing a, except possibly at a, then the $\lim_{x \to a} f(x) = L$ (read "the **limit** of f as x approaches a equals L") if for every number $\varepsilon > 0$, there exists a number $\delta > 0$ such that if $0 < |x - a| < \delta$, then $|f(x) - L| < \varepsilon$. The limit is said to *exist* only if the following conditions are satisfied: (i) the limit L is a single finite real number; and (ii) the limit as x approaches a from the left equals the limit as x approaches a from the right; that is, $\{ \lim_{x \to a^+} f(x) = \lim_{x \to a^-} f(x) \}$. If no such L exists, then we say that $\lim_{x \to a} f(x)$ *does not exist*.

Common situations that occur when the limit of a function f as x approaches a does *not* exist are (i) $\lim_{x \to a^+} f(x) \neq \lim_{x \to a^-} f(x)$, (ii) $f(x)$ increases or decreases without bound as x approaches a, or (iii) $f(x)$ oscillates between two fixed values as x approaches a.

Informally, the "ε-δ" definition of limit given here means that if the values of $f(x)$ get arbitrarily close to a single value L as x approaches a from either side, then $\lim_{x \to a} f(x) = L$. When $\lim_{x \to a} f(x)$ exists, the limit is unique. Furthermore, its value is independent of the value of f at a. When $\lim_{x \to a} f(x)$ exists, three situations might occur at a: (i) $f(a) = \lim_{x \to a} f(x)$; (ii) $f(a)$ is undefined; or (iii) $f(a)$ is defined, but $f(a) \neq \lim_{x \to a} f(x)$.

When $\lim_{x \to a} f(x)$ exists and $\lim_{x \to a} f(x) = f(a)$, you can find the limit by direct substitution. Here are some common limits that can be evaluated using direct substitution.

$$\lim_{x \to a} b = b \qquad\qquad \lim_{x \to a} x^n = a^n, \text{ for } n \text{ a positive integer.}$$

$$\lim_{x \to a} x = a \qquad\qquad \lim_{x \to a} \sqrt[n]{x} = \sqrt[n]{a}, \text{ for } n \text{ a positive integer with the restriction that if } n \text{ is even, } a > 0.$$

$\lim\limits_{x \to a} \dfrac{1}{x} = \dfrac{1}{a}, a \neq 0$ If f is a polynomial function given by $f(x) = a_n x^n + a_{n-1} x^{n-1} + a_{n-2} x^{n-2} + \ldots + a_1 x^1 + a_0$, $\lim\limits_{x \to a} f(x) = f(a)$

$\lim\limits_{x \to a} \sqrt{x} = \sqrt{a}, a > 0$ If f is a rational function given by $f(x) = \dfrac{p(x)}{q(x)}$, $\lim\limits_{x \to a} f(x) = \dfrac{p(a)}{q(a)}$, provided $q(a) \neq 0$

For a in the domain of the function,

$$\lim\limits_{x \to a} \sin x = \sin a \qquad \lim\limits_{x \to a} \cos x = \cos a$$

$$\lim\limits_{x \to a} \tan x = \tan a \qquad \lim\limits_{x \to a} \cot x = \cot a$$

$$\lim\limits_{x \to a} \sec x = \sec a \qquad \lim\limits_{x \to a} \csc x = \csc a$$

Limit of a composite function: If f and g are functions such that $\lim\limits_{x \to a} g(x) = L$, and $\lim\limits_{x \to L} f(x) = f(L)$, then $\lim\limits_{x \to a} f \circ g(x) = \lim\limits_{x \to a} f\left(g(x)\right) = f(L)$.

If $\lim\limits_{x \to a} p(x) = 0$ and $\lim\limits_{x \to a} q(x) = 0$, then direct substitution into $\lim\limits_{x \to a} \dfrac{p(x)}{q(x)}$ yields $\dfrac{0}{0}$, which is called an **indeterminate form.** When this problem occurs, try factoring $x - a$ from $p(x)$ and $q(x)$, reducing the algebraic fraction $\dfrac{p(x)}{q(x)}$, and then finding the limit of the resulting expression, if it exists. Another and more efficient way to approach problems of this type is to apply *L'Hôpital's* **rule,** which says that if p and q are differentiable (See the next section, "Derivatives," in this chapter for a discussion of the term *differentiable*) at every number a in some interval, except possibly at a, and $\lim\limits_{x \to a} p(x) = 0$ and $\lim\limits_{x \to a} q(x) = 0$, then $\lim\limits_{x \to a} \dfrac{p(x)}{q(x)} = \lim\limits_{x \to a} \dfrac{p'(x)}{q'(x)}$, provided $q'(x) \neq 0$ in the interval and the limit on the right exists. (The notation $p'(x)$ and $q'(x)$ will be explained in "Derivatives.") L'Hôpital's rule also applies when $\lim\limits_{x \to a} p(x) = \pm\infty$ and $\lim\limits_{x \to a} q(x) = \pm\infty$.

A word of caution: **If you use your graphing calculator to help you evaluate a limit as the variable approaches a particular value, you run the risk of obtaining an incorrect answer. Remember, you cannot always trust the sketch of a function that is produced by your graphing calculator. For instance, for most graphing calculators, the graph of $y = \sin(1/x)$ at values near x equal zero will never be correct. Thus, using your graphing calculator to aid in finding $\lim\limits_{x \to 0} \sin(1/x)$ likely would lead you to a completely wrong conclusion.**

Assuming that the functions f and g have limits that exist as x approaches a, the following fundamental properties have to do with the limits of various combinations of f and g.

Properties of Limits	
Sum or Difference	$\lim\limits_{x \to a} [f(x) \pm g(x)] = \lim\limits_{x \to a} f(x) \pm \lim\limits_{x \to a} g(x)$
Product	$\lim\limits_{x \to a} [f(x) \cdot g(x)] = \lim\limits_{x \to a} f(x) \cdot \lim\limits_{x \to a} g(x)$
Quotient	$\lim\limits_{x \to a} \dfrac{f(x)}{g(x)} = \dfrac{\lim\limits_{x \to a} f(x)}{\lim\limits_{x \to a} g(x)}$, provided $g(x) \neq 0$ and $\lim\limits_{x \to a} g(x) \neq 0$
Power	$\lim\limits_{x \to a} [f(x)]^n = [\lim\limits_{x \to a} f(x)]^n$
Root	$\lim\limits_{x \to a} \sqrt[n]{f(x)} = \sqrt[n]{\lim\limits_{x \to a} f(x)}$, for n a positive integer and $\lim\limits_{x \to a} f(x) > 0$ when n is even
Scalar Multiplication	$\lim\limits_{x \to a} k f(x) = k \lim\limits_{x \to a} f(x)$, for any real number k

Derivatives

For this topic, you must demonstrate an understanding of the derivative of a function as a limit, as the slope of a curve, and as a rate of change (for example, velocity, acceleration, growth, decay) (*Mathematics: Content Knowledge (0061) Test at a Glance*, page 4).

The **derivative** f' (read "f prime") of the function f at the number x is defined as $f'(x) = \lim_{h \to 0} \frac{f(x+h) - f(x)}{h}$, if this limit exists. If this limit does not exist, then f does not have a derivative at x. A *differentiable* function is a function that has a derivative. If $f'(c)$ exists, then f is **differentiable** at c; otherwise, f does not have a derivative at c. Various symbols are used to represent the derivative of a function f. If you use the notation $y = f(x)$, then the derivative of f can be symbolized by $f'(x)$, $D_x f(x)$, y', $D_x y$, $\frac{dy}{dx}$, or $\frac{d}{dx}f(x)$.

The derivative f' is called the **first derivative** of f. The derivative of f' is called the **second derivative** of f and is denoted f''. Similarly, the derivative of f'' is called the **third derivative** of f and is denoted f''', and so on.

If $f'(a)$ exists, then the **tangent line** to the graph of the function f at the point $P(a, f(a))$ is the line through P that has **slope** $m = f'(a)$.

If $f'(t)$ exists, then the (instantaneous) **rate of change** of f at t is $f'(t)$. For example, if $s(t)$ is the position function of a moving object, then the **velocity** (the instantaneous rate of change) of the object at time t is $s'(t)$. Additionally, the **acceleration** of the object at time t is $s''(t)$.

Continuity

For this topic, you must be able to show that a particular function is continuous and demonstrate an understanding of the relationship between continuity and differentiability (*Mathematics: Content Knowledge (0061) Test at a Glance*, page 4).

The function f is **continuous** at the point a in the domain of f if all three of the following conditions are met: (i) $f(a)$ is defined; (ii) $\lim_{x \to a} f(x)$ exists; and (iii) $\lim_{x \to a} f(x) = f(a)$; otherwise, the function f is **discontinuous** at x. A function f is continuous in an open interval if it is continuous at each point in the interval. If a function is continuous on the entire real line, the function is **everywhere continuous;** that is to say, its graph has no holes, jumps, or gaps in it.

The following types of functions are continuous at every point in their domains.

Continuous Functions	
Constant functions	$f(x) = k$, where k is a constant
Power functions	$f(x) = x^n$, where n is a positive integer
Polynomial functions	$f(x) = a_n x^n + a_{n-1} x^{n-1} + a_{n-2} x^{n-2} + \ldots + a_1 x^1 + a_0$
Rational functions	$f(x) = \frac{p(x)}{q(x)}$, provided $q(x) \neq 0$
Radical functions	$f(x) = \sqrt[n]{x}$, $x \geq 0$, where n is a positive integer
Trigonometric functions	$f(x) = \sin x$, $f(x) = \cos x$, $f(x) = \tan x$, $f(x) = \cos x$, $f(x) = \cot x$, $f(x) = \csc x$

If f is continuous at c and f is continuous at $g(c)$, then $f \circ g(x) = f\big(g(x)\big)$ is continuous at c.

If a function g is differentiable at c, then f is continuous at c; in other words, *differentiability implies continuity*. Therefore, if f is *not* continuous at c, then f is also *not* differentiable at c. *Caution:* Continuity does *not* imply differentiability. A function can be continuous at a point a even though $f'(x)$ does not exist at a. This circumstance occurs when there is a cusp (a sharp corner) or a vertical tangent line at a.

Analyzing the Behavior of a Function

For this topic, you must be able to analyze the behavior of a function (for example, find relative maxima and minima, concavity), solve problems involving related rates, and solve applied minima-maxima problems (*Mathematics: Content Knowledge (0061) Test at a Glance*, page 4).

If f is continuous on a closed interval $[a, b]$ and differentiable on the open interval (a, b), then (i) f is **increasing** on $[a, b]$ if $f'(x) > 0$ on (a, b); (ii) f is **decreasing** on $[a, b]$ if $f'(x) < 0$ on (a, b); and (iii) f is **constant** on $[a, b]$ if $f'(x) = 0$ on (a, b).

Let f be defined on an interval containing c, then $f(c)$ is a **minimum** (also, called the **absolute minimum**) of f in the interval if $f(c) \leq f(x)$ for every number x in the interval; similarly, $f(c)$ is a **maximum** (also, called the **absolute maximum**) of f in the interval if $f(c) \geq f(x)$ for every number x in the interval. The minimum and maximum values of a function in an interval are the **extreme values,** or **extrema,** of the function in the interval.

The Extreme Value Theorem states that if f is continuous on a closed interval $[a, b]$, then f has both a minimum and a maximum value in $[a, b]$.

> **Tip: The Extreme Value Theorem tells you when the minimum and maximum of a function exist, but not how to find these values. You can use the minimum-maximum feature of your graphing calculator to find the extreme values of a function.**

The number $f(c)$ is a **relative minimum** of a function f if there exists an open interval containing c in which $f(c)$ is a minimum; similarly, the number $f(c)$ is a **relative maximum** of a function f if there exists an open interval containing c in which $f(c)$ is a maximum. If $f(c)$ is a relative minimum or maximum of f, it is called a **relative extremum** of f.

If c is a number in the domain of f, c is called a **critical number** of f if either $f'(c) = 0$ or $f'(c)$ does not exist. The critical numbers determine points at which $f'(x)$ can change signs.

If f has a relative extremum at c, then either $f'(c) = 0$ or $f'(c)$ does not exist.

A **sign diagram** for $f'(x)$ is a diagram along the real line showing the signs for $f'(x)$ between critical numbers for f. You can use a sign diagram to predict the shape of the graph of f.

The **First Derivative Test** provides that if c is a critical number of a function f that is continuous on an open interval (a, b) containing c, then (i) if $f'(x)$ changes sign from negative to positive as x increases through c, then $f(c)$ is a relative minimum of f; and (ii) if $f'(x)$ changes sign from positive to negative as x increases through c, then $f(c)$ is a relative maximum of f.

The **Second Derivative Test** provides that if $f'(c) = 0$ and $f''(c)$ exists on an open interval containing c, then (i) $f(c)$ is a relative minimum of f if $f''(c) > 0$; and (ii) $f(c)$ is a relative maximum of f if $f''(c) < 0$. If $f''(c) = 0$, the test is inconclusive.

If f is a function whose first and second derivatives exist on some open interval containing the number c, then (i) the graph of f is **concave upward** at $(c, f(c))$ if $f''(c) > 0$, and (ii) the graph of f is **concave downward** at $(c, f(c))$ if $f''(c) < 0$.

The point $(c, f(c))$ is a **point of inflection** if the concavity of the graph of f changes at $(c, f(c))$.

> **Tip: A methodical way to analyze the behavior of a function is to proceed as follows: First, find the critical number(s) of f by solving $f'(x) = 0$ or for which $f'(x)$ does not exist; next, use the First Derivative Test, a sign diagram, and, if applicable, the Second Derivative Test to find relative extrema; and then use $f''(c)$, if it exists, to investigate concavity and identify points of inflection.**

The Mean Value Theorem and the Fundamental Theorem of Calculus

For this topic, you must demonstrate an understanding of and ability to use the Mean Value Theorem and the Fundamental Theorem of Calculus (*Mathematics: Content Knowledge (0061) Test at a Glance*, page 4).

The Mean Value Theorem states that if the function f is continuous in the closed interval $[a, b]$ and $f'(x)$ exists on the open interval (a, b), then there exists a number c in (a, b) such that $f(b) - f(a) = (b - a)f'(c)$.

The function F is called an **antiderivative** (or **indefinite integral**) of the function f if $F' = f$.

The **Fundamental Theorem of Calculus** states that if f is continuous on the closed interval $[a, b]$ and F is an anti-derivative of f on $[a, b]$, then the evaluation of the **definite integral** $\int_a^b f(x)\,dx$ is given by $\int_a^b f(x)\,dx = F(b) - F(a)$. (Note: See the next section titled "Integration as a Limiting Sum" for a discussion of definite integrals).

The following notation is used when applying the Fundamental Theorem of Calculus: $\int_a^b f(x)\,dx = F(x)\big|_a^b = F(b) - F(a)$.

If the function f is continuous and has an antiderivative on the closed interval $[a, b]$, then the **average value** of f on $[a, b]$ is $\frac{1}{b-a}\int_a^b f(x)\,dx$.

The **Second Fundamental Theorem of Calculus** states that if f is continuous on an open interval containing c, then for every x in the interval $\frac{d}{dx}\int_c^x f(x)\,dx = f(x)$.

Properties of Integrals
If f is defined at $x = a$, then $\int_a^a f(x)\,dx = 0$.
If f is integrable on $[a, b]$, then $\int_a^b f(x)\,dx = -\int_b^a f(x)\,dx$.
If f is integrable on $[a, b]$ and k is a constant, then the function kf is integrable on $[a, b]$ and $\int_a^b kf(x)\,dx = k\int_a^b f(x)\,dx$.
If f and g are integrable on $[a, b]$, then the functions $f \pm g$ are integrable on $[a, b]$ and $\int_a^b \big(f(x) \pm g(x)\big)\,dx = \int_a^b f(x)\,dx \pm \int_a^b g(x)\,dx$.
If f is integrable on $[a, b]$, $[a, c]$, and $[c, b]$, then $\int_a^b f(x)\,dx = \int_a^c f(x)\,dx + \int_c^b f(x)\,dx$.
If f is integrable on $[-a, a]$ and f is even, then $\int_{-a}^a f(x)\,dx = 2\int_0^a f(x)\,dx$.
If f is integrable on $[-a, a]$ and f is odd, then $\int_{-a}^a f(x)\,dx = 0$.

Integration as a Limiting Sum

For this topic, you must demonstrate an intuitive understanding of integration as a limiting sum that can be used to compute area, volume, distance, or other accumulation processes (*Mathematics: Content Knowledge (0061) Test at a Glance*, page 5).

If a function f is defined on the closed interval $[a, b]$, then the **definite integral** of f from a to b is defined as a limiting sum given by: $\int_a^b f(x)\,dx = \lim\limits_{\max \Delta x_i \to 0} \sum\limits_{i=1}^n f(c_i)\Delta x_i$, where $[a, b]$ is divided into n subintervals (not necessarily equal), c_i is a point in the ith subinterval $[x_{i-1}, x_i]$, and $\Delta x_i = x_i - x_{i-1}$, provided this limit exists. The limiting sum, $\lim\limits_{\max \Delta x_i \to 0} \sum\limits_{i=1}^n f(c_i)\Delta x_i$, in the definition of definite integral is called a **Riemann Sum.** For the Mathematics CK, you will not have to use the definition of definite integral to evaluate integrals; however, it is important that you understand integration as a limiting sum.

If f is a nonnegative, continuous function on the closed interval $[a, b]$, then the area of the region bounded by the graph of f, the x-axis, and the vertical lines $x = a$ and $x = b$ is given by: Area $= \int_a^b f(x)\,dx$.

> **Tip: Your graphing calculator has a numerical integration feature that you can use to find the area under a curve to a close approximation.**

If f and g are continuous functions on the closed interval $[a, b]$ and $f(x) \geq g(x)$ on $[a, b]$, then the area of the region bounded by $y = f(x)$, $y = g(x)$, and the vertical lines $x = a$ and $x = b$ is given by: Area $= \int_a^b \left(f(x) - g(x) \right) dx$.

> **Tip: For the Mathematics CK, if asked to find the area enclosed by two curves, first, you might need to find the points of intersection of the two curves to determine a and b. Your graphing calculator has features that will allow you to find where the curves intersect, or you might elect to find the points of intersection algebraically. After determining a and b, you can numerically evaluate the integral using the numerical integration feature of your calculator.**

The definite integral can be used to compute area under a curve or between two curves as shown in this section. It can also be used to compute the volume of three-dimensional figures, accumulated distance, accumulated production, the total of a continuous income stream, and the results of other limiting sum processes.

Approximation of Derivatives and Integrals

For this topic, you must be able to numerically approximate derivatives and integrals (*Mathematics: Content Knowledge (0061) Test at a Glance*, page 4).

If $f'(x)$ exists, then the numerical value of f' at c is $f'(c)$. Analytically, this means that to find the numerical value of the derivative of a function at a point c, you must first find the derivative of the function, and then evaluate the derivative of the function at the point c. For the Mathematics CK, the most efficient way to find the numerical value of the derivative of a function at a point c is to use the numerical derivative feature of your graphing calculator to obtain a close approximation of the answer.

Analytically, since $\int_a^b f(x)\,dx = F(x)\big|_a^b = F(b) - F(a)$, to find the numerical value of the integral $\int_a^b f(x)\,dx$, you would first find an antiderivative (say F) for f, evaluate that antiderivative at a and b, and then find the difference, $F(b) - F(a)$. This approach is very time-consuming, so for the Mathematics CK, the most efficient way to find the numerical value of the derivative of an integral is to use the numerical integration feature of your graphing calculator to obtain a close approximation of the answer—*provided you are confident that* f *can be integrated using a formula*. If f is a function that cannot be integrated using a formula, a graphing calculator might give an approximation that is totally incorrect. (See the Trapezoid Rule and Simpson's Rule later in this chapter for two techniques for dealing with integrals containing functions that cannot be integrated using a formula.)

> **Tip: For the Mathematics CK, you are expected to bring a graphing calculator that can compute both derivatives of functions numerically and definite integrals numerically. The time limitations for the test have been determined based on the assumption that you will be using such a calculator. Therefore, it is vital that you practice using the time-saving numerical derivative and numerical integration features of your calculator as you encounter such problems in the practice tests in this CliffsTestPrep book—so that you will become adept at using these features before you take the official Mathematics CK.**

You should be aware that some functions cannot be integrated by using a formula. In addition to the Riemann sum formula, the following two techniques are **numerical integration methods** that can be used to approximate a definite integral for a function f that is continuous on a closed interval $[a, b]$.

Trapezoid Rule: $\int_a^b f(x)\,dx \doteq \frac{b-a}{2n}[f(x_0) + 2f(x_1) + 2f(x_2) + \ldots + 2f(x_{n-1}) + f(x_n)]$, where $[a, b]$ is divided into n subdivisions.

Simpson's Rule: $\int_a^b f(x)\,dx \doteq \frac{b-a}{3n}[f(x_0) + 4f(x_1) + 2f(x_2) + 4f(x_3) + \ldots + 2f(x_{n-2}) + 4f(x_{n-1}) + f(x_n)]$, where $[a, b]$ is divided into an even number n of equal subdivisions.

Differentiation and Integration Techniques

For this topic, you must be able to use standard differentiation and integration techniques (*Mathematics: Content Knowledge (0061) Test at a Glance*, page 4).

The process of finding a derivative is called **differentiation.** You will need to know the following differentiation formulas for the Mathematics CK test.

Differentiation Formulas

$$\frac{d}{dx}k = 0, \text{ for } k \text{ a real number} \qquad \frac{d}{dx}x = 1 \qquad \frac{d}{dx}x^n = n\,x^{n-1}, \text{ for } n \text{ a rational number}$$

$$\frac{d}{dx}\sin x = \cos x \qquad \frac{d}{dx}\cos x = -\sin x \qquad \frac{d}{dx}\tan x = \sec^2 x$$

$$\frac{d}{dx}\sec x = \sec x \tan x \qquad \frac{d}{dx}\csc x = -\csc x \cot x \qquad \frac{d}{dx}\cot x = -\csc^2 x$$

$$\frac{d}{dx}\ln x = \frac{1}{x} \qquad \frac{d}{dx}e^x = e^x$$

If f and g are differentiable at x,

$$\frac{d}{dx}kf(x) = kf'(x), \text{ for } k \text{ a real number}$$

$(f(x) \pm g(x))' = f'(x) \pm g'(x)$ (Sum and Difference Formulas)

$(f(x)g(x))' = f'(x) \cdot g(x) + f(x) \cdot g'(x)$ (Product Formula)

$\left(\dfrac{f(x)}{g(x)}\right)' = \dfrac{f'(x)\,g(x) - f(x)\,g'(x)}{\left(g(x)\right)^2}$, provided $g(x) \neq 0$ (Quotient Formula)

$(f(g(x)))' = f'(g(x)) \cdot g'(x)$ (Chain Rule)

Note: The formulas for $(f(x)g(x))'$, $\left(\dfrac{f(x)}{g(x)}\right)'$, and $(f(g(x)))'$ are given in the Notation, Definitions, and Formulas pages at the beginning of the Mathematics CK test booklet.

The process of integrating a function is called **integration.** You will need to know the following integration formulas for the Mathematics CK test. The constant C in the formulas is called the **constant of integration.**

Integration Formulas

$$\int 0\,dx = C \qquad\qquad \int k\,dx = kx + C \qquad\qquad \int x^n\,dx = \frac{x^{n+1}}{n+1} + C, n \neq 1$$

$$\int \cos x\,dx = \sin x + C \qquad \int \sin x\,dx = -\cos x + C \qquad \int \sec^2 x\,dx = \tan x + C$$

$$\int \sec x \tan x\,dx = \sec x + C \qquad \int \csc x \cot x\,dx = -\csc x + C \qquad \int \csc^2 x\,dx = -\cot x + C$$

$$\int \frac{1}{x}\,dx = \ln|x| + C \qquad\qquad \int e^x\,dx = e^x + C$$

Change of Variable: $\int_a^b f\left(g(x)\right)g'(x)\,dx = \int_{g(a)}^{g(b)} f(u)\,du$, where $u = g(x)$ and $du = g'(x)dx$

Integration by Parts: $\int u\,dv = uv - \int v\,du$

> **Note: The formula for integration by parts is given in the Notation, Definitions, and Formulas pages at the beginning of the Mathematics CK test booklet.**

Limits of Sequences and Series

For this topic, you must be able to determine the limits of sequences and simple infinite series (*Mathematics: Content Knowledge (0061) Test at a Glance*, page 5).

A **sequence** is a function whose domain is the set of positive integers. The notation a_n denotes the image of the integer n, and a_n is called the **nth term** (or **element**) of the sequence. We use $\{a_n\}$ or $a_1, a_2, \ldots, a_n, \ldots$, to denote a sequence with nth term a_n.

The sequence $a_1, a_2, \ldots, a_n, \ldots$, has **limit** L, written $\lim_{n \to \infty} a_n = L$, if for every number $\varepsilon > 0$, there exists a number M such that $|a_n - L| < \varepsilon$ whenever $n > M$. A sequence that has a limit is said to **converge** to that limit. Sequences that do not converge are said to **diverge.**

Three important limits of sequences you need to know for the Mathematics CK are the following:

$$\lim_{n \to \infty} k = k, \text{ for } k \text{ a real number} \qquad \lim_{n \to \infty} \frac{1}{n} = 0 \qquad \lim_{n \to \infty} \frac{k}{n^p} = 0, \text{ for } k \text{ a real number and } p \text{ any positive rational number}$$

Assuming that the sequences $\{a_n\}$ and $\{b_n\}$ have limits that exist, the following fundamental properties hold.

Properties of Limits of Sequences

Sum or Difference $\qquad \lim_{n \to \infty}[a_n \pm b_n] = \lim_{n \to \infty} a_n \pm \lim_{n \to \infty} b_n$

Product $\qquad\qquad\quad \lim_{n \to \infty}[a_n \cdot b_n] = \lim_{n \to \infty} a_n \cdot \lim_{n \to \infty} b_n$

Quotient $\qquad\qquad\quad \lim_{n \to \infty} \frac{a_n}{b_n} = \frac{\lim_{n \to \infty} a_n}{\lim_{n \to \infty} b_n}$, provided $b_n \neq 0$ and $\lim_{n \to \infty} b_n \neq 0$

Scalar Multiplication $\quad \lim_{n \to \infty} ka_n = k \lim_{n \to \infty} a_n$, for any real number k

Some useful theorems about limits of sequences are the following:

If $a_n \leq c_n \leq b_n$ for each integer n and if $\lim_{n \to \infty} a_n = \lim_{n \to \infty} b_n = L$, then $\lim_{n \to \infty} c_n = L$. (The **Squeeze Theorem**)

If $\lim_{n \to \infty} a_n = L$, then $\lim_{n \to \infty} |a_n| = |L|$.

If $\lim_{n \to \infty} |a_n| = 0$, then $\lim_{n \to \infty} a_n = 0$.

A sequence is **monotonic** if either (i) its terms are **nondecreasing** $a_1 \leq a_2 \leq a_3 \ldots \leq a_n \leq \ldots$ or (ii) its terms are **nonincreasing** $a_1 \geq a_2 \geq a_3 \ldots \geq a_n \geq \ldots$.

A sequence is **bounded above** if there is a real number b_{upper} such that $a_n \leq b_{upper}$ for all n. A sequence is **bounded below** if there is a real number b_{lower} such that $b_{lower} \leq a_n$ for all n. A sequence is **bounded** if it is bounded above and bounded below.

If a sequence is monotonic and bounded, then it converges.

If $\{a_n\}$ is an infinite sequence, then $\sum_{n=1}^{\infty} a_n = a_1 + a_2 + a_3 + \ldots + a_n + \ldots$ is an **infinite series** (also called **series**). The notation a_n denotes the **nth term** of the series. You can also represent the series $\sum_{n=1}^{\infty} a_n$ as $\sum a_n$.

Associated with each infinite series is its **sequence of partial sums:** $S_1 = a_1$, $S_2 = a_1 + a_2$, $S_3 = a_1 + a_2 + a_3, \ldots, S_n = a_1 + a_2 + a_3 + \ldots + a_n, \ldots$. An infinite series with partial sums $S_1, S_2, S_3, \ldots, S_n, \ldots$ is said to **converge** if and only if $\lim_{n \to \infty} S_n$ exists. If the limit does not exist, then the infinite series is said to **diverge**. For a convergent series, if $\lim_{n \to \infty} S_n = S$, the number S is called the **sum of the series.**

If $\sum_{n=1}^{\infty} a_n$ and $\sum_{n=1}^{\infty} b_n$ converge, then the following properties hold.

Properties of Convergent Series

Sum or Difference $\qquad \sum_{n=1}^{\infty} (a_n \pm b_n) = \sum_{n=1}^{\infty} a_n \pm \sum_{n=1}^{\infty} b_n.$

Scalar Multiplication $\qquad \sum_{n=1}^{\infty} ka_n = k \sum_{n=1}^{\infty} a_n,$ for any real number k.

An infinite series of the form $\sum_{n=1}^{\infty} ar^{n-1} = a_1 + a_2 r + a_3 r^2 + \ldots + a_n r^{n-1} + \ldots$ is called a **geometric series** with ratio r. This series diverges if $|r| \geq 1$ and converges if $0 < |r| < 1$. The sum of a geometric series that converges is given by: $\sum_{n=1}^{\infty} ar^{n-1} = \frac{a}{1-r},$ where $0 < |r| < 1$.

If the series $\sum a_n$ converges, then the sequence $\{a_n\}$ converges to 0. Thus, if the sequence $\{a_n\}$ does *not* converge to 0, then $\sum a_n$ diverges. This latter statement is sometimes called "the ***nth* term test for divergence.**" That is, if the limit of the *n*th term of the series does *not* converge to 0, then the series diverges. *Caution:* Do not interpret this to mean that if the *n*th term of the series does converge to 0, that the series converges. When the limit of the *n*th term of a series converges to 0, you can draw no conclusions about convergence or divergence of the series based solely on that information.

Tip: Sometimes it is convenient to begin an infinite sequence or series at $n = 0$ instead of $n = 1$, so be sure to check for the starting value of *n* when you work problems involving sequences or series on the Mathematics CK.

Note: See the section titled "Arithmetic and Geometric Sequences and Series" in the chapter titled "Discrete Mathematics" for an additional discussion of sequences and series.

Data Analysis and Statistics

According to the *Mathematics: Content Knowledge Test (0061) at a Glance* (www.ets.org/Media/Tests/PRAXIS/pdf/ 0061.pdf), the Data Analysis and Statistics content category of the Mathematics CK tests your knowledge and skills in seven topic areas:

- Organizing data
- Measures of central tendency and dispersion
- Regression
- Normal distributions
- Informal inference
- Types of studies
- Characteristics of well-designed studies

This review discusses the key ideas and formulas in each topic area that are most important for you to know for the Mathematics CK.

Organizing Data

For this topic, you must be able to organize data into a suitable form (for example, construct a histogram and use it in the calculation of probabilities) (*Mathematics: Content Knowledge (0061) Test at a Glance*, page 5).

There are several ways to record, organize, and present data. On the Mathematics CK, you will be expected to perform data analysis by reading and interpreting information from **charts** and **tables, pictographs, circle graphs, line graphs, dotplots, stem-leaf plots, bar graphs, histograms,** and **scatterplots.**

Charts and **tables** organize information in columns and rows. Each column or row is labeled to explain the entries. A **frequency table** is a tabular representation of data that shows the frequency of each value in the data set. A **relative frequency table** shows the frequency of each value as a proportion of the whole set. The total of all relative frequencies should be 100 percent, but instead might be very close to 100 percent, due to round-off error.

In a **pictograph,** pictures or symbols are used to represent numbers. Each symbol represents a given number of a particular item. The symbol, its meaning, and the quantity it represents should be stated on the graph. To read a pictograph, count the number of symbols in a row and multiply this number by the scale indicated on the graph. Sometimes, a fraction of a symbol is shown. In that case, approximate the fraction and use it accordingly.

A **circle graph,** or **pie chart,** is a graph in the shape of a circle. Circle graphs are used to display the relationship of each type or class of data within a whole set of data in a visual form. It is also called a "pie" chart because it looks like a pie cut into wedge-shaped slices. The wedges are labeled to show the categories for the graph. Each sector angle represents a specific part of the whole. Usually percents are used to show the amount of the graph that corresponds to each category. The total amount in percentage shown on the graph is 100 percent. The graph is made by dividing the 360 degrees of the circle into portions that correspond to the percentages for each category. Reading a circle graph is a simple matter of reading the percents displayed on the graph for the different categories.

A **line graph** uses lines or broken lines for representing data. It has both a horizontal and a vertical scale. The data points for the graph are plotted as ordered pairs of numbers, according to the two scales. Line segments are used to connect consecutive points. Sometimes, two or more sets of data are plotted on the same graph. The slant of the line between the points shows whether the data values are increasing, decreasing, or remaining at a constant value. If the line slants upward, the data values are increasing; if the line slants downward, the data values are decreasing; and a horizontal line (no slant) means that the data values remain constant. Line graphs are useful for showing change over time.

A **dotplot** (or **line plot**) is a graph in which the possible values of the data are indicated along the horizontal axis, and points (or dots) are placed above each value to indicate the number of times that that value occurs in the data.

A **stem and leaf plot** is a graphical representation of data in which each data value is separated into two parts: a stem (such as the leftmost digit for data consisting of two-digit numbers) and a leaf (such as the rightmost digit for data consisting of two-digit numbers). The stems are listed once (commonly) vertically (from smallest to largest), and the corresponding leaves for the data values are listed horizontally (from smallest to largest) beside the appropriate stem.

A **bar graph** uses bars to represent frequencies, percents, or amounts. The bars correspond to different categories that are labeled at the base of the bars. The bars in a bar graph may be displayed vertically or horizontally. The widths of the bars are equal. The length or height of the bar indicates the number, percent, or amount for the category for that particular bar. A scale (usually beginning with 0) marked with equally spaced values will be shown on the graph. To read a bar graph, examine the scale to determine the units and the amount between the marked values. Then determine where the endpoints of the bars fall in relation to the scale.

A **histogram** is a special type of bar graph that summarizes data by using totals within intervals. The intervals are of equal length and cover from the lowest to the highest data value. The range of the data is divided into class intervals for which the frequency of occurrence is represented by a rectangular column. The height of the column is proportional to the frequency of observations within the interval. Unlike the bars in other bar graphs, the bars in a histogram are side-by-side with no space in between. In a **relative frequency histogram** the vertical scale is marked with relative frequencies instead of actual frequencies (or counts). The total of the relative frequencies should be 100 percent, but might instead be very close to 100 percent due to round-off error.

A **scatterplot** is a graph of **bivariate data,** paired values of data from two variables, plotted on a coordinate grid. The data are paired in a way that matches each value from one variable with a corresponding value from the other variable. The pattern of the plot can be helpful in determining whether there is a relationship between the two variables; and, if there is, the nature of that relationship.

Drawing valid conclusions from graphical representations of data requires that you have read the graph accurately and analyzed the graphical information correctly. Sometimes a graphical representation will distort the data in some way, leading you to draw an invalid conclusion.

When you have to interpret graphical information on the Mathematics CK, follow these suggestions:

- Make sure that you understand the title of the graph.
- Read the labels on the parts of the graph to understand what is being represented.
- Make sure that you know what each picture in a pictograph represents.
- Examine carefully the scale of bar graphs, line graphs, histograms, and scatterplots.
- Look for trends such as increases (rising values), decreases (falling values), and periods of inactivity (constant values, horizontal lines) in line graphs.
- Look for concentrations of data points and the shape of the data for dotplots, stem-leaf plots, bar graphs, histograms, and scatterplots.
- Make sure that the numbers add up correctly.
- Be prepared to do some simple arithmetic calculations.
- Use only the information in the graph. Do not answer based on your personal knowledge or opinion.
- Mark and draw on the graphs in the test booklet.

Measures of Central Tendency and Dispersions

For this topic, you must know and be able to find the appropriate uses of common measures of central tendency (for example, population mean, sample mean, median, mode) and dispersion (for example, range, population standard deviation, sample standard deviation, population variance, sample variance) (*Mathematics: Content Knowledge (0061) Test at a Glance*, page 5).

A **measure of central tendency** is a numerical value that describes a data set by providing a "central" or "typical" value of the data set. The three most common measures of central tendency are the **mean, median,** and **mode.** Each of these measures represents a different way of describing a typical value of a set of data. Measures of central tendency should have the same units as those of the data values from which they are determined. If no units are specified, as in test scores, then the measure of central tendency will not specify units.

The **mean** of a data set is another name for the arithmetic average of the data values. To calculate the mean: first, sum the data values; and then, divide by the number of data values that are in the data set; that is, the mean = $\dfrac{\text{the sum of the data values}}{\text{the number of data values in the data set}}$.

> **Tip: Using the statistical features of your graphing calculator is a quick and efficient way to calculate the mean of a data set.**

The **median** is the middle value or the average of the two middle values in an *ordered* set of data. Determining the median of a data set is a two-step process: First, put the data values in order from least to greatest (or greatest to least). Find the middle data value. If there is no single middle data value, find the mean of the two middle data values.

> **Tip: Using the statistical features of your graphing calculator is a quick and efficient way to calculate the median of a data set. If you determine the median without using your graphing calculator, don't make the common mistake of neglecting to put the numbers in order first.**

The **mode** is the data value or values that occur most frequently in a data set; there can be one mode, more than one mode, or no mode. If two or more values occur most frequently, then each will be a mode. When each value in the data set appears the same number of times, there is no mode.

The mean, median, and mode are ways to describe a central value of a data set. To know which of these measures of central tendency you should use to describe a data set, consider their characteristics.

The **mean** has several important characteristics.

- Although the mean represents a central or typical value of a data set, the mean does not have to be one of the values in the data set.
- The actual data values are used in the computation of the mean. If any one value is changed, the value of the mean will change.
- A disadvantage of the mean is that it is influenced by outliers, especially in a small data set. An **outlier** is a data value that is extremely high or extremely low in comparison to most of the other data values. If a data set contains extremely high values that are not balanced by corresponding low values, the mean will be misleadingly high. Similarly, if a data set contains extremely low values that are not balanced by corresponding high values, the mean will be misleadingly low.

The **median** is the most useful alternative to the mean as a measure of central tendency.

- Like the mean, the median does not have to be one of the values in the data set. If the data set contains an odd number of data values, the median will be the middle value; however, for an even number of data values, the median is the arithmetic mean of the two middle values.
- The median is not influenced by outliers.
- A disadvantage of the median as an indicator of a central value is that it is based on relative size rather than on the actual values in the data set.

The **mode** is the simplest measure of central tendency to calculate.

- If a data set has a mode, the mode (or modes) is one of the data values.
- The mode is the only appropriate measure of central tendency for data that are strictly nonnumeric.
- A disadvantage of the mode as an indicator of a central value is that it is based on relative frequency rather than on all the values in the set.

A **measure of dispersion** is a value that describes the spread of the data about the central value. Although measures of central tendency are important for describing data sets, their interpretation is enhanced when the spread or dispersion about the central value is known. For the Mathematics CK test, measures of dispersion you need to know are the **range, standard deviation,** and **variance.**

The **range** for a data set is the difference between the **maximum value** (the greatest value) and the **minimum value** (least value) in the data set: range = maximum value – minimum value. The range should have the same units as those of the data values from which it is computed. If no units are specified, then the range will not specify units.

The range gives some indication of the spread of the values in a data set, but its value is determined by only two of the data values. The extent of spread of the other numbers is not considered. A measure of dispersion that takes into account all the data values is the **standard deviation.** The formula for the **standard deviation,** σ (pronounced "sig-muh"), **of a population** (see the section titled "Informal Inference" in this chapter for a definition of the term *population*) with mean $\mu = \frac{\sum x}{N}$ (pronounced "mew") is given by: $\sigma = \sqrt{\frac{\sum(x-\mu)^2}{N}}$, where N is the number of elements in the population. The formula for the **standard deviation, s, of a sample** (see the section titled "Informal Inference" in this chapter for a definition of the term *sample*) with mean $\bar{x}$ (pronounced "eks-bar") is given by: $s = \sqrt{\frac{\sum(x-\bar{x})^2}{n-1}}$, where n is the number of elements in the sample. The **standard deviation** is a measure of the dispersion of a set of data values about the mean of the data set. If there is no dispersion in a data set, each data value equals the mean, giving a standard deviation of zero. The more the data values vary from the mean, the greater the standard deviation, meaning the data set has more spread. The standard deviation should have the same units as those of the data values from which it is computed. If no units are specified, then the standard deviation will not specify units.

The **variance of a population,** σ^2, is the square of the standard deviation of the population. The **variance of a sample,** s^2, is the square of the standard deviation of the sample.

Tip: Your graphing calculator will calculate the standard deviation and variance for a *sample*. For the Mathematics CK, if a problem requires that you calculate a standard deviation or variance, assume that you are calculating values for a sample unless you are told specifically otherwise.

Other measures that are used to describe a data set are percentiles and quartiles. The *P*th percentile is a value at or below which *P* percent of the data fall. For example, the median is the 50th percentile because 50 percent of the data fall below the median. **Quartiles** are values that divide an ordered data set into four portions, each of which contains approximately one-fourth of the data. Twenty-five percent of the data values are below the **first quartile** (also called the **25th percentile**); 50 percent of the data values are below the **second quartile** (also called the **50th percentile**), which is the same as the median; and 75 percent of the data values are below the **third quartile** (also called the **75th percentile**).

For a set of data, the **5-number summary** consists of the minimum value, the first quartile, the median, the third quartile, and the maximum value. A **box-and-whiskers plot** is a graphical representation of the 5-number summary for a data set.

A data set can be described in terms of the skewness of its distribution. **Skewness** describes the "lopsidedness" of the distribution. A distribution that is symmetric has no skew. A distribution that has a longer tail to the right is **positively skewed.** A distribution that has a longer tail to the left is **negatively skewed.** In a distribution with no skew, the mean, median, and mode are equal. In a positively skewed distribution the mean will lie to the right of the median. In a negatively skewed distribution, the mean will lie to the left of the median.

Regression

For this topic, you must be able to analyze data from specific situations to determine what type of function (for example, linear, quadratic, exponential) would most likely model that particular phenomenon; use the regression feature of the calculator to determine the curve of best fit; and interpret the regression coefficients, correlation, and residuals in context (*Mathematics: Content Knowledge (0061) Test at a Glance*, page 5).

Simple regression is an area of statistics in which a relation between an **independent variable** x (also called the **predictor** or **explanatory variable**) and a **dependent variable** y (also called the **response variable**) is explained through an equation.

Scatterplots are used to help determine the type of relationship that exists between the two variables. (See the section titled "Organizing Data" in this chapter for a description of the term *scatterplot*.) For the Mathematics CK, you will be expected to examine scatterplots and distinguish between those indicating linear and those indicating nonlinear relationships between two variables as illustrated here.

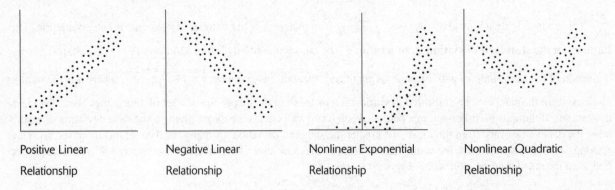

Positive Linear
Relationship

Negative Linear
Relationship

Nonlinear Exponential
Relationship

Nonlinear Quadratic
Relationship

If the scatterplot of the data seems approximately linear, the **line of best fit** is the line that fits the data best and is given by the equation: $\hat{y} = ax + b$, where a and b are called the **regression coefficients.** The **residuals** are the differences between the actual y-values in the scatterplot and the $\hat{y}$-values predicted by the linear equation. The line of best fit minimizes the sum of squares of the residuals and is called the **least-squares regression line.**

For the Mathematics CK, you will be expected to use your graphing calculator to compute the equation of the least-squares regression line and the correlation coefficient r between the x and y values. Consult your owner's manual for details on how to use the regression features of your graphing calculator. *Note:* Most calculators will use y instead of $\hat{y}$ in the regression equation.

The **correlation coefficient** is a numerical measure that describes the strength of the linear relationship between the two variables under consideration. Correlation coefficients range between −1 and +1, with −1 indicating a "perfect" negative correlation, and +1 indicating a "perfect" positive correlation. Correlation values very close to either −1 or +1 indicate very *strong* correlations. If the two variables have no relationship to each other, then the correlation coefficient will be zero. The further the correlation coefficient is from zero, the stronger is the relationship. (Remember, however, that you cannot have correlation coefficients below −1 or above +1.) Since the **correlation coefficient** is a measure of the strength of the linear relationship between the independent and dependent variables of the linear regression equation, it can be used as an estimate of the "goodness of fit" of the regression line. The closer $|r|$ is to 1, the more perfect is the linear relationship between x and y. If r is close to zero, there is little or no linear relationship, so the line is not a good fit for the data.

Normal Distributions

For this topic, you must demonstrate an understanding of and be able to apply normal distributions and their characteristics (for example, mean, standard deviation) (*Mathematics: Content Knowledge (0061) Test at a Glance*, page 5).

According to the **68-95-99.7 rule**, approximately 68 percent of the values of a random variable that is normally distributed falls within 1 standard deviation of the mean, about 95 percent falls within two standard deviations of the mean, and about 99.7 percent falls within 3 standard deviations of the mean. A result of the 68-95-99.7 rule is that a normal distribution with mean μ and standard deviation σ can be subdivided as shown in the following figure.

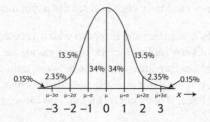

The numbers written horizontally along the bottom of the figure are simply measures of standard deviations from the mean, called **z-scores**. In working problems involving a normally distributed random variable X, you will often find it necessary to convert into units of standard deviations from the mean using the formula $z\text{-score} = \dfrac{x\text{-value} - \mu}{\sigma}$.

> **Tip:** Using the statistical features of your graphing calculator is an efficient and time-saving way to work problems involving the normal distribution. Consult your owner's manual for detailed instructions on how to find percentages and probabilities using areas under a normal curve and how to find a z-score corresponding to a known probability obtained from a normal distribution.

Informal Inference

For this topic, you must demonstrate an understanding of how sample statistics reflect the values of population parameters and use sampling distributions as the basis for informal inference (*Mathematics: Content Knowledge Test (0061) at a Glance*, page 5).

A **population** is the set of all elements (subjects, experimental units) under investigation. A **parameter** is a numerical value that describes some aspect of a population. Customary symbols for the two population parameters, mean and standard deviation, are μ and σ, respectively.

A **sample** is a subset of the population. A **statistic** is a numerical measurement that is computed from a sample. Customary symbols for the two sample statistics, mean and standard deviation, are $\bar{x}$ and s, respectively.

In **inferential statistics** information from samples is used to make estimates, predictions, decisions, or generalizations about a population. Statistics from samples are used to estimate population parameters. For convenience, this chapter uses x to represent a numerical measurement on a population or sample element.

A **sampling distribution** is the probability distribution of the values of a sample statistic obtained from all possible samples of the same size.

The **sampling distribution of the mean** ($\bar{x}$) has the following properties: (i) the mean of the sampling distribution of $\bar{x}$ = the mean of the sampled population; (ii) the standard deviation of the sampling distribution of $\bar{x}$ = $\dfrac{\text{Standard deviation of the sampled population}}{\text{Square root of the sample size}}$, (provided the standard deviation is positive); and (iii) the sampling distribution of $\bar{x}$ approaches the normal distribution as the sample size increases (**Central Limit Theorem**).

Types of Studies

For this topic, you must demonstrate an understanding of the differences among various kinds of studies and which types of inferences can legitimately be drawn from each (*Mathematics: Content Knowledge (0061) Test at a Glance*, page 5).

Quantitative studies fall into four broad categories: **survey, correlational, experimental,** or **observational.**

In **survey** studies, the purpose is to gather information from a representative sample in order to generalize to a population of interest. Examples of this type of study include opinion surveys, fact-finding surveys, and questionnaire and interview studies. Results are summarized and reported. Generalization of the survey results to the population would be appropriate only when the sample has been randomly chosen from the population and is of adequate size.

In **correlational** studies, the purpose is to investigate the extent to which variations in one variable correspond with variations in another variable. Example of such studies include investigating the relationship between performance on a standardized reading test and time spent reading independently, between college grades and high school GPA, and between income and years of education. It is very important to note that correlational studies *cannot* show causation. In other words, if two variables are correlated, it does not mean that one causes the other.

In **experimental** studies, the purpose is to investigate possible cause-and-effect relationships by exposing an experimental group to a treatment condition and comparing the results to a control group not receiving the treatment. The study is set up in such a way that one group of experimental units get the treatment (the experimental group) and another group (the control group) does not, and then comparisons are made to see whether the treatment had an influence on the variable of interest. In order for such comparisons to be valid, other sources of variation must be controlled. Examples of such studies include investigating the effectiveness of a new method of teaching reading on reading ability, the effect of a new drug on cancer patients, and the effect of a type of fertilizer on plant growth. In a well-designed experimental study, experimental units are randomly assigned to either the treatment or control group to assure that groups are similar in all respects *except* for the treatment. Therefore, any difference in the two groups can be attributed to the treatment. Only when investigators conduct a well-designed experimental study would a cause-and-effect conclusion be valid.

Observational studies involve collecting and analyzing data without changing existing conditions. Observational studies are conducted when it is not possible (or, perhaps, not appropriate) to randomly assign experimental units to some treatment condition (for example, being a smoker). Such studies are conducted in a setting that does not permit the investigator to manipulate or control all relevant variables. The nonrandomness in sampling and the constraint imposed by observing a predetermined condition limit drawing cause-and-effect conclusions from observational studies because there is a possibility that results are due to some variables other than the variables being studied.

Characteristics of Well-Designed Studies

For this topic, you must know the characteristics of well-designed studies, including the role of randomization in surveys and experiments (*Mathematics: Content Knowledge (0061) Test at a Glance*, page 5).

A **sample** is a portion of a population that is examined to gain information about the whole population. A **random sample** is one in which the members of the sample are randomly selected from the population. A **representative sample** is one in which the characteristics of the sample entities mirror the characteristics of the population under investigation. The **sample size** is the number of entities in the sample. Statistical formulas or guidelines are available for determining adequate sample size for various types of studies. In general, increasing the sample size leads to more accurate results. A sample is most likely to be a representative sample when it has been chosen randomly from the population, and it is of adequate size.

Tip: Conclusions from a study should not be based on samples that are far too small (for example, a survey that uses less than 10 subjects). For the Mathematics CK, consider this aspect if you are asked to critique the results of a study.

Bias in a study is a type of systematic error that favors particular results.

Extraneous variables are unwanted variables that are not themselves being studied but, nevertheless, might influence study outcomes.

In order to provide results worthy of consideration, carefully plan **well-designed studies,** investigate issues that are clear and unambiguous, clearly identify populations of the study, use randomization in selecting representative samples of adequate size, use well-defined variables of interest, avoid bias of various types, and control outside factors, such as extraneous variables, that could jeopardize the validity of conclusions. Only when investigators use well-designed studies can conclusions that are reliable and valid be drawn.

Probability

According to the *Mathematics: Content Knowledge Test (0061) at a Glance* (www.ets.org/Media/Tests/PRAXIS/pdf/0061.pdf), the Probability content category of the Mathematics CK tests your knowledge and skills in four topic areas:

- Sample spaces and probability distributions
- Conditional probability and independent and dependent events
- Expected value
- Empirical probability

This review discusses the key ideas and formulas in each topic area that are most important for you to know for the Mathematics CK.

Sample Spaces and Probability Distributions

For this topic, you must demonstrate an understanding of concepts of sample space and probability distribution and be able to construct sample spaces and distributions in simple cases (*Mathematics: Content Knowledge Test (0061) at a Glance*, page 5).

A **sample space** S is the set of all possible outcomes of an experiment. Each member of S is called an **outcome** (or simple event, sample point, or elementary outcome).

Note: A sample space can be finite or infinite. For the Mathematics CK, only finite sample spaces are considered.

An **event** E is a collection of outcomes from S; that is, an event E is a subset of the sample space S. An event E is said **to occur** if a member of E occurs when the experiment is performed. For example, if the sample space is the experiment of drawing one tile from a box containing 5 wooden 1-inch-×-1-inch tiles, numbered 1 through 5, and E is the event that the tile drawn shows an odd number; then $S = \{1, 2, 3, 4, 5\}$ and $E = \{1, 3, 5\}$.

A **probability measure** on a sample space S is a function that assigns to each outcome in S a real number between 0 and 1, inclusive, so that the values assigned to the outcomes in S sum to 1. The value assigned to an outcome in S is called the **probability** of that outcome.

The **probability of an event** is the sum of the probabilities of the individual outcomes that are members of the event. The probability of an event is a numerical value between 0 and 1, inclusive, that quantifies the chance or likelihood that the event will occur.

Outcomes are **equally likely** if each outcome is as likely to occur as any other outcome.

If all the outcomes in the sample space are equally likely, the probability of an event E, denoted $P(E)$, is given by:

$$P(E) = \frac{\text{Number of ways } E \text{ can occur}}{\text{Total number of outcomes in the sample space}}$$

For example, if the sample space is the experiment of drawing one tile from a box containing 5 wooden 1-inch-×-1-inch tiles, numbered 1 through 5, and E is the event that the tile drawn shows an odd number, then $S = \{1, 2, 3, 4, 5\}$ and $E = \{1, 3, 5\}$ and $P(E) = \dfrac{\text{Number of ways } E \text{ can occur}}{\text{Total number of outcomes in the sample space}} = \dfrac{3}{5}$.

An event is **certain** to occur if and only if the probability of the event is 1. An event is **impossible** if and only if the probability of the event is 0. The probability of any event is a number between 0 and 1, inclusive.

Determining the outcomes in a sample space is a critical step in solving a probability problem. For simple experiments, counting techniques such as making a **tree diagram** or an **organized chart** are two useful ways to generate a list of the outcomes. More sophisticated techniques, which include the **multiplication principle, permutations,** and **combinations,** are needed for problems that are less straightforward. See the topic "Counting Techniques" in the chapter titled "Discrete Mathematics" for a discussion of these methods.

A **random variable** is a function X that assigns a real number x, determined by chance, to each outcome in a sample space. The number x is referred to as a value of the **random variable.**

A **probability distribution** is a graph, chart, table, or formula that gives the probability for each value of the random variable.

Suppose in the numbered tile-drawing experiment given previously, the random variable X assigns the value 3 to the outcomes that show an odd number on the drawn tile and the value 2 to the outcomes that show an even number on the drawn tile. Then, the following table is the probability distribution for X:

x	3	2
$P(x)$	$\frac{3}{5}$	$\frac{2}{5}$

Conditional Probability and Independent and Dependent Events

For this topic, you must demonstrate an understanding of concepts of conditional probability and independent and dependent events and be able to compute the probability of a compound event (*Mathematics: Content Knowledge Test (0061) at a Glance*, page 5).

The **complement of an event A,** denoted $\overline{A}$, is the event that A does not occur. The probability of the complement of an event A is given by $P(\overline{A}) = 1 - P(A)$.

A **compound event** is any event combining two or more given events.

In probability the word *or* is used in the inclusive sense. Thus, $P(A \text{ or } B)$ is the probability that event A occurs or event B occurs or that both events occur simultaneously on one trial of an experiment.

The **Addition Rule** states that $P(A \text{ or } B) = P(A) + P(B) - P(A \text{ and } B \text{ occur simultaneously})$. This rule applies to one trial of an experiment.

> **Tip:** For the Mathematics CK, it is not necessary to memorize the Addition Rule for probabilities. The most efficient and straightforward way to find *P*(*A* or *B*) on the test is to sum the number of ways that event *A* can occur and the number of ways that event *B* can occur, *being sure to add in such a way that no outcome is counted twice*, and then divide by the total number of outcomes in the sample space.

Two events are **mutually exclusive** if they cannot occur at the same time; that is, they have no outcomes in common.

Two events *A* and *B* are **independent** if the occurrence of one does not affect the probability of the occurrence of the other. If events *A* and *B* are not independent, they are said to be **dependent.**

The probability of an event *B*, given that an event *A* has occurred, is called a **conditional probability** and is denoted *P*(*B*|*A*). In other words, you compute the probability of event *B* by taking into account that the event *A* has already occurred.

The **Multiplication Rule** states that $P(A \text{ and } B) = P(A)\,P(B|A)$. This rule applies when two trials are performed.

If the events *A* and *B* are independent, then $P(A \text{ and } B) = P(A)\,P(B)$.

> **Tip:** For the Mathematics CK, to find the probability that event *A* occurs on the first trial and event *B* occurs on the second trial, multiply the probability of event *A* times the probability of event *B* ,where you have determined the probability of *B* by taking into account that the event *A* has already occurred.

To find the probability that **at least one** of something occurs, use the multiplication rule and the rule of complements as follows: $P(\text{at least one}) = 1 - P(\text{none})$.

The **odds in favor** of an event *A* are given by $\dfrac{P(A)}{1 - P(A)}$, usually expressed in the form *p*: *q* (or *p* to *q*), where *p* and *q* are integers with no common factors and $\dfrac{1 - P(A)}{P(A)} = \dfrac{p}{q}$.

The **odds against** an event *A* are given by $\dfrac{1 - P(A)}{P(A)}$, usually expressed in the form *q*: *p* (or *q* to *p*), where *p* and *q* are integers with no common factors and $\dfrac{1 - P(A)}{P(A)} = \dfrac{q}{p}$.

Expected Value

For this topic, you must be able to compute and interpret the expected value of random variables in simple cases (for example, fair coins, expected winnings, expected profit) (*Mathematics: Content Knowledge Test (0061) at a Glance*, page 5).

If *X* is a discrete random variable that takes on values $x_1, x_2, \ldots, x_n$ with probabilities $P(x_1), P(x_2), \ldots, P(x_n)$, the **expected value, denoted *E*(*X*),** is the theoretical **mean** μ of *X* and is given by:

$$\mu = E(X) = x_1 P(x_1) + x_2 P(x_2) + \ldots + x_n P(x_n)$$

For the random variable, developed from the numbered tile-drawing experiment, that has the following probability distribution,

x	3	2
$P(x)$	$\dfrac{3}{5}$	$\dfrac{2}{5}$

$$\mu = E(X) = x_1 P(x_1) + x_2 P(x_2) = 3 \cdot \frac{3}{5} + 2 \cdot \frac{2}{5} = 2.6$$

You can use your understanding of probability distributions and expected value to decide whether a game is fair. For instance, suppose that you pay 3 chips to play a game with the numbered tiles. You win 3 chips if the tile drawn shows an odd number and 2 chips if the tile drawn shows an even number. Your expected value for the game is 2.6 chips. Since you are paying a 3-chip fee to play the game, on average, you lose 0.4 chips. The game is not fair, since you, the player, can expect to lose.

Empirical Probability

For this topic, you must be able to use simulations to construct empirical probability distributions and to make informal inferences about the theoretical probability distribution (*Mathematics: Content Knowledge Test (0061) at a Glance*, page 5).

When a probability is determined by observing outcomes of an experiment, it is called empirical probability. In **empirical probability,** the probability of an event E is defined by conducting the experiment a large number of times, called **trials,** and counting the number of times that event E actually occurred. Based on these results, the probability of E is *estimated* as follows:

Empirical Probability of $E = P(E) = \dfrac{\text{Number of times } E \text{ occurred}}{\text{Total number of trials}}$.

As the numbers of trials increases, the empirical probability approaches the true probability of the event. The empirical probability of an event is also called its **relative frequency probability** or **experimental probability.**

In some situations, empirical probability is the only feasible way to assign a probability to an event. For instance, insurance companies set premiums based on empirical probabilities.

Matrix Algebra

According to the *Mathematics: Content Knowledge Test (0061) at a Glance* (www.ets.org/Media/Tests/PRAXIS/pdf/0061.pdf), the Matrix Algebra content category of the Mathematics CK tests your knowledge and skills in six topic areas:

- Vectors and matrices
- Operations with matrices
- Solving systems of linear equations
- Determinants
- Representation of geometric transformations

This review discusses the key ideas and formulas in each topic area that are most important for you to know for the Mathematics CK.

Vectors and Matrices

For this topic, you must demonstrate an understanding of vectors and matrices as systems that have some of the same properties as the real number system (for example, identity, inverse, and commutativity under addition and multiplication) (*Mathematics: Content Knowledge Test (0061) at a Glance*, page 5).

A **matrix** is a rectangular array of elements. For the Mathematics CK test, the elements of a matrix are real or complex numbers or expressions representing real or complex numbers. A matrix with m **rows** and n **columns** is called an $m \times n$ matrix. Matrices are commonly denoted by uppercase letters and their elements by the corresponding lowercase letters, which are subscripted to indicate the location of the elements in the matrix. For a matrix A, the notation a_{ij} denotes the element in the ith row and jth column of the matrix. It is also customary to denote an $m \times n$ matrix A by $[a_{ij}]_{(m,n)}$, or simply by $[a_{ij}]$, if the order is clear.

> **Tip:** Your graphing calculator has a Matrix menu that allows you to define, edit, or display a matrix. Most graphing calculators will allow up to 99 rows or columns, depending on available memory.

The **order** of a matrix is the number of rows and columns it contains; thus, an $m \times n$ matrix has order $m \times n$. A $1 \times n$ matrix is called a **row vector of order n.** An $m \times 1$ matrix is called a **column vector of order m.** If $m = n$, the matrix is called a **square matrix of order n.**

The **main diagonal** of a square matrix of order n is the diagonal of elements $a_{11}, a_{22}, \ldots, a_{nn}$ from the top-left corner to the bottom-right corner of the matrix.

A **diagonal matrix** is a square matrix whose only nonzero elements are on the main diagonal. A diagonal matrix that has only ones on the main diagonal is called the **identity matrix.** The identity matrix of order n is denoted I_n.

A **zero matrix** is a matrix containing only zero elements.

The **negative** of a matrix $A = [a_{ij}]$ is the matrix $-A = [-a_{ij}]$, whose elements are the negatives of their corresponding elements in A.

Two matrices A and B are equal if and only if they have the same order and their corresponding elements are equal. Therefore, if two matrices $A = [a_{ij}]$ and $B = [b_{ij}]$ are equal, then $a_{ij} = b_{ij}$, for $1 \le i \le m$ and $1 \le j \le n$.

The **transpose** of an $m \times n$ matrix A is an $n \times m$ matrix, denoted A^T (read as "A transpose"), obtained by interchanging the rows and columns of A. The transpose of a matrix A is also denoted A'.

Tip: Your graphing calculator has a matrix feature that will return the transpose of a matrix.

A matrix A is said to be **symmetric** if $A = A^T$.

With respect to arithmetic operations with matrices (which will be defined in the next section, "Operations with Matrices"), matrices *that contain elements that are complex numbers or real numbers* have some properties in common with the properties of their elements. With respect to the operation of matrix addition the set of $m \times n$ matrices is closed, is commutative, and associative, and has an additive identity and an additive inverse for each $m \times n$ matrix. For the operation of matrix multiplication, certain restrictions on the order of the matrices involved in the multiplication must be met before the operation is defined. For situations in which matrix multiplication is defined, matrix multiplication is closed, associative, and distributes over addition. In general, matrix multiplication is *not* commutative, nor does there always exist a multiplicative identity element or multiplicative inverses.

Operations with Matrices

For this topic, you must be able to perform scalar multiplication and add, subtract, and multiply vectors and matrices and find inverses of matrices (*Mathematics: Content Knowledge Test (0061) at a Glance*, page 5).

A **scalar** is a number or numerical quantity.

The **scalar product, kA,** of an $m \times n$ matrix $A = [a_{ij}]$ and a scalar k is the $m \times n$ matrix $C = [c_{ij}]$, where $c_{ij} = ka_{ij}$.

Tip: You can use the multiplication key on the keyboard of your graphing calculator to find a scalar product.

The **sum, $A + B$,** of two $m \times n$ matrices $A = [a_{ij}]$ and $B = [b_{ij}]$ is the $m \times n$ matrix $C = [c_{ij}]$, where $c_{ij} = a_{ij} + b_{ij}$. With respect to matrix addition, the zero matrix is the additive **identity element** and $-A$ is the **additive inverse.** The difference, $A - B$, of two matrices is defined to be $A + (-B)$.

Two matrices are **conformable** for matrix addition or subtraction if they have the same order. *Addition or subtraction of matrices with unlike orders is not defined.*

Tip: Provided the matrices have the same order, you can use the addition key on the keyboard of your graphing calculator to perform matrix addition. Practice using this helpful feature of your calculator before you take the Mathematics CK.

The **inner product** (also called the **dot product**), $A \cdot B$, *in that order* of a $1 \times m$ row vector $A = [a_{11}\ a_{12}\ a_{13} \ldots a_{1m}]$ and an $m \times 1$ column vector $B = \begin{bmatrix} b_{11} \\ b_{21} \\ \vdots \\ b_{m1} \end{bmatrix}$ is the scalar $a_{11}b_{11} + a_{12}b_{21} + \ldots + a_{1m}b_{m1}$. Notice that you multiply *row by column*: multiply each element of the row times the corresponding element of the column and then sum the products.

The **product, AB,** *in that order* of an $m \times k$ matrix $A = [a_{ij}]$ and a $k \times n$ matrix $B = [b_{ij}]$ is the $m \times n$ matrix $C = [c_{ij}]$, where $c_{ij} = a_{i1}b_{1j} + a_{i2}b_{2j} + \ldots + a_{ik}b_{kj}$, for $1 \leq i \leq m$ and $1 \leq j \leq n$. Notice that the element c_{ij} is the inner product of the ith row of A and the jth column of B.

Two matrices, A and B, are **conformable** for matrix multiplication in the order AB, only if the number of columns of matrix A is equal to the number of rows of matrix B. In the product, AB, we say B is **premultiplied** by A and A is **postmultipled** by B. *Multiplication of matrices that are not conformable is not defined.*

Tip: Provided the matrices are conformable for multiplication, you can use the multiplication key on the keyboard of your graphing calculator to perform matrix multiplication. However, because of the distinctive way that matrix multiplication is defined, in general, matrix multiplication is *not* commutative, not even for square matrices of the same order. Because of this noncommutative feature of matrix arithmetic, you must pay careful attention to the order of the factors in any product of matrices when you are taking the Mathematics CK.

If A is a square matrix of order n and there exists a square matrix B of order n such that $AB = BA = I$, then B is called the **inverse** of A and is designated A^{-1}. Not all square matrices have inverses, but when the inverse for a square matrix exists, the inverse is unique. A matrix that has an inverse is said to be **nonsingular.**

The inverse of a 2×2 nonsingular matrix $A = \begin{bmatrix} a_{11} & a_{12} \\ a_{21} & a_{22} \end{bmatrix}$ is given by $A^{-1} = \begin{bmatrix} \frac{a_{22}}{\triangle} & \frac{-a_{12}}{\triangle} \\ \frac{-a_{21}}{\triangle} & \frac{a_{11}}{\triangle} \end{bmatrix}$, where $\triangle = a_{11}a_{22} - a_{12}a_{21} \neq 0$.

The scalar $\triangle = a_{11}a_{22} - a_{12}a_{21}$ is called the **determinant of A** (See the section "Determinants" in this chapter for an additional discussion on determinants.) The matrix A has an inverse if and only if $\triangle = a_{11}a_{22} - a_{12}a_{21} \neq 0$.

If you use a graphing calculator, finding the inverse of a nonsingular 2×2 matrix is relatively easy. However, it is important that you know and understand how to find the inverse of a 2×2 matrix *without the use of a graphing calculator*. The procedure can be stated in four steps: (1) Compute $\triangle = a_{11}a_{22} - a_{12}a_{21}$, (2) switch a_{11} and a_{22}, (3) Change the signs of a_{12} and a_{21} (but don't switch them!), (4) divide each element by $\triangle$. The reason you must understand the process is that a question might ask about the process rather than for you to find the inverse.

Another process for finding the inverse of a nonsingular 2×2 matrix $A = \begin{bmatrix} a_{11} & a_{12} \\ a_{21} & a_{22} \end{bmatrix}$ is to (1) create the 2×4 **partitioned matrix** $= \begin{bmatrix} a_{11} & a_{12} : 1 & 0 \\ a_{21} & a_{22} : 0 & 1 \end{bmatrix}$, which contains A as a **submatrix** on the left and I as a submatrix on the right, and (2) through a series of **elementary row operations** (interchanging two rows, multiplying a row by a nonzero scalar, adding two rows, multiplying a row by a scalar and adding the result to a row—all of which can be performed using the Matrix menu of your graphing calculator), convert the submatrix A into an identity matrix. This process will yield the matrix $\begin{bmatrix} 1 & 0 : \frac{a_{22}}{a_{11}a_{22} - a_{12}a_{21}} & \frac{-a_{12}}{a_{11}a_{22} - a_{12}a_{21}} \\ 0 & 1 : \frac{-a_{21}}{a_{11}a_{22} - a_{12}a_{21}} & \frac{a_{11}}{a_{11}a_{22} - a_{12}a_{21}} \end{bmatrix}$, which shows I on the left and A^{-1} on the right. This latter process will also work for higher-order matrices. Again, it's more important that you understand the process, rather than how you would actually use it to find the inverse of a matrix when you are taking the Mathematics CK. For the test if you need to find the inverse of a matrix, you should use the reciprocal key on the keyboard of your graphing calculator to obtain the inverse so as to avoid tedious calculations that can waste valuable time.

Tip: When you determine an inverse for a matrix using your graphing calculator, if the entries in the inverse matrix are in decimal form, if needed, use the feature of your calculator that changes decimals to fractions to display the matrix entries as their fractional equivalents. If the answer cannot be simplified or the resulting denominator is more than three digits, most graphing calculators will return the decimal equivalent.

Solving Systems of Linear Equations

For this topic, you must be able to use matrix techniques to solve systems of linear equations (*Mathematics: Content Knowledge Test (0061) at a Glance*, page 5).

A system of three equations with three unknowns is given by:

$$a_{11}x + a_{12}y + a_{13}z = c_1$$
$$a_{21}x + a_{22}y + a_{23}z = c_2$$
$$a_{31}x + a_{32}y + a_{33}z = c_3$$

This system can be solved using the algebraic methods of substitution and elimination (which are presented in the section "Systems of Equations and Inequalities" in the chapter titled "Algebra and Number Theory") or the system can be solved using a technique called **transformation of the augmented matrix,** which will be presented in this section. The system is said to be **consistent** if it has a solution; otherwise, the system is said to be **inconsistent.**

The augmented matrix for the system is the matrix $\begin{bmatrix} a_{11} & a_{12} & a_{13} & c_1 \\ a_{21} & a_{22} & a_{23} & c_2 \\ a_{31} & a_{32} & a_{33} & c_3 \end{bmatrix}$.

To solve the system, you use elementary row operations (interchanging two rows, multiplying a row by a nonzero scalar, adding two rows, multiplying a row by a scalar and adding the result to a row) to transform the submatrix of coefficients a_{ij} as closely as possible into the identity matrix. When the system is consistent, the results will be one of the following **reduced row-echelon forms:**

$\begin{bmatrix} 1 & 0 & 0 & x_0 \\ 0 & 1 & 0 & y_0 \\ 0 & 0 & 1 & z_0 \end{bmatrix}$, which yields the unique solution $x = x_0, y = y_0, z = z_0$;

$\begin{bmatrix} 1 & 0 & k_1 & x_0 \\ 0 & 1 & k_2 & y_0 \\ 0 & 0 & 0 & 0 \end{bmatrix}$, which yields the nonunique solution $x = x_0 - k_1z, y = y_0 - k_2z$; or

$\begin{bmatrix} 1 & j_1 & k_1 & x_0 \\ 0 & 0 & 0 & 0 \\ 0 & 0 & 0 & 0 \end{bmatrix}$, which yields the nonunique solution $x = x_0 - j_1y - k_1z$.

The process of reducing the augmented matrix to reduced row-echelon form can be very time-consuming and tedious. Since the Mathematics CK is a timed test, you should use your graphing calculator to find the solution. Enter the elements of the augmented matrix into the calculator, have the calculator produce the reduced row-echelon form of the augmented matrix, and then "read" the solution from the display.

The technique of solving a system of linear equations by transformation of the augmented matrix can be applied to a **system of n equations with n unknowns** such as

$$a_{11}x_1 + a_{12}x_2 + \ldots + a_{1n}x_n = c_1$$
$$a_{21}x_1 + a_{22}x_2 + \ldots + a_{2n}x_n = c_2$$
$$\ldots \quad \ldots \quad \ldots \quad \ldots \quad \ldots$$
$$a_{n1}x_1 + a_{n2}x_2 + \ldots + a_{nm}x_n = c_n$$

You would proceed in the same manner as shown for systems with three equations and three unknowns.

Determinants

For this topic, you must be able to use determinants to reason about inverses of matrices and solutions to systems of equations (*Mathematics: Content Knowledge Test (0061) at a Glance*, page 5).

For every square matrix A there is a unique corresponding scalar called the **determinant of A,** denoted $|A|$, which is a well-defined combination of products of the elements of A. Notice that only square matrices have determinants.

The determinant of a 2×2 matrix $A = \begin{bmatrix} a_{11} & a_{12} \\ a_{21} & a_{22} \end{bmatrix}$ is given by $|A| = \begin{vmatrix} a_{11} & a_{12} \\ a_{21} & a_{22} \end{vmatrix} = a_{11}a_{22} - a_{12}a_{21}$.

One way to obtain the determinant of a 3×3 matrix $A = \begin{bmatrix} a_{11} & a_{12} & a_{13} \\ a_{21} & a_{22} & a_{23} \\ a_{31} & a_{32} & a_{33} \end{bmatrix}$ is given by $|A| = a_{11} \begin{vmatrix} a_{22} & a_{23} \\ a_{32} & a_{33} \end{vmatrix} - a_{12} \begin{vmatrix} a_{21} & a_{23} \\ a_{31} & a_{33} \end{vmatrix} +$

$a_{13} \begin{vmatrix} a_{21} & a_{22} \\ a_{31} & a_{32} \end{vmatrix} = a_{11}(a_{22}a_{33} - a_{23}a_{32}) - a_{12}(a_{21}a_{33} - a_{23}a_{31}) + a_{13}(a_{21}a_{32} - a_{22}a_{31})$.

Tip: You can calculate determinants for 2×2, 3×3, and higher-order matrices using your graphing calculator. Always double-check your entries to make sure you have entered the matrix correctly before finding the determinant.

If a square matrix has a row or column consisting of only zeroes, the determinant of the matrix equals zero.

If A is a square matrix, then $|kA| = k|A|$.

A matrix has an inverse if and only if its determinant does *not* equal zero.

If the coefficient matrix $A = [a_{ij}]$ of the system of n linear equations with n unknowns given by:

$$a_{11}x_1 + a_{12}x_2 + \ldots + a_{1n}x_n = c_1$$
$$a_{21}x_1 + a_{22}x_2 + \ldots + a_{2n}x_n = c_2$$
$$\ldots \quad \ldots \quad \ldots \quad \ldots \quad \ldots$$
$$a_{n1}x_1 + a_{n2}x_2 + \ldots + a_{nn}x_n = c_n$$

has a nonzero determinant (that is, if $|A| \neq 0$), then the system has exactly one solution. If $|A| = 0$, then the system might have no solution or infinitely many solutions.

Representation of Geometric Transformations

For this topic, you must be able to represent translations, reflections, rotations, and dilations of objects in the plane by using sketches, coordinates, vectors, and matrices (*Mathematics: Content Knowledge Test (0061) at a Glance*, page 5).

The four **geometric transformations** are **translations, reflections, rotations,** and **dilations.** You can think of geometric transformations as ways to change geometric figures without changing their basic properties. (See the section, "Geometric Transformations," in the chapter titled "Geometry" for an additional discussion of geometric transformations.)

A convenient way to represent geometric transformations is by using matrices. A geometric figure in the plane can be represented by a $2 \times n$ matrix whose columns elements are the n vertices of the figure. For instance, a triangle T with vertices (x_1, y_1), (x_2, y_2), and (x_3, y_3) can be represented as $T = \begin{bmatrix} x_1 & x_2 & x_3 \\ y_1 & y_2 & y_3 \end{bmatrix}$.

A **translation h units horizontally and k units** vertically is accomplished by adding the 2×3 translation matrix $\begin{bmatrix} h & h & h \\ k & k & k \end{bmatrix}$ to T: $\begin{bmatrix} h & h & h \\ k & k & k \end{bmatrix} + \begin{bmatrix} x_1 & x_2 & x_3 \\ y_1 & y_2 & y_3 \end{bmatrix} = \begin{bmatrix} h+x_1 & h+x_2 & h+x_3 \\ k+y_1 & k+y_2 & k+y_3 \end{bmatrix}$.

A **reflection over the line $y = x$** is accomplished by premultiplying T by the 2×2 matrix $\begin{bmatrix} 0 & 1 \\ 1 & 0 \end{bmatrix}$: $\begin{bmatrix} 0 & 1 \\ 1 & 0 \end{bmatrix}\begin{bmatrix} x_1 & x_2 & x_3 \\ y_1 & y_2 & y_3 \end{bmatrix} =$

$\begin{bmatrix} y_1 & y_2 & y_3 \\ x_1 & x_2 & x_3 \end{bmatrix}$. A **reflection over the y-axis** is accomplished by premultiplying T by the 2×2 matrix $\begin{bmatrix} -1 & 0 \\ 0 & 1 \end{bmatrix}$:

$\begin{bmatrix} -1 & 0 \\ 0 & 1 \end{bmatrix} \begin{bmatrix} x_1 & x_2 & x_3 \\ y_1 & y_2 & y_3 \end{bmatrix} = \begin{bmatrix} -x_1 & -x_2 & -x_3 \\ y_1 & y_2 & y_3 \end{bmatrix}$. A **reflection over the x-axis** is accomplished by premultiplying T by the

2×2 matrix $\begin{bmatrix} 1 & 0 \\ 0 & -1 \end{bmatrix}$: $\begin{bmatrix} 1 & 0 \\ 0 & -1 \end{bmatrix} \begin{bmatrix} x_1 & x_2 & x_3 \\ y_1 & y_2 & y_3 \end{bmatrix} = \begin{bmatrix} x_1 & x_2 & x_3 \\ -y_1 & -y_2 & -y_3 \end{bmatrix}$.

A **rotation of θ degrees about the origin** is accomplished by premultiplying T by the 2×2 matrix $\begin{bmatrix} \cos\theta & -\sin\theta \\ \sin\theta & \cos\theta \end{bmatrix}$. For

instance, for a 90° counterclockwise rotation, premultiply T by $\begin{bmatrix} 0 & 1 \\ -1 & 0 \end{bmatrix}$: $\begin{bmatrix} 0 & 1 \\ -1 & 0 \end{bmatrix} \begin{bmatrix} x_1 & x_2 & x_3 \\ y_1 & y_2 & y_3 \end{bmatrix} = \begin{bmatrix} y_1 & y_2 & y_3 \\ -x_1 & -x_2 & -x_3 \end{bmatrix}$.

A **dilation by a scale factor k** is accomplished by premultiplying T by the 2×2 matrix $\begin{bmatrix} k & 0 \\ 0 & k \end{bmatrix}$: $\begin{bmatrix} k & 0 \\ 0 & k \end{bmatrix} \begin{bmatrix} x_1 & x_2 & x_3 \\ y_1 & y_2 & y_3 \end{bmatrix} =$
$\begin{bmatrix} kx_1 & kx_2 & kx_3 \\ ky_1 & ky_2 & ky_3 \end{bmatrix}$.

To accomplish translations in combination with rotations, reflections, or dilations using one transformation matrix, write the vertex matrix as a $3 \times n$ matrix with ones as the elements in the third row. Then, for example, to translate

h units horizontally and k units vertically and reflect over the line $y = x$, premultiply by the 3×3 matrix $\begin{bmatrix} 0 & 1 & h \\ 1 & 0 & k \\ 0 & 0 & 1 \end{bmatrix}$:
$\begin{bmatrix} 0 & 1 & h \\ 1 & 0 & k \\ 0 & 0 & 1 \end{bmatrix} \begin{bmatrix} x_1 & x_2 & x_3 \\ y_1 & y_2 & y_3 \\ 1 & 1 & 1 \end{bmatrix} = \begin{bmatrix} y_1+h & y_2+h & y_3+h \\ x_1+k & x_2+k & x_3+k \\ 1 & 1 & 1 \end{bmatrix}$.

The technique of premultiplying the vertex matrix by either a 2×2 or a 3×3 transformation matrix can be applied when the number of vertices is extended to $n > 3$. You would proceed in the same manner as shown for a figure with three vertices.

Tip: When you are working problems involving geometric transformations on the Mathematics CK, sketch a figure to help you visualize the situation, in conjunction with using your graphing calculator to check the results of pre-multiplying by the transformation matrix.

Discrete Mathematics

According to the *Mathematics: Content Knowledge Test (0061) at a Glance* (www.ets.org/Media/Tests/PRAXIS/pdf/ 0061.pdf), the Discrete Mathematics content category of the Mathematics CK tests your knowledge and skills in six topic areas:

- Counting techniques
- Recursive functions
- Equivalence relations
- Arithmetic and geometric sequences and series
- Discrete and continuous representations
- Modeling and solving problems

This review discusses the key ideas and formulas in each topic area that are most important for you to know for the Mathematics CK.

Counting Techniques

For this topic, you must be able to solve basic problems that involve counting techniques, including the multiplication principle, permutations, and combinations and use counting techniques to understand various situations (for example, number of ways to order a set of objects, to choose a subcommittee from a committee, to visit *n* cities) (*Mathematics: Content Knowledge Test (0061) at a Glance*, page 6).

The **Fundamental Counting Principle** states that if one event can occur in any one of *m* ways, and, after it has occurred, a second event can occur in any one of *n* ways, then both events can occur, in the order given, in $m \cdot n$ ways. This principle can be extended to any number of events. This counting technique produces results in which order determines different outcomes.

The **Addition Principle** states that if one task can be done in any one of *m* ways and a second task can be done in any one of *n* ways and if the two tasks *cannot* be done at the same time, then the number of ways to do the first *or* the second task is $(m + n)$ ways.

The Addition Principle can be modified in the following way for situations in which two tasks overlap; that is, when the two tasks can be done at the same time: If one task can be done in any one of *m* ways and a second task can be done in any one of *n* ways, and if the two tasks *can* be done at the same time, then the number of ways to do the first *or* the second task is $(m + n)$ – (the number of ways the two tasks can be done at the same time).

A **permutation** is an ordered arrangement of a set of distinct items. The number of permutations of *n* distinct items is $n! = n(n-1)(n-2) \cdot \ldots \cdot 3 \cdot 2 \cdot 1$.

Note: The notation *n*! is read "*n* factorial." By definition 0! = 1.

The number of permutations of *r* items selected from *n* distinct items is $_nP_r = \dfrac{n!}{(n-r)!}$. It is important when you apply the formula $_nP_r$, that you make sure that the following conditions are met: the *n* items must be *n different* items, the *r* items must be selected *without replacement*, and you must count different orderings of the same items *separately*.

The number of permutations of *n* items for which n_1 of the *n* items are alike, n_2 of the *n* items are alike, . . . , n_k of the *n* items are alike is $\dfrac{n!}{n_1! n_2! \cdots n_k!}$.

A **combination** is an arrangement of a set of distinct items in which different orderings of the same items are considered to be the same.

The number of combinations of r items selected from n distinct items is $_nC_r = \dfrac{n!}{r!(n-r)!}$. It is important when you apply the formula $_nC_r$ that you make sure that the following conditions are met: the n items must be n *different* items, the r items must be selected *without replacement*, and you must consider different orderings of the same items to be *the same*.

Note: The notation $_nC_r$ is also written $\begin{pmatrix} n \\ r \end{pmatrix}$.

Tip: When different orderings of the same items are counted as separate results, you have a permutation problem, but when different orderings of the same items are *not* counted as separate results, you have a combination problem.

Your graphing calculator is designed to numerically evaluate both $_nP_r$ and $_nC_r$. Make a point to practice using this time-saving feature of your graphing calculator before you take the Mathematics CK.

Recursive Functions

For this topic, you must be able to find values of functions defined recursively and understand how recursion can be used to model various phenomena and translate between recursive and closed-form expressions for a function (*Mathematics: Content Knowledge Test (0061) at a Glance*, page 6).

A **sequence** is a function whose domain is the set of positive integers. The notation a_n denotes the image of the integer n, and a_n is called the **general term,** or **nth term** (or **element**), of the sequence. You use $\{a_n\}$ or $a_1, a_2, \ldots, a_n, \ldots,$ to denote a sequence with nth term a_n. (See the chapter titled "Functions" for a discussion of functions in general.)

A **recursive definition** for a sequence is a definition that includes the value of one or more initial terms of the sequence and a formula that tells how to find each term from previous terms.

The terms of the **Fibonacci sequence** are given by the recursive definition: $a_1 = 1$, $a_2 = 1$, and $a_n = a_{n-1} + a_{n-2}$, $n \geq 3$.

A **closed-form expression** for the general term a_n of a recursive sequence is a formula that can be used to find a_n without knowing any of the previous terms. Note: Not all recursive sequences have a closed-form expression for the general term.

Tip: Sometimes it is convenient to begin a recursive sequence at $n = 0$ instead of $n = 1$, so be sure to check for the starting value of n when you work problems involving sequences on the Mathematics CK.

Equivalence Relations

For this topic, you must be able to determine whether a binary relation on a set is reflexive, symmetric, or transitive and determine whether a relation is an equivalence relation (*Mathematics: Content Knowledge Test (0061) at a Glance*, page 6).

The **Cartesian product** of two sets A and B, denoted $A \times B$, is the set of all ordered pairs (x, y) such that $x \in A$ and $y \in B$.

A **binary relation** (also called simply **relation**) from a set A to a set B is a subset of $A \times B$. If $A = B$, then we say the relation is on A. In other words, a relation on the set A is a subset of $A \times A$.

79

For a relation $\mathfrak{R}$, the notation $x \mathfrak{R} y$ (read as "x is related to y") is used to denote that the ordered pair $(x, y) \in \mathfrak{R}$.

A relation $\mathfrak{R}$ on a set S is

> **reflexive** if $x \mathfrak{R} x$ for all $x \in S$
>
> **symmetric** if $x \mathfrak{R} y \Rightarrow y \mathfrak{R} x$ for all $x, y \in S$
>
> **transitive** if $(x \mathfrak{R} y$ and $y \mathfrak{R} z) \Rightarrow x \mathfrak{R} z$ for all $x, y, z \in S$
>
> **antisymmetric** if $(x \mathfrak{R} y$ and $y \mathfrak{R} x) \Rightarrow x = y$ for all $x, y \in S$

An **equivalence relation** is a reflexive, symmetric, and transitive relation.

Note: The definitions for reflexive, symmetric, transitive, antisymmetric, and equivalence relation are given in the Notation, Definitions, and Formulas pages at the beginning of the Mathematics CK test booklet.

Arithmetic and Geometric Sequences and Series

For this topic, you must be able to use finite and infinite arithmetic and geometric sequences and series to model simple phenomena (for example, compound interest, annuity, growth, decay) (*Mathematics: Content Knowledge Test (0061) at a Glance*, page 6).

A **sequence** is a function whose domain is the set of positive integers. The notation a_n denotes the image of the integer n, and a_n is called the **nth term** (or **element**) of the sequence.

An **arithmetic sequence** (also called **arithmetic progression**) is a sequence of the form $a_1, a_1 + d, a_1 + 2d, \ldots, a_1 + (n-1)d, \ldots$, where d is the **common difference** between terms and the **general term** is $a_n = a_1 + (n-1)d$.

The sum of the first n terms of an arithmetic sequence is given by: $s_n = \dfrac{n}{2}(a_1 + a_n)$.

A **geometric sequence** (also called **geometric progression**) is a sequence of the form $a_1, a_1 r, a_1 r^2, \ldots, a_1 r^{n-1}, \ldots$, where r is the **common ratio** between terms and the **general term** is $a_n = a_1 r^{n-1}$.

The sum of the first n terms of a geometric sequence with common ratio r is given by: $s_n = \dfrac{a_1(1 - r^n)}{1 - r}$, provided that $r \neq 1$.

Tip: Sometimes it is convenient to begin an arithmetic or geometric sequence at $n = 0$ instead of $n = 1$, so be sure to check for the starting value of n when you work problems involving sequences on the Mathematics CK.

Note: See the section titled "Limits of Sequences and Series" in the chapter titled "Calculus" for an additional discussion of sequences and series.

Discrete and Continuous Representations

For this topic, you must demonstrate an understanding of the relationship between discrete and continuous representations and how they can be used to model various phenomena (*Mathematics: Content Knowledge Test (0061) at a Glance*, page 6).

Discrete mathematics (also called **finite** mathematics) is the study of processes with discrete or unconnected objects. Discrete mathematics does not require the notion of continuity. (See the section titled "Continuity" in the chapter titled "Calculus" for a discussion of the term *continuity*.) Generally, processes studied in discrete mathematics have a finite (or countable) number of objects. Discrete mathematics has widespread uses in a variety of areas such as number theory, computer security, networking, robotics, social choice theory, and linear programming.

The techniques of algebra and the powerful tools of calculus are needed for dealing with continuous processes. For example, functions with graphs that have no gaps, jumps, or holes are continuous functions. Applications of continuous functions are found in many fields such as in the sciences and in business and industry.

Modeling and Solving Problems

For this topic, you must be able to use difference equations, vertex-edge graphs, trees, and networks to model and solve problems (*Mathematics: Content Knowledge Test (0061) at a Glance*, page 6).

A **difference equation** is an equation that describes sequential, step-by-step change. A difference equation has the form $f(n + 1) - f(n) = g(n)$, where n is a positive integer.

> **Note: A difference equation is the discrete mathematics analog to the first derivative equation given by $f'(x) = g(x)$.** **(See the section titled "Derivatives" in the chapter titled "Calculus" for a discussion of the first derivative $f'(x)$.)**

A difference equation for the first difference, call it $\triangle a_n$, of a sequence $\{a_n\}$ is given by $a_{n+1} - a_n = \triangle a_n$. The first difference describes the rate of growth or decline of the sequence. When $\triangle a_n$ is positive, the terms of the sequence are increasing; when $\triangle a_n$ is negative, the terms of the sequence are decreasing. When $\triangle a_n$ is constant, the sequence is growing or declining at a constant rate and the relationship between terms is linear. The **second difference** of a sequence is given by $\triangle a_{n+1} - \triangle a_n$. When the second difference is constant, the relationship between terms of the sequence is quadratic.

A **vertex-edge graph** is a discrete structure consisting of a nonempty, finite set of **vertices** (also called **nodes**) and a set of **edges** (also called **lines**) **connecting** these vertices. Vertex-edge graphs are commonly used to model and solve problems involving optimal situations for networks, paths, schedules, and relationships among finitely many objects. The following figure is a vertex-edge graph with six vertices and seven edges.

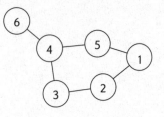

A **vertex** that meets an edge is an **endpoint** of that edge, and the edge is said to be **incident** with that vertex.

Two edges are **adjacent** if they share a common vertex. Two vertices are **adjacent** if they are joined by a common edge.

A **loop** is an edge that is incident with exactly one vertex; that is, both endpoints of the edge are the same.

A **link** is an edge that has two different endpoints.

The **degree** of a vertex is the number of edges that are incident to that vertex (with loops being counted twice).

The **Degree Sum Formula** states that the sum of the degrees of the vertices of a graph is an even number equal to twice the number of edges of the graph. Consequently, there are no graphs with an odd number of vertices of odd degree.

A **path** in a vertex-edge graph is a sequence of vertices such that from each of its vertices there is an edge to the next vertex. A **simple path** is a path in which no edge is repeated.

A **circuit** in a vertex-edge graph is a path that begins and ends at the same vertex. A **simple circuit** is a circuit in which no edge is repeated.

A **Euler path** in a vertex-edge graph is a path that uses each edge exactly once. There is no Euler path for a graph that has more than two vertices of odd degree.

A **Hamiltonian path** in a vertex-edge graph is a path that uses each vertex exactly once.

A vertex-edge graph is **connected** if there is a path between each pair of vertices.

A **tree** is a connected vertex-edge graph that contains no simple circuits. The following figure is a tree with six vertices and five edges.

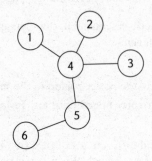

PART II

3 FULL-LENGTH PRACTICE TESTS

Answer Grid for Practice Test 1

(Remove This Sheet and Use It to Mark Your Answers)

1 Ⓐ Ⓑ Ⓒ Ⓓ		26 Ⓐ Ⓑ Ⓒ Ⓓ
2 Ⓐ Ⓑ Ⓒ Ⓓ		27 Ⓐ Ⓑ Ⓒ Ⓓ
3 Ⓐ Ⓑ Ⓒ Ⓓ		28 Ⓐ Ⓑ Ⓒ Ⓓ
4 Ⓐ Ⓑ Ⓒ Ⓓ		29 Ⓐ Ⓑ Ⓒ Ⓓ
5 Ⓐ Ⓑ Ⓒ Ⓓ		30 Ⓐ Ⓑ Ⓒ Ⓓ
6 Ⓐ Ⓑ Ⓒ Ⓓ		31 Ⓐ Ⓑ Ⓒ Ⓓ
7 Ⓐ Ⓑ Ⓒ Ⓓ		32 Ⓐ Ⓑ Ⓒ Ⓓ
8 Ⓐ Ⓑ Ⓒ Ⓓ		33 Ⓐ Ⓑ Ⓒ Ⓓ
9 Ⓐ Ⓑ Ⓒ Ⓓ		34 Ⓐ Ⓑ Ⓒ Ⓓ
10 Ⓐ Ⓑ Ⓒ Ⓓ		35 Ⓐ Ⓑ Ⓒ Ⓓ
11 Ⓐ Ⓑ Ⓒ Ⓓ		36 Ⓐ Ⓑ Ⓒ Ⓓ
12 Ⓐ Ⓑ Ⓒ Ⓓ		37 Ⓐ Ⓑ Ⓒ Ⓓ
13 Ⓐ Ⓑ Ⓒ Ⓓ		38 Ⓐ Ⓑ Ⓒ Ⓓ
14 Ⓐ Ⓑ Ⓒ Ⓓ		39 Ⓐ Ⓑ Ⓒ Ⓓ
15 Ⓐ Ⓑ Ⓒ Ⓓ		40 Ⓐ Ⓑ Ⓒ Ⓓ
16 Ⓐ Ⓑ Ⓒ Ⓓ		41 Ⓐ Ⓑ Ⓒ Ⓓ
17 Ⓐ Ⓑ Ⓒ Ⓓ		42 Ⓐ Ⓑ Ⓒ Ⓓ
18 Ⓐ Ⓑ Ⓒ Ⓓ		43 Ⓐ Ⓑ Ⓒ Ⓓ
19 Ⓐ Ⓑ Ⓒ Ⓓ		44 Ⓐ Ⓑ Ⓒ Ⓓ
20 Ⓐ Ⓑ Ⓒ Ⓓ		45 Ⓐ Ⓑ Ⓒ Ⓓ
21 Ⓐ Ⓑ Ⓒ Ⓓ		46 Ⓐ Ⓑ Ⓒ Ⓓ
22 Ⓐ Ⓑ Ⓒ Ⓓ		47 Ⓐ Ⓑ Ⓒ Ⓓ
23 Ⓐ Ⓑ Ⓒ Ⓓ		48 Ⓐ Ⓑ Ⓒ Ⓓ
24 Ⓐ Ⓑ Ⓒ Ⓓ		49 Ⓐ Ⓑ Ⓒ Ⓓ
25 Ⓐ Ⓑ Ⓒ Ⓓ		50 Ⓐ Ⓑ Ⓒ Ⓓ

CUT HERE

Mathematics: Content Knowledge Practice Test 1

Directions: Each of the questions or incomplete statements is followed by four suggested answers or completions. Select the one that is best in each case and then fill in the corresponding lettered space on the answer sheet.

1. Rose took a cab from the bus station to her home. She gave the cab driver $20, which included the fare and a tip of $2. The cab company charges $3 for the first mile and 75 cents for each additional ½ mile. How many miles is Rose's home from the bus station?

   A. 10 miles
   B. 11 miles
   C. 20 miles
   D. 21 miles

2. For which of the following expressions is $a + b$ a factor?

   I. $a^2 - b^2$
   II. $a^2 + b^2$
   III. $a^3 - b^3$
   IV. $a^3 + b^3$

   A. I and II only
   B. I and IV only
   C. II and III only
   D. III and IV only

3. A student needs an average of at least 80 on four tests to earn a grade of B in algebra. The student has grades of 78, 91, and 75 on the first three tests. What is the *lowest* grade the student can make on the fourth test and still receive a B in the algebra class?

   A. 99
   B. 82
   C. 80
   D. 76

4. Which of the following statements can be proven using the principle of mathematical induction?

   A. $\sin^2\theta + \cos^2\theta = 1$, where θ is a real number.
   B. $\lim_{x \to 0} \frac{\sin x}{x} = 1$, where x is a real number.
   C. $\sum_{k=1}^{n} k = \frac{n(n+1)}{2}$, where n is a natural number.
   D. $\int_{a}^{b} f(x)\,dx = F(b) - F(a)$, where $F'(b) = f(x)$ and a, b are real numbers.

5. Which of the following expressions is equivalent to the expression $\left(m^2 + 4\right)^{-\frac{1}{2}}$?

   A. $-\dfrac{m^2 + 4}{2}$
   B. $-\sqrt{m^2 + 4}$
   C. $\dfrac{1}{\sqrt{m^2 + 4}}$
   D. $\dfrac{1}{m + 2}$

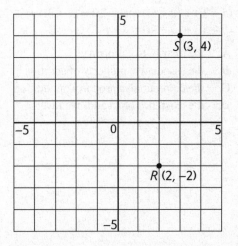

6. What is the distance between the two points R and S in the graph shown here?

   A. $\sqrt{37}$ units
   B. $\sqrt{29}$ units
   C. 7 units
   D. $\sqrt{49}$ units

GO ON TO THE NEXT PAGE

7. Which of the following statements is true about the solution set of the system of equations represented by the graphs shown?

    A. The system of equations has no solution because the two graphs do not intersect.

    B. The solution set is $\{-4, 4, 7\}$.

    C. An x-value that satisfies the system is $\frac{7}{2} + i\frac{\sqrt{41}}{2}$.

    D. An x-value that satisfies the system is $\frac{7}{2} - i\frac{\sqrt{17}}{2}$.

8. Which property of the complex numbers is illustrated here?

$$(5 - 3i) + (2 + 6i) + (1 - 2i) = (7 + 3i) + (1 - 2i) =$$
$$(5 - 3i) + (3 + 4i) = 8 + i$$

    A. the distributive property
    B. the associative property of addition
    C. the commutative property of addition
    D. the existence of an additive inverse

9. Using a digital thermometer, every morning at 8 A.M. for 5 days, a scientist measures the temperature in degrees Celsius of a lake. The temperature readings are 10.6°, 9.2°, 9.1°, 10.8°, and 10.3°. Before the temperature measurements are numerically summarized, the scientist discovers that the digital thermometer used is off by 0.7 degrees. Which of the following is a true statement that can be made about the scientist's data?

    A. The data are unreliable.
    B. The data are imprecise.
    C. The data are inconclusive.
    D. The data are inaccurate.

10. A rectangular-shaped swimming pool is 50 feet wide and 60 feet long with an uneven bottom surface. The table that follows shows the depth of the water at intervals of 10 feet.

Interval	Depth
0 feet	3.0
10 feet	5.1
20 feet	7.5
30 feet	9.6
40 feet	10.5
50 feet	11.5
60 feet	12.0

Using the data in the table, the best approximation of the volume of the water in the pool is:

    A. 22,500 ft^3.
    B. 23,600 ft^3.
    C. 25,850 ft^3.
    D. 28,100 ft^3.

11. A pharmacist measures the mass of a medical substance and uses the appropriate number of significant figures to record the mass as 7 grams, to the nearest gram. Which of the following ways most accurately expresses the range of possible values of the mass of the substance?

    A. 7 grams ± 1.0 grams

    B. 7 grams ± 0.5 grams

    C. 7 grams ± 0.1 grams

    D. 7 grams

12. A carpenter needs to drill a hole in a triangular piece of wood. The center of the hole needs to be equidistant from each side of the triangle. Which of the following constructions should the carpenter do to determine the location of the hole?

    A. Find the intersection of the bisectors of the three angles.

    B. Find the intersection of the three altitudes of the triangle.

    C. Find the intersection of the perpendicular bisectors of the three sides.

    D. Find the intersection of the three medians of the triangle.

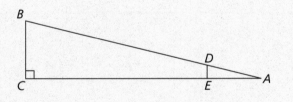

13. In triangle *ABC,* segment *CE* has length 50 units, segment *EA* has length 25 units, and segment *DE* has length 10 units. What is the area of triangle *ABC*?

    A. 750 square units

    B. 1125 square units

    C. 1500 square units

    D. 2250 square units

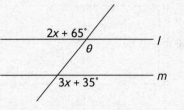

14. In the figure, lines *l* and *m* are parallel. What is the measure of angle θ?

    A. 125°

    B. 97°

    C. 30°

    D. 16°

15. A length of cable is attached to the top of a 24-foot pole. The cable is anchored 7 feet from the base of the pole. What is the length of the cable?

    A. 23 feet

    B. 25 feet

    C. 31 feet

    D. 625 feet

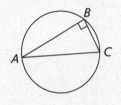

16. In the figure, the circle circumscribed about the right triangle *ABC* has a radius of 4.5 cm. What is the length of the hypotenuse *AC* of right triangle *ABC*?

    A. It cannot be determined from the information given.

    B. 9π cm

    C. 4.5π cm

    D. 9 cm

GO ON TO THE NEXT PAGE

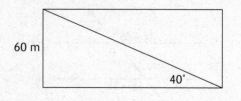

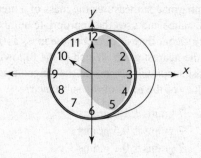

17. In the rectangle shown, what is the length of the diagonal, to the nearest tenth of a meter?

    A. 71.5 m
    B. 78.3 m
    C. 80.5 m
    D. 93.3 m

18. If $y + 4 = 10 \cos x$, what is the maximum value of y?

    A. −14
    B. −6
    C. 6
    D. 14

20. The diagram shows a clock on an x-y coordinate system with the center of the clock at the origin. If the hour hand has length 5 centimeters, what are the coordinates of the tip of the hour hand at 10 o'clock?

    A. $\left(5 \cos \frac{\pi}{6}, 5 \sin \frac{\pi}{6}\right)$
    B. $\left(5 \cos \frac{5\pi}{6}, 5 \sin \frac{5\pi}{6}\right)$
    C. $\left(5 \sin \frac{\pi}{6}, 5 \cos \frac{\pi}{6}\right)$
    D. $\left(5 \sin \frac{5\pi}{6}, 5 \cos \frac{5\pi}{6}\right)$

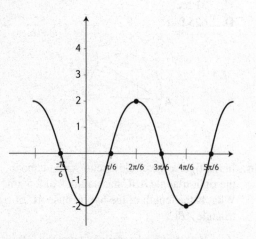

19. The graph above shows a representation of a sound wave on an oscilloscope. Which of the following functions best represents the curve?

    A. $2 \cos\left(x - \frac{\pi}{6}\right)$
    B. $2 \sin\left(x - \frac{\pi}{6}\right)$
    C. $2 \cos\left(3x - \frac{\pi}{2}\right)$
    D. $2 \sin\left(3x - \frac{\pi}{2}\right)$

GO ON TO THE NEXT PAGE

21. Water is poured at a constant rate into the container shown in the diagram. Which of the following graphs best represents the height of the water in the container as a function of time?

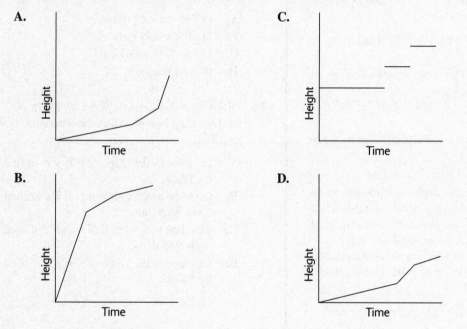

A.

B.

C.

D.

GO ON TO THE NEXT PAGE

22. Which of the following sets of ordered pairs represents a function?

   I. $\{(4, 5), (3, 1), (3, 10), -(2, 0)\}$
   II. $\{(5, 5), (5, 5^2), (5, 5^3), (5, 5^4)\}$
   III. $\{(2, 3), (4, 3), (8, 3), (16, 3)\}$

   A. II only
   B. III only
   C. II and III only
   D. I, II, and III

23. The profit function for a manufacturing company is given by the function $y = \dfrac{x^2 + x - 2000}{100}$, where y is the profit in 1000 dollars per month and x is the number of units sold. If the company sells between 100 units and 400 units per month, which of the following represents the domain D_f and the range R_f of the function?

   A. $D_f = \{x \mid 100 < x < 400\}$; $R_f = \{y \mid 81 < y < 1584\}$
   B. $D_f = \{y \mid 81{,}000 < y < 1{,}584{,}000\}$; $R_f = \{x \mid 100 < x < 400\}$
   C. $D_f = \{y \mid 81 < y < 1584\}$; $R_f = \{x \mid 100 < x < 400\}$
   D. $D_f = \{x \mid 100 < x < 400\}$; $R_f = \{y \mid 81{,}000 < y < 1{,}584{,}000\}$

24. Using data collected through experimentation, an electrical engineer develops a function that relates the electric current that passes through a material to the temperature of the material in a given temperature range. In addition to being a relation, which of the following statements must be true about the function?

   A. It has a smooth graph with no cusps or jagged edges.
   B. It is continuous and takes on values at all points in the temperature range.
   C. It is differentiable at all points in the temperature range.
   D. It gives a single value for the current at each point in the temperature range.

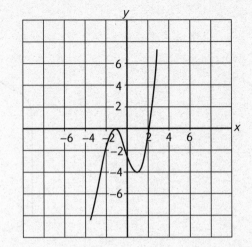

25. The graph shows a relation R between x and y. On which domain is R a function of x?

   A. $\{x \mid -6 < x < 6\}$ only
   B. $\{x \mid 0 < x < 4\}$ only
   C. $\{x \mid x < 0 \cup x > 4\}$ only
   D. the real numbers

26. Given the cubic function $f(x) = x^3$, which of the following best describes the function $f(x) = (x - 5)^3$?

   A. the same as the graph of $f(x) = x^3$ shifted up by 5 units
   B. the same as the graph of $f(x) = x^3$ shifted down by 5 units
   C. the same as the graph of $f(x) = x^3$ shifted right by 5 units
   D. the same as the graph of $f(x) = x^3$ shifted left by 5 units

27. In 2005, recreational fishing lake *A* had a bass population of 1000. Over the previous 10 years, the bass have increased an average of 20 fish each year. Recreational fishing lake *B* had an average bass population decrease of 15 bass per year during the same period and by 2005 had reached a population of 2000. If *t* = the number of years after 2005, which of the following equations can be used to determine the year in which the two lakes will have equal bass populations, assuming the current trends continue?

   A. $1000 - 20t = 2000 + 15t$

   B. $1000 + 20t = 2000 - 15t$

   C. $1000 - 15t = 2000 + 20t$

   D. $1000 + 15t = 2000 + 20t$

28. If $f(x) = \dfrac{2x+6}{x+2}$ and $g(x) = x + 2$, then $(g \circ f)(x) = g(f(x)) =$

   A. $\dfrac{4x+10}{x+2}$.

   B. $\dfrac{2x+10}{x+4}$.

   C. $\dfrac{4x+8}{x+2}$.

   D. $\dfrac{2x+8}{x+4}$.

29. A quality control engineer has determined that a machine can produce $Q(d)$ units per day after *d* days in operation, where $Q(d) = \dfrac{5(6d+14)}{d+7}$. Assuming the machine continues to work efficiently, approximately how many components is the machine able to produce per day after being in operation for a long extended period of time?

   A. 6 units

   B. 10 units

   C. 14 units

   D. 30 units

30. The value of the first derivative at points x_1, x_2, x_3, and x_4 on the graph of an acceleration curve $a(t)$ are as follows:

   $a'(x_1) = -0.8$

   $a'(x_2) = -0.35$

   $a'(x_3) = 0.5$

   $a'(x_4) = 0.72$

At which point is the acceleration changing most rapidly?

   A. point x_1

   B. point x_2

   C. point x_3

   D. point x_4

31. Find the area of the region in the plane bounded by the curve $y = \dfrac{x^2}{2}$ and the line $y = 2$.

   A. $\dfrac{8}{3}$

   B. $\dfrac{16}{3}$

   C. $\dfrac{24}{3}$

   D. $\dfrac{40}{3}$

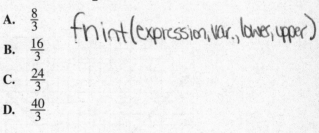

fnint(expression, var., lower, upper)

GO ON TO THE NEXT PAGE

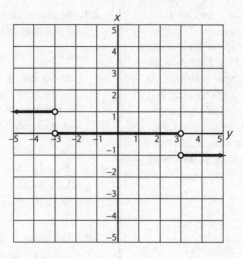

32. The figure is a graph of $y = f'(x)$. Which of the following graphs is a possible representation of f?

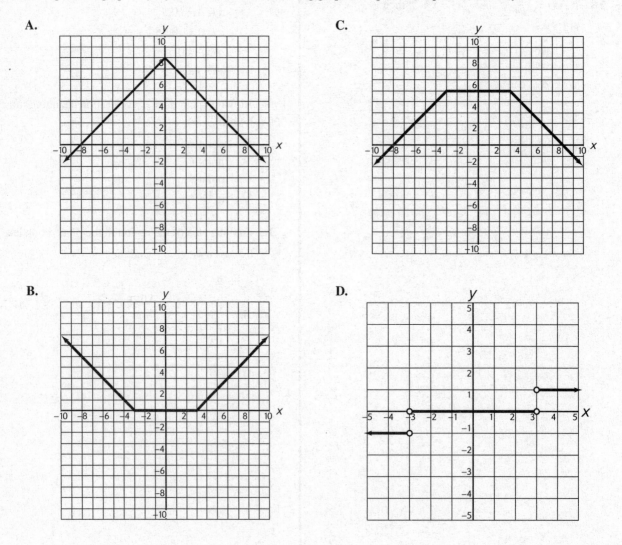

33. The velocity in feet per second of a car during the first 10 seconds of a test run is given by $v(t) = 0.9t^2$. What is the distance the car has traveled after 10 seconds?

    A. 30 feet
    B. 90 feet
    C. 300 feet
    D. 900 feet

34. A rectangular pen is to be adjacent to a brick wall and is to have fencing on three sides, the side on the brick wall requiring no fencing. If 550 yards of fencing are available, find the length of the pen with the largest area.

    A. 110 yds
    B. 137.5 yds
    C. 183.3 yds
    D. 275 yds

35. Richard has participated in eight track meets so far this season. His running times for the 440-meter race have been 73, 63, 68, 64, 69, 61, 66, and 64 seconds. What is Richard's median running time for the eight meets?

    A. 64 seconds
    B. 65 seconds
    C. 66 seconds
    D. 66.5 seconds

Book Genre Preference	
Genre	**Number of Students**
Biography/Historical Nonfiction	22
Historical Fiction	29
Mystery	32
Science/Nature Informational	25
Science Fiction/Fantasy	52
Total	**160**

36. The table above shows the results of a poll of young readers regarding what genre of books they read most often. If a pie chart is constructed using the data in the table, what central angle should be used to represent the category science fiction/fantasy?

    A. 49.5°
    B. 52°
    C. 117°
    D. 187.2°

Results of the Experiment Based on 5 Trials		
Group	**Mean**	**Standard Deviation**
A	30 cm	5 cm
B	30 cm	8 cm
C	25 cm	10 cm
D	25 cm	9 cm

37. The data in the table above are based on five repetitions of the same experiment performed by four different groups of students: Group A, Group B, Group C, and Group D. The data of which group are most reliable?

    A. Group A
    B. Group B
    C. Group C
    D. Group D

GO ON TO THE NEXT PAGE

38. The lifetime of a certain type of disposable razor is normally distributed with a mean of 16.8 shavings and a standard deviation of 2.4 shavings. What percentage of disposable razors of this type will last more than 19.2 shavings?

    A. 2.5%

    B. 16%

    C. 34%

    D. 68%

39. A researcher is analyzing data from an experiment using a simple linear regression model. Using the statistical features of a graphing calculator, the researcher entered the data into the calculator and ran a least squares linear regression. In addition to providing the regression coefficients, the calculator gave a correlation coefficient of –0.03. What should the researcher infer from this coefficient?

    A. The linear model is not a good fit for the data.

    B. The dependent and independent variables have a strong negative correlation.

    C. The slope of the linear model is –0.03.

    D. The intercept of the linear model is –0.03.

	Diagnosis is Positive	Diagnosis is Negative
Smoker	25	5
Non-Smoker	15	155

40. The data in the table above show the diagnosis of 200 subjects consisting of smokers and nonsmokers who were tested for lung cancer in a certain clinic. If one of the 200 subjects tested is randomly selected, what is the probability that the subject was positively diagnosed as having lung cancer, given that the subject is a smoker?

    A. $\frac{1}{5}$

    B. $\frac{1}{6}$

    C. $\frac{5}{8}$

    D. $\frac{5}{6}$

41. A meteorologist predicts that there is a 40% chance of a thunderstorm and a 10% chance that a thunderstorm will produce hail. What is the probability that if a thunderstorm occurs, it will produce hail?

    A. 4%

    B. 10%

    C. 30%

    D. 50%

42. Only one of 10 remote controls in a box is defective. The remote controls are tested one at a time. If the first three remote controls tested are not defective, what is the probability that the fourth remote control tested is defective?

    A. $\frac{99}{100}$

    B. $\frac{1}{10}$

    C. $\frac{1}{7}$

    D. $\frac{7}{10}$

$$7x - 8y + 5z = 5$$
$$-4x + 5y - 3z = -3$$
$$x - y + z = 0$$

43. Solve the system of equations for y.

    A. –2

    B. –1

    C. 0

    D. 1

44. Given $\triangle ABC$ with vertices $A(0, 0)$, $B(3, 0)$, and $C(0, 4)$ in the x-y plane, which of the following matrix transformations represents a dilation of $\triangle ABC$ with center $(0, 0)$ and scale factor 3?

    A. $\begin{bmatrix} 0 & 3 \\ 0 & 3 \end{bmatrix}\begin{bmatrix} 0 & 3 & 0 \\ 0 & 0 & 4 \end{bmatrix}$

    B. $\begin{bmatrix} 3 & 3 \\ 0 & 0 \end{bmatrix}\begin{bmatrix} 0 & 3 & 0 \\ 0 & 0 & 4 \end{bmatrix}$

    C. $\begin{bmatrix} 3 & 3 \\ 3 & 3 \end{bmatrix}\begin{bmatrix} 0 & 3 & 0 \\ 0 & 0 & 4 \end{bmatrix}$

    D. $\begin{bmatrix} 3 & 0 \\ 0 & 3 \end{bmatrix}\begin{bmatrix} 0 & 3 & 0 \\ 0 & 0 & 4 \end{bmatrix}$

45. For which of the following transformations will the magnitude of a vector be unchanged?

   I.   rotation of the vector by an angle θ

   II. translation of the vector by h units to the right and k units up

  III. dilation of the vector with center at the origin by a scale factor of m

   A. I and II only

   B. I and III only

   C. II and III only

   D. I, II, and III

$$\begin{bmatrix} 5 & 1.5 \\ 2 & d \end{bmatrix}$$

46. For what value of d is the 2×2 matrix shown NOT invertible?

   A. –0.6

   B. 0

   C. 0.6

   D. 3

47. Given the recursive function defined by

     $f(0) = 3,$

     $f(n) = 2f(n-1) + 3$ for $n \geq 1,$

what is the value of $f(3)$?

   A. 9

   B. 21

   C. 45

   D. 93

48. How many different license plates can be made consisting of two digits followed by four letters?

   A. $2 \cdot 4$

   B. $\left({}_{10}C_2 \right)\left({}_{26}C_4 \right)$

   C. $10^2 \cdot 26^4$

   D. 36^6

49. A civic club has 200 members. A committee of 5 members is to be selected to attend a national conference. How many different committees could be formed?

   A. ${}_{200}C_5$

   B. ${}_{200}P_5$

   C. 200^5

   D. $200!$

50. The relation "is a subset of" satisfies which of the following properties?

   I.   reflexive

   II. symmetric

  III. transitive

   A. II only

   B. III only

   C. I and III only

   D. II and III only

IF YOU FINISH BEFORE TIME IS CALLED, CHECK YOUR WORK ON THIS SECTION ONLY. DO NOT WORK ON ANY OTHER SECTION IN THE TEST.

Mathematics: Content Knowledge Practice Test 1 Answer Key

Question Number	Correct Answer	Content Category	Question Number	Correct Answer	Content Category
1.	B	Algebra and Number Theory	26.	C	Functions
2.	B	Algebra and Number Theory	27.	B	Functions
3.	D	Algebra and Number Theory	28.	A	Functions
4.	C	Algebra and Number Theory	29.	D	Calculus
5.	C	Algebra and Number Theory	30.	A	Calculus
6.	A	Algebra and Number Theory	31.	B	Calculus
7.	D	Algebra and Number Theory	32.	C	Calculus
8.	B	Algebra and Number Theory	33.	C	Calculus
9.	D	Measurement	34.	D	Calculus
10.	C	Measurement	35.	B	Data Analysis and Statistics
11.	B	Measurement	36.	C	Data Analysis and Statistics
12.	A	Geometry	37.	A	Data Analysis and Statistics
13.	B	Geometry	38.	B	Data Analysis and Statistics
14.	A	Geometry	39.	A	Data Analysis and Statistics
15.	B	Geometry	40.	D	Probability
16.	D	Geometry	41.	A	Probability
17.	D	Trigonometry	42.	C	Probability
18.	C	Trigonometry	43.	B	Matrix Algebra
19.	D	Trigonometry	44.	D	Matrix Algebra
20.	B	Trigonometry	45.	A	Matrix Algebra
21.	A	Functions	46.	C	Matrix Algebra
22.	B	Functions	47.	C	Discrete Mathematics
23.	A	Functions	48.	C	Discrete Mathematics
24.	D	Functions	49.	A	Discrete Mathematics
25.	D	Functions	50.	C	Discrete Mathematics

Answer Explanations for Practice Test 1

1. B. Analyze the problem. The fare is $3 for the first mile plus $0.75 for each additional ½ mile. Devise a plan. To solve the problem, you will need to break the distance into a 1-mile portion plus a portion composed of half-mile segments.

Method 1: You can write an equation that models the situation and solve it.

Let n = the number of half-mile segments

Distance from the bus station to Rose's home = 1 mile + ½ n miles

Fare = $3 + 0.75n$

$$\text{Fare} + \text{Tip} = \$20$$
$$\$3 + \$0.75n + \$2 = \$20$$
$$\$0.75n = \$15$$
$$n = \frac{\$15}{\$0.75}$$
$$n = 20 \text{ half-mile segments}$$

Distance from the bus station to Rose's home = 1 mile + ½ n miles = 1 mile + ½ (20) miles = 11 miles, Choice B.

Choice A results if you forget to add in the first mile to get the total distance. Choices C and D occur if you treat the 20 half-mile segments as miles.

Method 2: Another way to work this problem is to check the answer choices—a smart test-taking strategy for multiple-choice math tests.

Checking Choice A: If the distance to Rose's home is 10 miles, then the trip is broken into a 1-mile portion plus 9 miles = 1 mile + 18 half-miles. The fare for the trip = $3 (for the first mile) + $\left(\frac{\$0.75}{\text{half–mile}} \right)$(18 half-miles) = $3 + $13.50 = $16.50. When you add the $2 tip, the total is $18.50 ≠ $20, so eliminate A.

Checking Choice B: If the distance to Rose's home is 11 miles, then the trip is broken into a 1-mile portion plus 10 miles = 1 mile + 20 half-miles. The fare for the trip = $3 (for the first mile) + $\left(\frac{\$0.75}{\text{half–mile}} \right)$(20 half-miles) = $3 + $15.00 = $18.00. When you add the $2 tip, the total is $20, which is correct. Choice B is the correct response.

In a test situation, you should go on to the next question since you have obtained the correct answer. You would not have to check choices C and D; but for your information Choice C gives $21.50 and Choice D gives $23, both of which are too high.

2. B. This question is an example of a multiple-response set question. One approach to answering this type of question is to follow the following steps:

Step 1. Read the question carefully to make sure you understand what the question is asking.

Step 2. Identify choices that you know are incorrect from the Roman numeral options, and then draw a line through every answer choice that contains a Roman numeral you have eliminated.

Looking at the four expressions given in the Roman numeral options, you can immediately eliminate Roman II because $a^2 + b^2$ is *not* factorable over the real numbers. Draw a line through choices A and C because each of these answer choices contains Roman numeral II.

Step 3. Examine the remaining answer choices to determine which Roman numeral options you need to consider.

The remaining answer choices are B and D, which contain Roman numeral options I, III, and IV. Notice that both B and D contain Roman numeral IV, so you know that Roman numeral IV is correct and that there is no need to check it. Look at the factors of the two remaining Roman numeral options I and III, and draw a line through an answer choice that contains an incorrect Roman numeral option.

I. $a^2 - b^2 = (a + b)(a - b)$

III. $a^3 - b^3 = (a - b)(a^2 + ab + b^2)$

Roman numeral I is correct because $(a + b)$ is a factor of $a^2 - b^2$. Roman numeral III is incorrect because $(a + b)$ is *not* a factor of $a^3 - b^3$. Draw a line through answer Choice D. This leaves answer Choice B as the correct response because it includes every Roman numeral option that is correct and no incorrect Roman numeral options.

3. D. Analyze the problem. The question asks: What is the *lowest* grade the student can make on the fourth test and still receive a B in the course? The average of the student's four test grades must be at least 80. This means the sum of the four test grades divided by 4 must be at least 80. Devise a plan.

Method 1: You can find the answer by writing and solving an equation.

Let $x =$ the lowest grade the student can make on the fourth test and still have at least an 80 average.

$$\frac{\text{sum of 4 test grades}}{4} = \frac{78 + 91 + 75 + x}{4} = 80$$

Solve for x.

$$\frac{244 + x}{4} = 80 \qquad \text{Simplify the numerator.}$$

$$244 + x = 320 \qquad \text{Cross multiply.}$$

$$x = 76$$

The lowest grade that will yield an average of at least 80 is 76, Choice D.

Method 2: Another way to work this problem is to check the answer choices—a smart test-taking strategy for multiple-choice math tests. However, be careful with this problem. Because you have to find the *lowest* test score that will work, you must check all the answer choices even if you find an answer choice that gives an average in the 80s.

Checking A: $\frac{78 + 91 + 75 + 99}{4} = \frac{343}{4} = 85.75$

Checking B: $\frac{78 + 91 + 75 + 82}{4} = \frac{326}{4} = 81.5$

Checking C: $\frac{78 + 91 + 75 + 80}{4} = \frac{324}{4} = 81.0$

Checking D: $\frac{78 + 91 + 75 + 76}{4} = \frac{320}{4} = 80.0$, correct because 76 is the <u>lowest</u> grade needed.

The other answer choices are too high.

Tip: Most graphing calculators allow you to recall and edit the last expression you entered. Use this convenient feature of your calculator to save time with the checking process.

4. C. The **principle of mathematical induction** states that any set of counting numbers which contains the number 1 and which contains $k + 1$, whenever it contains the counting number k, contains all the counting numbers. Eliminate choices A, B, and D, which are statements about the real numbers. Choice C is a statement about the sum of the first n natural numbers. The natural numbers is another name for the counting numbers, so the statement in Choice C can be proven using the principle of mathematical induction. Choice A can be proven using trigonometric concepts and the Pythagorean theorem. Choices B and D can be proven using techniques from calculus.

5. C. The exponent for the quantity $\left(m^2 + 4\right)^{-\frac{1}{2}}$ is $-\frac{1}{2}$. Recall that negative exponents indicate reciprocals and fractional exponents indicate roots. Thus, the exponent $-\frac{1}{2}$ indicates to write the reciprocal of the square root of $m^2 + 4$, which is Choice C: $\frac{1}{\sqrt{m^2 + 4}}$. Choice A results if you mistakenly interpret the exponent to mean multiply $m^2 + 4$ by the exponent, $-\frac{1}{2}$. Choice B results if you mistakenly interpret the exponent to mean that you should write the negative of the square root of $m^2 + 4$. Choice D results if you correctly interpret the exponent, but mistakenly simplify the denominator $\sqrt{m^2 + 4}$ as $m + 2$. The quantity $m + 2$ is not the square root of $m^2 + 4$, because $(m + 2)^2 = m^2 + 4m + 4 \neq m^2 + 4$. Be mindful to avoid careless errors such as those shown in this answer explanation.

6. A. Mark on the diagram. Draw a line connecting the points $R(2, -2)$ and $S(3, 4)$.

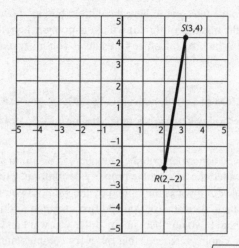

The formula for the distance between two points (x_1, y_1) and (x_2, y_2) is $\sqrt{\left(x_2 - x_1\right)^2 + \left(y_2 - y_1\right)^2}$. To find the distance between $(2, -2)$ and $(3, 4)$, let $x_1 = 2$, $y_1 = -2$, $x_2 = 3$, and $y_2 = 4$, and then plug these values into the formula:

$$\sqrt{\left(x_2 - x_1\right)^2 + \left(y_2 - y_1\right)^2} = \sqrt{\left(3 - 2\right)^2 + \left(4 - (-2)\right)^2} = \sqrt{\left(1\right)^2 + \left(6\right)^2} = \sqrt{1 + 36} = \sqrt{37}.$$

The distance between the points R and S is $\sqrt{37}$ units, Choice A. Choices B, C, and D result if you make a computation error.

7. D. Analyze the problem. The figure shows a circle centered at 0 with radius 4 units and a line that passes through the points $(0, 7)$ and $(7, 0)$. Devise a plan. First, write an equation that represents each of the graphs shown. Next, use algebraic techniques to find the simultaneous solution of the two equations.

Step 1. Write an equation for the circle. The equation of a circle centered at 0 with radius 4 is $x^2 + y^2 = 16$.

Step 2. Write an equation for the line. The line passes through the points $(0, 7)$ and $(7, 0)$. You can use the slope-intercept form of the equation of the line, $y = mx + b$, to write the equation. To find the slope, use the formula for the slope of a line $= \frac{y_2 - y_1}{x_2 - x_1} = \frac{0 - 7}{7 - 0} = \frac{-7}{7} = -1$. The y-intercept b is 7. The equation of the line is $y = -x + 7$.

Step 3. Solve the system of two equations:

$x^2 + y^2 = 16$

$y = -x + 7$

You can solve this system using the technique of substitution. Substitute $y = -x + 7$ into the equation $x^2 + y^2 = 16$.

$$x^2 + (-x + 7)^2 = 16$$
$$x^2 + x^2 - 14x + 49 = 16$$
$$2x^2 - 14x + 33 = 0$$

Use the quadratic formula: $\qquad\qquad x = \dfrac{-b \pm \sqrt{b^2 - 4ac}}{2a}$.

Tip: You should program the quadratic formula into your calculator beforehand to save time during the test. When using your calculator to solve a quadratic formula, *always* set the calculator in complex number mode. Complex number mode will display both real solutions and complex solutions.

$a = 2$, $b = -14$, $c = 33$

$$x = \frac{-(-14) \pm \sqrt{(-14)^2 - 4 \cdot 2 \cdot 33}}{2 \cdot 2} = \frac{14 \pm \sqrt{196 - 264}}{4} = \frac{14 \pm \sqrt{-68}}{4} = \frac{14 \pm 2i\sqrt{17}}{4} = \frac{7}{2} \pm i\frac{\sqrt{17}}{2}.$$

Thus, $\frac{7}{2} - i\frac{\sqrt{17}}{2}$ is an x-value that satisfies the system, making Choice D the correct response. Choice A is the mistake of thinking the graphs must intersect to have a solution; but, as shown here, such a system can have a complex solution. Choice B is the mistake of thinking that the points where the graphs cross the x-axis are the solution set; clearly, this notion is incorrect. Choice C results if you mistakenly write the equation of the circle centered at 0 with radius 4 as $x^2 + y^2 = 4$.

Caution: When an equation or a system of equations has real solutions, you can use the Trace feature of a graphing calculator to find a solution. This method will <u>not</u> work when the graphs do not intersect as in this problem.

8. **B.** The illustration shows that you can group complex numbers in a sum in any way you want and still get the same answer. This property is called the associative property of addition, Choice B. The distributive property, Choice A, is used when a complex number is multiplied by the sum of two other numbers; the results will be the same whether you multiply first and then add, or you add first and then multiply. The commutative property, Choice C, tells you that you can add two numbers in any order you want and still get the same answer. The existence of an additive inverse, Choice D, means that for every complex number there exists a partner that will add to that complex number to give zero as a sum.

9. **D.** In science and mathematics *accurate* refers to the degree to which a measurement is true or correct. The scientist's temperature data are inaccurate because each contains an error of 0.7 degrees, due to the miscalibrated digital thermometer. The measurements do not correctly reflect the true temperature of the lake on the given days. In science and mathematics *precise* refers to the degree to which a measurement is repeatable and reliable; that is, consistently getting the same or similar data each time the measurement is taken. The precision of a measurement depends on the magnitude of the smallest measuring unit used to obtain the measurement (for example, to the nearest meter, to the nearest centimeter, to the nearest millimeter, and so on). In theory, the smaller the measurement unit used, the more precise the measurement. Even though the measurements are inaccurate, they are precise (eliminate Choice B) and reliable (eliminate Choice A) because they are consistently determined within close specified limits. The scientist's data are not *inconclusive* since the scientist can draw conclusions, although the conclusions will be inaccurate due to the faulty measuring device (eliminate Choice C).

10. **C.** Draw a sketch to help you understand the problem.

Analyze the problem. From the information given in the problem, you can know that the swimming pool has an uneven bottom surface. Thus, none of the standard formulas for the volume of a geometric solid can be used to directly calculate the volume of the water in the pool. However, you know that methods of successive approximation can be used to approximate the volume of such geometric figures. With one such method, the volume of the figure is partitioned in two different ways—so that one partitioning overestimates the volume, yielding an upper bound, and the other partitioning underestimates the volume, yielding a lower bound. The average of the upper and lower bounds will yield a good approximation of the volume of the geometric figure. Devise a plan. To approximate the volume of water in the pool will take three steps. First, find an upper bound using the right endpoint values; next, find a lower bound using the left endpoint values; and then, average the upper and lower bounds.

Step 1. Find an upper bound for the volume of water in the pool using the *right* endpoint values. Do this by partitioning the water in the pool into six 10 ft (length) × 50 ft (width) rectangular prisms, whose heights, in order, are 5.1 ft, 7.5 ft, 9.6 ft, 10.5 ft, 11.5 ft, and 12.0 ft as shown here.

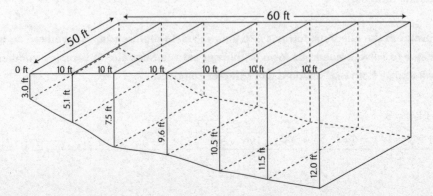

The sum of the volumes of these six rectangular prisms is an upper bound for the volume of the water in the pool.

Upper bound for the volume of water in the pool = 10 ft × 50 ft × 5.1 ft + 10 ft × 50 ft × 7.5 ft + 10 ft × 50 ft × 9.6 ft + 10 ft × 50 ft × 10.5 ft + 10 ft × 50 ft × 11.5 ft + 10 ft × 50 ft × 12.0 ft = 10 ft × 50 ft × (5.1 ft + 7.5 ft + 9.6 ft + 10.5 ft + 11.5 ft + 12.0 ft) = 10 ft × 50 ft × (56.2 ft) = 28,100 ft^3.

> **Tip: Notice that you can simplify the calculation by factoring out 10 ft × 50 ft from each term.**

Step 2. In a similar manner, find a lower bound for the volume of water in the pool using the *left* endpoint values.

Lower bound for the volume in the pool = 10 ft × 50 ft × (3.0 ft + 5.1 ft + 7.5 ft + 9.6 ft + 10.5 ft + 11.5 ft) = 10 ft × 50 ft × (47.2 ft) = 23,600 ft^3.

> **Tip: Most graphing calculators allow you to recall and edit the last expression you entered. To save keystrokes (and, importantly, time), you can recall the calculation you performed in Step 1 and replace 12.0 with 3.0 to find the lower bound.**

Step 3. Average the upper and lower bounds.

$$\frac{28,100 \text{ ft}^3 + 23,600 \text{ ft}^3}{2} = 25,850 \text{ ft}^3, \text{ Choice C.}$$

> **Note: Of course, sequences of increasingly accurate approximations can be obtained by refining the precision of the partitioning (for example, measuring the depth of the water at 5 feet intervals, rather than 10 feet intervals). The upper and lower bounds get increasingly close to each other, and their average will approach the true volume of the geometric figure.**

The other answer choices are not as good approximations as that obtained by averaging an upper and lower bound. Choice A results if you use the formula for the volume of a trapezoidal prism to calculate the volume of water in the pool, where the bases of the trapezoid are 3 ft and 12 ft, the width of the prism is 50 ft, and the height is 60 ft. The sketch of the pool indicates this approach would underestimate the volume to a greater degree than the lower bound obtained by using the left endpoints. Choice B is the lower bound obtained by using the left endpoint values. Choice C is the upper bound obtained by using the right endpoint values.

11. **B.** The **maximum possible error** of a measurement is half the magnitude of the smallest measurement unit used to obtain the measurement. The most accurate way of expressing the measurement is as an interval. Thus, a measurement of 7 grams, to the nearest gram, should be reported as 7 grams ± 0.5 grams, Choice B. Choice A is incorrect because this interval indicates a greater possible error than is necessary. Choice C is incorrect because this interval indicates an error that is less than what should be indicated. Choice D is incorrect because no measurement is exactly correct.

12. **A.** The angle bisectors of a triangle are concurrent in a point that is equidistant from the three sides, which means Choice A is the correct response. Choice B is incorrect because the altitudes of a triangle are concurrent in a point, called the orthocenter of the triangle; but, in general, the point of concurrency is not equidistant from the three sides. Choice C is incorrect because the perpendicular bisectors of a triangle are concurrent in a point that is equidistant from the vertices of the triangle; but, in general, the point of concurrency is not equidistant from the three sides. Choice D is incorrect because the medians of a triangle are concurrent in a point, called the centroid of the triangle; but, in general, the point of concurrency is not equidistant from the three sides.

13. **B.** Mark on the diagram.

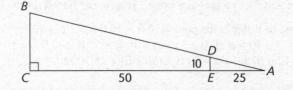

Analyze the problem. From the figure, you can see that triangle *ABC* is a right triangle. To find the area of a right triangle, you find ½ the product of the lengths of the two legs. You can determine the length of leg *CA* by adding the lengths of the two segments, *CE* and *EA*. The length of *BC* can be determined by using properties of the two similar triangles *ABC* and *ADE*. Devise a plan. To find the area of triangle *ABC* will take three steps. First, find the length of leg *CA* by adding the lengths of the two segments, *CE* and *EA*. Next, find the length of leg *BC* by using the proportionality of corresponding sides of the two similar triangles *ABC* and *ADE*. Then, find the area of triangle *ABC* by calculating ½ (length of *CA*)(length of *BC*).

Step 1. Find the length of leg *CA*.

CA = length of *CE* + length of *EA* = 50 units + 25 units = 75 units

Step 2. Find the length of *BC*; call it *x*:

Set up a proportion and solve it:

$$\frac{x}{75} = \frac{10}{25}$$

$$25x = 750 \quad \text{Cross multiply.}$$

$$x = 30 \text{ units}$$

Step 3. Find the area of triangle *ABC*.

area of triangle $ABC = \frac{1}{2}$(30 units)(75 units) = 1125 square units, Choice B.

Choice A results if you use 50 units as the length of leg *CA* when calculating the area. Choice C results if you use 50 units as the length of leg *CA* when calculating the area, and you omit ½ in the area formula. Choice D results if you omit ½ in the area formula.

14. A. Analyze the problem. From the figure, you can see that angles $2x + 65°$ and θ are vertical angles, so they are equal. Angles θ and $3x + 35°$ are corresponding angles of parallel lines, so they are equal. Thus, angles $2x + 65°$ and $3x + 35°$ are equal. Devise a plan. To find the measure of θ will take two steps. First, set the angle expressions $2x + 65°$ and $3x + 35°$ equal to each other, and then solve the resulting equation for *x*. Next, substitute the value obtained for *x* into one of the angle expressions, $2x + 65°$ or $3x + 35°$, to find θ.

Step 1. Solve for *x*.

$$2x + 65° = 3x + 35°$$

$$30° = x$$

Step 2. Substitute the value obtained for *x* into $2x + 65°$.

$2x + 65° = 2(30°) + 65° = 125°$, Choice A.

Choice B results if you mistakenly conclude that angles $2x + 65°$ and $3x + 35°$ are supplementary. Choice C results if you fail to do Step 2. Choice D results if you conclude that angles $2x + 65°$ and $3x + 35°$ are supplementary, and you also fail to do Step 2.

15. B. First sketch a diagram to illustrate the problem.

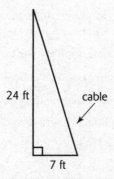

Analyze the problem. The pole, the cable, and the ground form a right triangle. From the diagram, you can see that the length of the cable is the hypotenuse of a right triangle that has legs of 24 feet and 7 feet. You can use the Pythagorean theorem to find the hypotenuse. Devise a plan. To find the length of the cable, plug into the formula for the Pythagorean theorem and solve for the hypotenuse, denoted by c:

$$c = \text{hypotenuse} = ?, \ a = 24 \text{ ft}, \text{ and } b = 7 \text{ ft}$$

$$c^2 = a^2 + b^2 = (24 \text{ ft})^2 + (7 \text{ ft})^2 = 576 \text{ ft}^2 + 49 \text{ ft}^2 = 625 \text{ ft}^2$$

$c = 25$ ft, Choice B. Choice A results if you mistakenly decide that 24 feet is the length of the hypotenuse, instead of the length of a leg of the right triangle. Choice C results if you mistakenly decide to solve the problem by adding the lengths of the two legs to find the length of the hypotenuse. Choice D results if you fail to find the square root of 625.

16. D. Analyze the problem. From the figure, you can see that right angle ABC is an inscribed angle. The measure of an inscribed angle is half the degree measure of its intercepted arc. Thus, the degree measure of arc AC is 180°, making the chord AC, which is the hypotenuse of right triangle ABC, a diameter of the circle. Devise a plan. To find the length of the hypotenuse, multiply the radius by 2. Length of the hypotenuse = 2(4.5 cm) = 9 cm, Choice D. Answer Choice B is the circumference of the circle. Answer Choice C is the length of arc AC.

17. D. Mark on the diagram. Label the diagonal d.

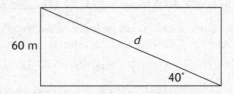

Analyze the problem. From the figure, you can see that the diagonal divides the rectangle into two right triangles. In the lower right triangle, the side 60 m is opposite the angle 40°. Devise a plan. To find d, use the definition of the sine function, and then solve for d.

$$\sin 40° = \frac{\text{length of side opposite 40° angle}}{\text{length of hypotenuse}} = \frac{60 \text{ m}}{d}$$

$d = \dfrac{60 \text{ m}}{\sin 40°} = 93.3$ m (rounded to nearest tenth of a meter), Choice D. Choice A results if you mistakenly use the tangent function, instead of the sine function. Choice B results if you mistakenly use the cosine function, instead of the sine function. Choice C results if you correctly use the sine function, but your calculator is set to radian mode instead of degree mode.

Tip: Be sure to check that your calculator is in degree mode when the angle given is in degrees.

18. C. First, solve for y: $y = 10 \cos x - 4$. The maximum value of the cosine function is 1, so the maximum value of $10 \cos x$ is 10. Thus, the maximum value of $y = 10 \cos x - 4 = 10 - 4 = 6$, Choice C. Choice A results if you mistakenly use −10 as the maximum value for $10 \cos x$. Choices B and D result if you make a sign error.

19. D. From the shape of the graph, you know the graph can be viewed as either a sine or a cosine function. If $b > 0$, the general forms for the sine and cosine functions, $y = a\sin(bx - c) + k$ and $y = a\cos(bx - c) + k$, have graphs with **amplitude** = $|a|$, **period** = $\frac{2\pi}{b}$, a horizontal or **phase shift** of $\frac{c}{b}$ units (to the right of the origin if $\frac{c}{b}$ is positive; to the left of the origin if $\frac{c}{b}$ is negative), and a **vertical shift** of $|k|$ units (up from the origin if k is positive; down from the origin if k is negative). Analyze the graph. Regardless whether you view the graph as a sine or a cosine function, the graph has amplitude 2, period = $\frac{2\pi}{3}$, and no vertical shift (that is, $k = 0$). Solve for b in the general formula by setting $\frac{2\pi}{b} = \frac{2\pi}{3}$, which yields $b = 3$. Eliminate choices A and B because $b = 1$ in each of these expressions. Examine the remaining answer choices. Each has a phase shift = $\frac{c}{b} = \frac{\frac{\pi}{2}}{3} = \frac{\pi}{6}$ to the right of the origin. Looking at the graph, you can see that if you view the graph as a sine function, the graph has a phase shift of $\frac{\pi}{6}$ units to the right of the origin, making Choice D the correct response. Choice C is incorrect because if you view the graph as a cosine function, the phase shift is $\frac{\pi}{3}$ units, not $\frac{\pi}{6}$ units, to the right of the origin.

20. B. Mark on the diagram. Since the hour hand is at 10, the angle from the positive x-axis to the hour hand is $120° = \frac{5\pi}{6}$. The length of the hour hand is 5 cm.

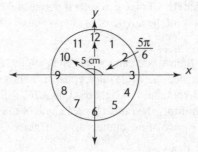

In polar coordinates, the tip of the hour hand is located at $(5, \frac{5\pi}{6})$. To change from polar (r, θ) to rectangular (x, y) use $x = r\cos\theta$; $y = r\sin\theta$. (These formulas are included in the Notation, Definitions, and Formulas pages at the beginning of your test booklet.) Substituting into the formulas, you have the coordinates of the tip of the hour hand are $(5\cos\frac{5\pi}{6}, 5\sin\frac{5\pi}{6})$, Choice B. Choice A results if you mistakenly use the angle $\frac{\pi}{6}$, instead of $\frac{5\pi}{6}$. Choice C results if you mistakenly switch sine and cosine in the conversion formulas. Choice D results if you mistakenly switch sine and cosine in the formulas, and you use the wrong angle.

21. A. Analyze the problem. From the figure, you can see that as water is poured into the container at a constant rate, the height of the water rises at a constant rate until it reaches the point near the top where the bottle narrows. At that point, the water rises at a faster, but still constant rate, until it reaches the neck of the bottle, where it rises at an even faster rate. The graph that corresponds to this analysis is given in Choice A. Choice B is incorrect because it indicates that the rate at which the water rises slows down as the water reaches the top of the bottle. Choice C is incorrect because it indicates that the height of the water in the bottle is constant at first, then suddenly leaps to a higher level and remains constant at that level for a while, and, finally, leaps to an even higher level, where it remains. Choice D is incorrect because it indicates that the rate at which the water rises initially is the same as the rate at which it rises when it reaches the neck of the bottle.

22. B. A **function** is a relation in which each first component is paired with *one and only one* second component. Only the relation in Roman numeral III satisfies this requirement, Choice B. In Roman I, the first component 3 is paired with two different second components, namely, 1 and 10. In Roman II, the first component 5 is paired with four different second components.

23. A. The domain of $y = \frac{x^2 + x - 2000}{100}$ is the set consisting of all its possible x-values; that is, $D_f = \{x \mid 100 < x < 400\}$. The range of $y = \frac{x^2 + x - 2000}{100}$ is the set consisting of all its possible y-values; that is, $R_f = \{y \mid \frac{100^2 + 100 - 2000}{100} < y < \frac{400^2 + 400 - 2000}{100}\} = R_f = \{y \mid 81 < y < 1584\}$. Thus, Choice A is the correct response.

> **Tip:** After you compute the y-value corresponding to $x = 100$, use the Recall Entry feature of your graphing calculator to compute the y-value corresponding to $x = 400$.

Choices B and C are incorrect because these choices use y-values for the domain instead of x-values. Choice D is incorrect because the range of the function is incorrect in this answer choice.

24. D. Only the statement given in Choice D will always be true about the engineer's function. By definition, each first component (temperature value) is paired with one and only one second component (current value). None of the other statements are guaranteed to be true about the engineer's function.

25. D. A graph of a function must pass the vertical line test: If any vertical line can be drawn so that it cuts the graph of a relation in more than one point, the relation is *not* a function. Examining the graph, you can see that the graph passes the vertical line test when x is any real number. Therefore, R is a function on the domain $= \{x \mid x$ is a real number$\}$, Choice D. The relation R fails the vertical line test for the domains given in the other answer choices, which are too restrictive.

26. C. Subtracting a positive constant h from x will result in a horizontal shift of h units to the right. The graph of $f(x) = (x - 5)^3$ is the same as the graph of $f(x) = x^3$ shifted right by 5 units. Eliminate choices A and B because these shifts are vertical. Eliminate D because the shift is to the left, not to the right.

> **Tip:** If you are unsure whether the shift is to the right or left, graph the two functions on your graphing calculator to check.

27. B. Analyze the problem. Lake A starts at a population of 1000 (in 2005) and increases an average of $20t$ fish after t years. Lake B starts at a population of 2000 (in 2005) and decreases an average of $15t$ fish after t years. Devise a plan. Write an expression that represents the bass population in each lake t years after 2005, and set the two expressions equal to each other: $1000 + 20t = 2000 - 15t$, Choice B. The other answer choices result if you analyze the problem incorrectly.

28. A. Everywhere you have x in $g(x) = x + 2$, you must substitute $\frac{2x + 6}{x + 2}$, and then simplify, if possible:

$$(g \circ f)(x) = g(f(x)) = g\left(\frac{2x + 6}{x + 2}\right) = \frac{2x + 6}{x + 2} + 2 = \frac{2x + 6}{x + 2} + \frac{2(x + 2)}{x + 2} = \frac{2x + 6}{x + 2} + \frac{2x + 4}{x + 2} = \frac{4x + 10}{x + 2}, \text{ Choice A.}$$

Choice B is what you get if you find $(f \circ g)(x) = f(g(x))$ instead of $(g \circ f)(x) = g(f(x))$. Choice C results if you make a simplifying error when finding $(g \circ f)(x) = g(f(x))$. Choice D results if you make the mistake of finding $f(g(x))$ instead of $g(f(x))$, and you make a simplifying error as well.

29. D. Analyze the problem. The phrase "a long extended period of time" is a clue that this is a calculus problem in which you need to find the limit of a function as the variable approaches infinity. Devise a plan. To answer the question, you will need to find the limit of the function $Q(d) = \frac{5(6d + 14)}{d + 7}$ as d approaches infinity:

$$\lim_{d \to \infty} \frac{5(6d + 14)}{d + 7} = \lim_{d \to \infty} \frac{30d + 70}{d + 7} = \lim_{d \to \infty} \frac{30 + \frac{70}{d}}{1 + \frac{7}{d}} = \frac{30 + 0}{1 + 0} = \frac{30}{1} = 30 \text{ units, Choice D. Choices A and C result if}$$

you evaluate the limit as d approaches infinity incorrectly. Choice B results if you find the limit as d approaches zero, instead of the limit as d approaches infinity.

30. A. The value of the first derivative at each point x_1, x_2, x_3, and x_4 is the instantaneous rate of change of the acceleration curve at that point. The acceleration is changing most rapidly at point x_1 because the magnitude of the change is greatest at this point, Choice A.

31. B. Make a quick sketch of the two graphs.

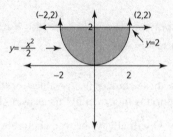

Analyze the problem. The two graphs intersect at the points $(-2, 2)$ and $(2, 2)$, and $y = 2$ lies above $y = \dfrac{x^2}{2}$ between $x = -2$ and $x = 2$. Devise a plan. To find the area of the region bounded by the two graphs, evaluate the following definite integral: $\displaystyle\int_{-2}^{2}\left(2 - \frac{x^2}{2}\right)dx$.

Method 1: The fastest and most efficient way to calculate this numerical integral is with your graphing calculator. Here are the steps using a TI-83 calculator. Before you enter functions, you must select Func mode, from the MODE menu. Enter the function $y = 2 - \dfrac{x^2}{2}$ into the Y = editor, which is where you define functions. As a precaution, clear any previously entered functions before you enter the function. Check the viewing WINDOW to make sure that the interval between –2 and 2 falls between Xmin and Xmax. If not, change Xmin and/or Xmax, as needed. Select $7: \int f(x)\,dx$ from the CALC (calculate) menu. Type –2 as the lower limit and then press ENTER. Type 2 as the upper limit and then press ENTER. The integral value is displayed as 5.3333333 and the graph is shaded (Note: the shaded region will be the mirror image of what you've shaded above because you entered the difference of the two functions into the function editor). Since the answer choices are given as fractions, select 1:Frac from the MATH menu. The display will show Ans►Frac. Press ENTER. The display shows $^{16}/_3$, Choice B.

Method 2: Integrate the function using methods of calculus.

$$\int_{-2}^{2}\left(2 - \frac{x^2}{2}\right)dx = \left(2x - \frac{x^3}{6}\right)\Bigg|_{-2}^{2} = \left(2\cdot2 - \frac{2^3}{6}\right) - \left(2\cdot-2 - \frac{(-2)^3}{6}\right) = \left(4 - \frac{8}{6}\right) - \left(-4 - \frac{-8}{6}\right) = 4 - \frac{4}{3} + 4 - \frac{4}{3} =$$

$8 - \dfrac{8}{3} = \dfrac{24}{3} - \dfrac{8}{3} = \dfrac{16}{3}$, Choice B. The other answer choices result if you make a mistake integrating the function.

32. C. Analyze the problem. Recall that the first derivative of a function at a point is equal to the slope of the graph at that point. By inspecting the graph of $y = f'(x)$, you can see that to the left of –3, the slope of the graph of f is a constant value of positive 1, indicating that to the left of –3 the graph of $y = f(x)$ is a straight line slanted to the right with slope of 1. Eliminate choices B and D because the graphs in these answer choices do not meet this condition. Between –3 and 3, according to the graph of $y = f'(x)$, the slope of the graph of f is a constant value of zero, indicating that between –3 and 3 the graph of $y = f(x)$ is a horizontal line. Eliminate Choice A because the graph in this answer choice does not have a horizontal component. By inspecting the graph of $y = f'(x)$, you can see that to the right of 3, the slope of the graph of f is a constant value of negative 1, indicating that to the right of 3 the graph of $y = f(x)$ is a straight line slanted to the left with slope of –1. Therefore, Choice C is the correct response because the graph in this answer choice is the only graph shown in the answer choices that is consistent with the behavior of $y = f'(x)$.

33. C. Analyze the problem. Recall that the first derivative of a position function is the velocity function. Devise a plan. To find the distance traveled after 10 seconds find the numerical integral of the velocity function between 0 and 10 seconds. That is, evaluate the following definite integral: $\int_{0}^{10} 0.9t^2 \, dt$.

Method 1: As in problem 31, the fastest and most efficient way to calculate this numerical integral is with your graphing calculator. Here are the steps using a TI-83 calculator. Before you enter functions, you must select Func mode, from the MODE menu. Enter the function $y = 0.9x^2$ into the Y = editor, which is where you define functions. Notice that you must use y and x for the variables instead of v and t. As a precaution, clear any previously entered functions before you enter the function. Check the viewing WINDOW to make sure that the interval between 0 and 10 falls between Xmin and Xmax. If not, change Xmin and/or Xmax, as needed. Select 7: $\int f(x) \, dx$ from the CALC (calculate) menu. Type 0 as the lower limit and then press ENTER. Type 10 as the upper limit and then press ENTER. The integral value is displayed as 300. Therefore, the distance the car has traveled after 10 seconds is 300 feet, Choice C.

Method 2: Integrate the function using methods of calculus.

$\int_{0}^{10} 0.9t^2 \, dt = \frac{0.9t^3}{3}\Big|_{0}^{10} = 0.3t^3\Big|_{0}^{10} = 0.3(10)^3 - 0.3(0)^3 = 0.3(1000) - 0.3(0) = 300 - 0 = 300$. Therefore, the distance the car has traveled after 10 seconds is 300 feet, Choice C. Choice A results if you make a calculation error. Choice B results if you fail to integrate the function. Choice D results if you fail to integrate the function, and you make a calculation error.

34. D. Analyze the problem. Let the two sides of the pen that are perpendicular to the brick wall each have length of x yards. Then the side parallel to the wall has length 550 yards – $2x$, since the sum of the three sides is 550 yards. Sketch a diagram to illustrate the problem:

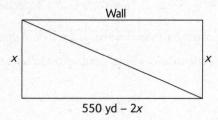

The area of the field is given by the function f, where $f(x) = x(550 - 2x) = 550x - 2x^2$

The pen will have maximum area when $f(x)$ is the maximum value of f. Devise a plan. To find the length of the pen with largest area will take three steps. First, solve $f'(x) = 0$ to find the critical point(s) for f. Check $f''(x)$ to determine whether a critical point is a maximum. If a critical point is a maximum, find the length of maximum area.

Step 1. Find the critical point(s) for f.

$f(x) = 550x - 2x^2$

$f'(x) = 550 - 4x = 0$

$x = 137.5$ yards.

Thus, $(137.5, f(137.5))$ is a critical point of f.

Step 2. Check $f''(137.5)$.

$f'(x) = 550 - 4x$

$f''(x) = -4 \Rightarrow f''(137.5) = -4 < 0$.

Thus, by the second derivative test, $f(137.5)$ will be the maximum area of the pen.

Step 3. Find the length of the pen that encloses the maximum area.

Length = 550 yd – 2(137.5 yd) = 275 yd, Choice D. Choice B results if you fail to do Step 3. The other answer choices result if you analyze the problem incorrectly.

35. B. In an ordered set of numbers, the median is the middle number if there is a middle number; otherwise, the median is the arithmetic average of the two middle numbers. First, put the running times in order from smallest to largest: 61 s, 63 s, 64 s, 64 s, 66 s, 68 s, 69 s, 73 s. Since there is no middle number, average the two running times, 64 s and 66 s that are in the middle of the list: $\frac{64\ s + 66\ s}{2} = \frac{130\ s}{2} = 65$ s, Choice B.

Choice A is the mode running time. Choice C is the mean running time. Choice D results if you forget to put the running times in order first.

36. C. A pie chart is made by dividing the 360 degrees of the circle that makes the pie chart into portions that correspond to the proportion for each category. The central angle that should be used to represent the category science fiction/fantasy $= \frac{52}{160}(360°) = 117°$, Choice C. Choice A is the central angle for the biography/historical nonfiction category. Choice B results if you use the number in the table for the degree measure. Choice D results if you treat the number in the table as a percentage of the total circle.

37. A. The standard deviation for the data obtained by Group A is less than the standard deviations of the data from the other groups, which means the data from Group A have less variability and are, therefore, more reliable.

38. B. Analyze the problem. According to the 68-95-99.7 rule, approximately 68 percent of the values of a random variable that is normally distributed falls within 1 standard deviation of the mean, about 95 percent falls within 2 standard deviations of the mean, and about 99.7 percent falls within 3 standard deviations of the mean. The mean number of shavings for the razors is 16.8 with standard deviation of 2.4 shavings. Devise a plan. To find the percentage of razors that will last more than 19.2 shavings will take two steps. First, determine the z-score for 19.2 shavings, and then find the percentage of the normal distribution that is above that z-score.

Step 1. Find the z-score for 19.2.

$z\text{-score} = \dfrac{\text{value} - \text{mean}}{\text{standard deviation}} = \dfrac{19.2 - 16.8}{2.4} = 1$. Therefore, 19.2 is 1 standard deviation above the mean.

Step 2. Find the percentage of the normal distribution that is 1 standard deviation above the mean.

You know that about 68% of the distribution is within standard deviation of the mean. Make a sketch to illustrate the problem.

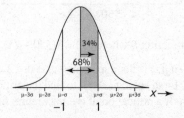

Since the normal curve is symmetric, about 34 percent ($\frac{1}{2}$ of 68 percent) of the distribution is between the mean and 1 standard deviation. Again, due to symmetry, 50 percent of the distribution is above the mean. Thus, approximately $50 - 34 = 16$ percent of the distribution is above 1 standard deviation above the mean. Thus, about 16 percent of the razors will last more than 19.2 shavings, Choice B. Choice A is the percentage of razors that will last more than 2 standard deviations above the mean. Choice C is the percentage of razors that will last between 16.8 shavings and 19.2 shavings. Choice D is the percentage of razors that will last within 1 standard deviation of the mean.

39. A. Since the correlation coefficient measures the linear relationship between the independent and dependent variables of the simple linear regression model, it can be used as an estimate of the "goodness of fit" of the regression model. Since the value –0.03 of the correlation coefficient is near zero, it fails to support a linear relationship between the variables of the linear regression, indicating that the linear model is not a good fit for the data, Choice A. Choice B is incorrect because the value –0.03 of the correlation coefficient implies little or no linear relationship between the dependent and independent variables. Choices C and D are incorrect because, in general, neither the slope nor the intercept for the regression model is the same as the correlation coefficient between the independent and dependent variables of the regression.

40. D. Analyze the problem. This question asks you to find a conditional probability; that is, you are to find the probability when you already know that the subject is a smoker. Thus, when computing the probability, the number of possible subjects under consideration is no longer 200 subjects, but is reduced to the total number of smokers. Devise a plan. To find the probability that if one of the 200 subjects is randomly selected, the subject was positively diagnosed with lung cancer, *given* that the subject is a smoker will take two steps. First, find the total number of smokers, and then, of these, find the probability that a smoker was diagnosed with lung cancer.

Step 1. Find the total number of smokers.

Total number of smokers = 25 + 5 = 30 smokers.

Step 2. Of the 30 smokers, find the probability that a smoker was diagnosed with lung cancer.

The probability the smoker was diagnosed with lung cancer = P(diagnosed with lung cancer|subject is a smoker) = $\frac{25}{30} = \frac{5}{6}$, Choice D. Choice A is the probability that a randomly selected subject is diagnosed with lung cancer, regardless whether the subject is or is not a smoker. Choice B is the probability that a randomly selected subject had a negative diagnosis of lung cancer, given that the subject is a smoker. Choice C is the probability that a randomly selected subject is a smoker, given the subject was diagnosed with lung cancer.

41. A. This problem requires an application of the Multiplication Rule, which states that $P(A \text{ and } B) = P(A) P(B|A)$. P(thunderstorm and hail) = P(thunderstorm) P(hail given that there is a thunderstorm) = $40\% \cdot 10\% = .4 \cdot .1 = 0.04 = 4\%$, Choice A. The other answer choices result if you analyze the problem incorrectly.

42. C. Analyze the problem. Since there are only 7 remote controls left in the box, one of which is defective, the probability that the next remote control is defective = $\frac{1}{7}$. The other answer choices result if you analyze the problem incorrectly.

43. B. The augmented matrix for the system is

$$\begin{bmatrix} 7 & -8 & 5 & 5 \\ -4 & 5 & -3 & -3 \\ 1 & -1 & 1 & 0 \end{bmatrix}$$

Although you can work this problem by using operations on the rows to transform the matrix so that the solution to the system is easily obtainable, the process is tedious and time-consuming. Since the Mathematics CK is a timed test, you should use your graphing calculator to find the solution. Enter the elements of the augmented matrix into the calculator, and then have the calculator produce the reduced row-echelon form of the augmented matrix. The display will show the following:

$$\begin{bmatrix} 1 & 0 & 0 & 1 \\ 0 & 1 & 0 & -1 \\ 0 & 0 & 1 & -2 \end{bmatrix}.$$ Thus, $x = 1$, $y = -1$, and $z = -2$ is the solution to the system.

Since $y = -1$, Choice B is the correct response. Choice A is the value of z in the solution set. Choice D is the value of x in the solution set. Choice C occurs if you make an error when determining the solution.

Tip: Be sure to use the negation key, not the subtraction key, when entering negative numbers as elements of the augmented matrix.

44. D. To answer this question, you will need to use your knowledge of matrix multiplication and transformations of geometric figures. You can represent the triangle ABC using a 2×3 matrix, with each column $\begin{bmatrix} x \\ y \end{bmatrix}$ representing a vertex: $\begin{bmatrix} 0 & 3 & 0 \\ 0 & 0 & 4 \end{bmatrix}$. The dilation of ABC, using a scale factor of 3, would be represented by the matrix $\begin{bmatrix} 0 & 9 & 0 \\ 0 & 0 & 12 \end{bmatrix}$. Looking at the answer choices, you can see that you need to select the 2×2 matrix that will multiply times $\begin{bmatrix} 0 & 3 & 0 \\ 0 & 0 & 4 \end{bmatrix}$ to give $\begin{bmatrix} 0 & 9 & 0 \\ 0 & 0 & 12 \end{bmatrix}$. A quick way to work this problem is to check the answer choices.

Checking A: $\begin{bmatrix} 0 & 3 \\ 0 & 3 \end{bmatrix}\begin{bmatrix} 0 & 3 & 0 \\ 0 & 0 & 4 \end{bmatrix} = \begin{bmatrix} 0 & 0 & \\ & & \end{bmatrix}$, eliminate A because the element in the first row second column is

not 9. There is no need to complete the multiplication.

Checking B: $\begin{bmatrix} 3 & 3 \\ 0 & 0 \end{bmatrix}\begin{bmatrix} 0 & 3 & 0 \\ 0 & 0 & 4 \end{bmatrix} = \begin{bmatrix} 0 & 9 & 12 \\ & & \end{bmatrix}$, eliminate B because the element in the first row third column is not

0. There is no need to complete the multiplication.

Checking C: $\begin{bmatrix} 3 & 3 \\ 3 & 3 \end{bmatrix}\begin{bmatrix} 0 & 3 & 0 \\ 0 & 0 & 4 \end{bmatrix} = \begin{bmatrix} 0 & 9 & 12 \\ 0 & 9 & \end{bmatrix}$, eliminate C because the element in the second row second column

is not 0. There is no need to complete the multiplication.

Thus, Choice D is the correct response since you've eliminated choices A, B, and C.

> **Tip: A quick way to check the answer choices is to do the multiplication with your graphing calculator. Enter the matrix $\begin{bmatrix} 0 & 3 & 0 \\ 0 & 0 & 4 \end{bmatrix}$ as matrix *B*. Then enter $\begin{bmatrix} 0 & 3 \\ 0 & 3 \end{bmatrix}$, Choice A, as matrix *A*. Next multiply [A] times [B], being sure to put [A] to the left of [B]. Now edit [A], so that it has elements $\begin{bmatrix} 3 & 3 \\ 0 & 0 \end{bmatrix}$, Choice B. Use the Recall Entry feature of the calculator to do the multiplication. Repeat for Choice C.**

45. A. This question is an example of a multiple-response set question. One approach to answering this type of question (as shown in a previous answer explanation) is to follow the following steps:

Step 1. Read the question carefully to make sure you understand what the question is asking.

A vector has magnitude and direction. The magnitude is the length of the vector, disregarding the direction.

Step 2. Identify choices that you know are incorrect from the Roman numeral options, and then draw a line through every answer choice that contains a Roman numeral you have eliminated.

Looking at the three transformations given in the Roman numeral options, you can immediately eliminate Roman III because dilating a vector would change its magnitude. Draw a line through choices B, C, and D because each of these answer choices contains Roman numeral III.

Choice A is correct because you've eliminated the other answer choices. You do not have to continue with the problem; but for your information, transformations and rotations are "rigid motions," meaning that magnitudes are preserved under these transformations.

46. C. Analyze the problem. The matrix $\begin{bmatrix} 5 & 1.5 \\ 2 & d \end{bmatrix}$ is not invertible if its determinant is equal to zero. Devise a plan. Set the determinant of the matrix equal to zero and solve for d.

$5d - (2)(1.5) = 5d - 3 = 0 \Leftrightarrow d = \frac{3}{5} = 0.6$, Choice C. The other answer choices result if you make a calculation error.

47. C. For the recursive formula given in the problem, you will need to find $f(2)$ and $f(1)$ before you can find $f(3)$. Since the problem tells you that $f(0) = 3$ and that $f(n) = 2f(n - 1) + 3$ for $n \geq 1$, then

$f(1) = 2f(0) + 3 = 2(3) + 3 = 6 + 3 = 9$

$f(2) = 2f(1) + 3 = 2(9) + 3 = 18 + 3 = 21$

$f(3) = 2f(2) + 3 = 2(21) + 3 = 42 + 3 = 45$, Choice C.

Choice A is $f(1)$, not $f(3)$. Choice B is $f(2)$, not $f(3)$. Choice D is $f(4)$, not $f(3)$.

48. C. Analyze the problem. Since there are six places to be filled, so to speak, on a license plate, you can work this problem by extending the Fundamental Counting Principle to six events. There are 10 possibilities for each of the two digits and 26 possible values for each of the four letters, which means the total number of possible license plates is $10 \cdot 10 \cdot 26 \cdot 26 \cdot 26 \cdot 26 = 10^2 \cdot 26^4$, Choice C. The other answer choices result if you analyze the problem incorrectly.

49. A. Since the order in which committee members are chosen does not make a difference as regards the composition of the committee, the number of different committees of size 5 that can be selected from the 200 members is $_{200}C_5$, Choice A. Choice B is incorrect because this answer counts different orders of selection of the same committee members as different committees. Choices C and D result if you analyze the problem incorrectly.

50. C. This question is an example of a multiple-response set question. One approach to answering this type of question (as shown in a previous answer explanation) is to follow the following steps:

Step 1. Read the question carefully to make sure you understand what the question is asking.

Recall that a set A is a subset of set B, written $A \subseteq B$, if and only if $x \in A \Rightarrow x \in B, \forall\, x \in A$.

Step 2. Identify choices that you know are incorrect from the Roman numeral options and then draw a line through every answer choice that contains a Roman numeral you have eliminated.

Looking at the three properties given in the Roman numeral options, you can immediately eliminate Roman II. The relation "is a subset of" is not symmetric because, for instance, $\{1, 3\} \subseteq$ Integers, but Integers $\subseteq \{1, 3\}$. Draw a line through choices A and D because each of these answer choices contains Roman numeral II.

Step 3. Examine the remaining answer choices to determine which Roman numeral options you need to consider.

The remaining answer choices are B and C, which contain Roman numeral options I and III. Notice that both B and C contain Roman numeral III, so you know that Roman numeral III is correct and that there is no need to check it. Look at the remaining Roman numeral option I. The relation "is a subset of" is reflexive because every set is a subset of itself; that is $A \subseteq A$.

Since Roman numeral I is correct, draw a line through answer Choice B. This leaves answer Choice C as the correct response because it includes every Roman numeral option that is correct and no incorrect Roman numeral options.

Answer Grid for Practice Test 2

(Remove This Sheet and Use It to Mark Your Answers)

1 Ⓐ Ⓑ Ⓒ Ⓓ	26 Ⓐ Ⓑ Ⓒ Ⓓ
2 Ⓐ Ⓑ Ⓒ Ⓓ	27 Ⓐ Ⓑ Ⓒ Ⓓ
3 Ⓐ Ⓑ Ⓒ Ⓓ	28 Ⓐ Ⓑ Ⓒ Ⓓ
4 Ⓐ Ⓑ Ⓒ Ⓓ	29 Ⓐ Ⓑ Ⓒ Ⓓ
5 Ⓐ Ⓑ Ⓒ Ⓓ	30 Ⓐ Ⓑ Ⓒ Ⓓ
6 Ⓐ Ⓑ Ⓒ Ⓓ	31 Ⓐ Ⓑ Ⓒ Ⓓ
7 Ⓐ Ⓑ Ⓒ Ⓓ	32 Ⓐ Ⓑ Ⓒ Ⓓ
8 Ⓐ Ⓑ Ⓒ Ⓓ	33 Ⓐ Ⓑ Ⓒ Ⓓ
9 Ⓐ Ⓑ Ⓒ Ⓓ	34 Ⓐ Ⓑ Ⓒ Ⓓ
10 Ⓐ Ⓑ Ⓒ Ⓓ	35 Ⓐ Ⓑ Ⓒ Ⓓ
11 Ⓐ Ⓑ Ⓒ Ⓓ	36 Ⓐ Ⓑ Ⓒ Ⓓ
12 Ⓐ Ⓑ Ⓒ Ⓓ	37 Ⓐ Ⓑ Ⓒ Ⓓ
13 Ⓐ Ⓑ Ⓒ Ⓓ	38 Ⓐ Ⓑ Ⓒ Ⓓ
14 Ⓐ Ⓑ Ⓒ Ⓓ	39 Ⓐ Ⓑ Ⓒ Ⓓ
15 Ⓐ Ⓑ Ⓒ Ⓓ	40 Ⓐ Ⓑ Ⓒ Ⓓ
16 Ⓐ Ⓑ Ⓒ Ⓓ	41 Ⓐ Ⓑ Ⓒ Ⓓ
17 Ⓐ Ⓑ Ⓒ Ⓓ	42 Ⓐ Ⓑ Ⓒ Ⓓ
18 Ⓐ Ⓑ Ⓒ Ⓓ	43 Ⓐ Ⓑ Ⓒ Ⓓ
19 Ⓐ Ⓑ Ⓒ Ⓓ	44 Ⓐ Ⓑ Ⓒ Ⓓ
20 Ⓐ Ⓑ Ⓒ Ⓓ	45 Ⓐ Ⓑ Ⓒ Ⓓ
21 Ⓐ Ⓑ Ⓒ Ⓓ	46 Ⓐ Ⓑ Ⓒ Ⓓ
22 Ⓐ Ⓑ Ⓒ Ⓓ	47 Ⓐ Ⓑ Ⓒ Ⓓ
23 Ⓐ Ⓑ Ⓒ Ⓓ	48 Ⓐ Ⓑ Ⓒ Ⓓ
24 Ⓐ Ⓑ Ⓒ Ⓓ	49 Ⓐ Ⓑ Ⓒ Ⓓ
25 Ⓐ Ⓑ Ⓒ Ⓓ	50 Ⓐ Ⓑ Ⓒ Ⓓ

CUT HERE

Directions: Each of the questions or incomplete statements is followed by four suggested answers or completions. Select the one that is best in each case, and then fill in the corresponding lettered space on the answer sheet.

1. Which of the following mathematical techniques is a key tool for converting the equation $y = ax^2 + bx + c$ into the form $y - k = a(x - h)^2$?

   A. solving quadratic equations
   B. differentiating
   C. completing the square
   D. squaring polynomials

   $$13 + 39 + 87 + 11 = 13 + 87 + 39 + 11 =$$
   $$100 + 50 = 150$$

2. Which of the following properties of the real numbers are illustrated by the preceding computation sequence?

   I. commutativity
   II. associativity
   III. distributive property

   A. I and II only
   B. I and III only
   C. II and III only
   D. I, II, and III

   input
   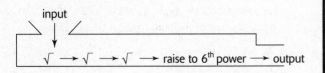
   $\sqrt{} \longrightarrow \sqrt{} \longrightarrow \sqrt{} \longrightarrow$ raise to 6th power $\longrightarrow$ output

3. If a positive number x is used as the input for the function machine shown, which of the following is equivalent to the output?

   A. $x^{\frac{1}{24}}$
   B. $x^{\frac{3}{4}}$
   C. x
   D. $x^{\frac{3}{2}}$

4. For what positive value of k will the graph of the function $y = \dfrac{5}{16x^2 + kx + 9}$ have exactly one vertical asymptote?

   A. 0
   B. 12
   C. 24
   D. 48

5. What is the equation of the line that is perpendicular to the line whose equation is $5x - 6y = 4$ and passes through the point $(3, 1)$?

   A. $5x - 6y = 9$
   B. $-6x + 5y = -13$
   C. $6x + 5y = 23$
   D. $6x + 5y = 21$

6. Given the recursive function defined by

   $$f(1) = 1,$$
   $$f(2) = 2,$$
   $$f(n) = 2f(n - 1) + f(n - 2) \text{ for } n \geq 3,$$

   what is the value of $f(5)$?

   A. 5
   B. 12
   C. 29
   D. 70

7. How many cups of water does a 5-gallon container of water hold?

   A. 20 cups
   B. 40 cups
   C. 60 cups
   D. 80 cups

GO ON TO THE NEXT PAGE

8. The exterior of a spherical tank with radius 12 feet is to be painted with one coat of paint. The paint sells for $22.40 per gallon and can be purchased in one gallon cans only. If a can of paint will cover approximately 400 square feet, what is the cost of the paint needed to paint the exterior of the tank?

   A. $22.40
   B. $44.80
   C. $101.36
   D. $112.00

9. A 26-foot cable is attached to a 30-foot pole. One end of the cable is anchored 10 feet from the base of the pole. How high up on the pole does the other end of the cable reach?

   A. 16 feet
   B. 24 feet
   C. 28 feet
   D. 30 feet

10. Kathryn runs the same distance each morning before going to work. For 10 days she records her running times for her target distance. Her recorded running times are 20 minutes, 35 minutes, 34 minutes, 30 minutes, 32 minutes, 36 minutes , 25 minutes, 35 minutes, 28 minutes, and 35 minutes. What is the difference between Kathryn's median running time and her mean running time for the 10 days?

   A. 0 minutes
   B. 2 minutes
   C. 3 minutes
   D. 4 minutes

11. Paul calls long distance to his friend J.D. in Germany. The first minute of the call costs $3.75, and each additional minute costs $0.55. The total cost of the call is $11.45. For how many minutes did the phone call between Paul and J.D. last?

   A. 13 minutes
   B. 14 minutes
   C. 15 minutes
   D. 16 minutes

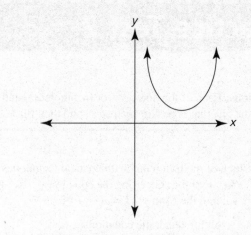

12. A quadratic function $y = ax^2 + bx + c$ with real coefficients has the graph shown. Which of the statements about the discriminant of the function, $b^2 - 4ac$, is true?

   A. $b^2 - 4ac = 0$.
   B. $b^2 - 4ac < 0$.
   C. $b^2 - 4ac > 0$.
   D. $b^2 - 4ac$ is undefined.

13. $(2 \cos 10° + 2\,i \sin 10°)^3$ equals

   A. $4\sqrt{3} + 4i$
   B. $4 + 4\sqrt{3}i$
   C. $8 \cos 1000° + 8\,i \sin 1000°$
   D. $8 \sin 1000° + 8\,i \cos 1000°$

14. Using a protractor, a student measures the three angles of a triangle, and then adds the three measurements to obtain a sum of 172°. What is the percent error of the sum to the nearest percent?

   A. 4%
   B. 5%
   C. 44%
   D. 47%

15. Triangle *ABC* has vertices (2, 1), (–3, 4), and (5, –3). Which of the following matrix multiplications would result in a reflection of △*ABC* over the *x*-axis?

A. $\begin{bmatrix} -1 & 0 \\ 0 & 1 \end{bmatrix}\begin{bmatrix} 2 & -3 & 5 \\ 1 & 4 & -3 \end{bmatrix}$

B. $\begin{bmatrix} 0 & 1 \\ -1 & 0 \end{bmatrix}\begin{bmatrix} 2 & -3 & 5 \\ 1 & 4 & -3 \end{bmatrix}$

C. $\begin{bmatrix} 0 & 1 \\ 1 & 0 \end{bmatrix}\begin{bmatrix} 2 & -3 & 5 \\ 1 & 4 & -3 \end{bmatrix}$

D. $\begin{bmatrix} 1 & 0 \\ 0 & -1 \end{bmatrix}\begin{bmatrix} 2 & -3 & 5 \\ 1 & 4 & -3 \end{bmatrix}$

16. Which of the following relations is NOT an equivalence relation?

A. "is similar to" over the set of all parallelograms
B. "is equal to" over the set of all $m \times n$ matrices
C. "is perpendicular to" over the set of all lines in the Cartesian coordinate plane
D. "is congruent to" over the set of all triangles

17. For which of the following data sets is the median clearly a preferred alternative to the mean as a measure of central tendency?

A. The data set contains some extremely high, without corresponding extremely low, data values.
B. The data set has a somewhat symmetrical distribution.
C. The data set is very large in number and has no mode.
D. The data set is very small in number and has no mode.

18. A box contains 50 1-inch-×-1-inch wooden tiles numbered 1 through 50. If one tile is drawn at random from the box, what is the probability that the number on the tile is a prime number?

A. $\dfrac{1}{50}$

B. $\dfrac{1}{15}$

C. $\dfrac{3}{10}$

D. $\dfrac{8}{25}$

19. To find the distance between two houses separated by a lake, a surveyor measures the angle between the houses from a distant point, *X,* on dry land. The surveyor then measures the straight line distance on dry land from *X* to each of the two houses. The distance from *X* to the first house is 60 ft and from *X* to the second house is 75 ft. If the angle measured at point *X* between the two houses is 60°, approximately how far apart are the two houses?

A. 39 ft
B. 69 ft
C. 96 ft
D. 4725 ft

20. The density of lead is 11.3 grams per cubic centimeter. What is the mass (to the nearest tenth of a gram) of a lead cube that measures 1.5 centimeters on a side?

A. 3.3 grams
B. 17.0 grams
C. 25.4 grams
D. 38.1 grams

21. A national health study estimates that 25% of the people over the age of 65 in the United States will get flu shots this year. According to the study, of the people who get flu shots, an estimated 2% will have some sort of adverse reaction. If *N* represents the number of people over the age of 65 in the United States, estimate how many people over age 65 will have an adverse reaction after getting flu shots this year.

A. 0.005*N*
B. 0.02*N*
C. 0.25*N*
D. 0.27*N*

22. Which of the following sets of ordered pairs represents a function?

I. {(4, 5), (4, 9), (3, 12), (–2, 0)}
II. {(3, 3), (3, 3^2), (3, 3^3), (3, 3^4)}
III. {(3, 3), (3^2, 3), (3^3, 3), (3^4, 3)}

A. II only
B. III only
C. II and III only
D. I, II, and III

GO ON TO THE NEXT PAGE

23. A team of biologists introduces a herd of 2500 deer onto an uninhabited island. If the deer population doubles every eight years, which of the following functions models the growth of the deer population on the island if t is the time in years?

   A. $(2500)^{0.125t}$

   B. $(2500)2^{0.125t}$

   C. $(2500)^{8t}$

   D. $(2500)2^{8t}$

24. Which of the following expressions is an identity for $\cos \theta \csc \theta$?

   A. 1

   B. $\cos^2 \theta$

   C. $\tan \theta$

   D. $\cot \theta$

25. If $f(x) = -x^{-2}$, then $f'(2)$ is

   A. -1

   B. $-\dfrac{1}{4}$

   C. $\dfrac{1}{4}$

   D. 1

26. Which of the following correlation coefficients shows the strongest relationship between two variables?

   A. $r = -0.88$

   B. $r = 0.03$

   C. $r = 0.50$

   D. $r = 0.72$

27. In general, with respect to matrix multiplication on the set of $n \times n$ matrices containing elements that are real numbers only, which of the following properties does NOT hold?

   A. closure

   B. commutativity

   C. associativity

   D. distributive property

28. If $f(x) = \dfrac{2x+6}{x+2}$ and $g(x) = x + 2$, then $(f \circ g)(x) = f(g(x)) =$

   A. $\dfrac{4x+10}{x+2}$

   B. $\dfrac{2x+10}{x+4}$

   C. $\dfrac{4x+8}{x+2}$

   D. $\dfrac{2x+8}{x+4}$

29. What are the units of the quantity $Y = \dfrac{Adv}{t}$, where A is measured in square centimeters (cm^2), d is expressed in grams per cm^3 ($\frac{g}{cm^3}$), v is expressed in centimeters per second ($\frac{cm}{s}$), and t is given in seconds (s)?

   A. g

   B. $\dfrac{g}{s^2}$

   C. $\dfrac{g - cm}{s}$

   D. $\dfrac{g - cm}{s^2}$

1 cm

30. The figure above consists of a semicircle of radius 1 cm and a right triangle with one leg equal to the radius of the semicircle as shown. What is the perimeter of the figure to the nearest tenth of a centimeter?

   A. 5.4 cm

   B. 5.9 cm

   C. 6.4 cm

   D. 9.5 cm

31. What is the product of the complex numbers $2 + 3i$ and $2 - 3i$?

   A. -5

   B. 13

   C. $13 - 12i$

   D. $13 + 12i$

32. What is the value of $\lim\limits_{x \to 3} \dfrac{2x - 6}{x^2 - 9}$?

   A. The limit does not exist.

   B. $\dfrac{1}{6}$

   C. $\dfrac{1}{3}$

   D. 1

33. The velocity in feet per second of a car during the first 5 seconds of a test run is given by $v(t) = 1.8t^2$. What is the distance the car has traveled after 5 seconds?

   A. 15 ft

   B. 45 ft

   C. 75 ft

   D. 225 ft

34. Find a, b, c, and d if $\begin{bmatrix} a & 5 \\ 4b & d \end{bmatrix} - \begin{bmatrix} 3a & 2c \\ -6 & -2d \end{bmatrix} = \begin{bmatrix} -8 & 7 \\ b & 9 \end{bmatrix}$

   A. $a = -4$, $b = -2$, $c = -1$, $d = 3$

   B. $a = 4$, $b = -2$, $c = -1$, $d = 3$

   C. $a = 4$, $b = -2$, $c = 1$, $d = -3$

   D. $a = -4$, $b = 2$, $c = 1$, $d = 3$

35. How many different license plates can be made consisting of four letters followed by two digits?

   A. $4 \cdot 2$

   B. $\left(_{26}C_4\right)\left(_{10}C_2\right)$

   C. $26^4 \cdot 10^2$

   D. 36^6

36. The equation of the line tangent to the graph of $y = 2x^3 - x + 3$ at the point where $x = 1$ is given by

   A. $6x - y = 2$.

   B. $5x - y = 1$.

   C. $5x - y = 5$.

   D. $5x - y = -1$.

37. What is the area of the region bounded by the graph of $f(x) = 3x^2 + 1$ and the x-axis over the closed interval $[1, 3]$?

   A. 26

   B. 28

   C. 30

   D. 32

38. The heights of a certain type of indoor plant are normally distributed with a mean of 24 inches and a standard deviation of 3.5 inches. What is the approximate probability a plant of this type chosen at random will be between 20.5 inches and 27.5 inches tall?

   A. 16%

   B. 34%

   C. 68%

   D. 84%

39. Given the cubic function $f(x) = x^3$, which of the following best describes the function $g(x) = (x - 2)^3 + 5$?

   A. the same as the graph of $f(x) = x^3$ shifted right by 2 units and up by 5 units

   B. the same as the graph of $f(x) = x^3$ shifted left by 2 units and up by 5 units

   C. the same as the graph of $f(x) = x^3$ shifted right by 2 units and down by 5 units

   D. the same as the graph of $f(x) = x^3$ shifted left by 2 units and down by 5 units

	Exam 1	Exam 2	Exam 3	Exam 4
Student's Grade	65	87	92	70
Class Mean	55	88	86	60
Class Standard Deviation	5	2	4	10

40. The data in the table above show a student's grades on four exams in a college statistics class along with the means and standard deviations of the grades for all the students in the class of 50 students. On which of the exams did the student perform best relative to the performance of the student's classmates?

   A. Exam 1

   B. Exam 2

   C. Exam 3

   D. Exam 4

GO ON TO THE NEXT PAGE

Practice Test 2

41. Which of the following graphs illustrates the solution to $\dfrac{2-x}{5} < 1$?

A. ![number line −8 to 8, shaded left of −3, filled point at −3]

B. ![number line −8 to 8, shaded right of −3, filled point at −3]

C. ![number line −8 to 8, shaded left of −3, open point at −3]

D. ![number line −8 to 8, shaded right of −3, open point at −3]

Time (minutes)	Population
0	1000
10	5000

42. The table above gives the population of a deadly bacterium at two different times. The growth of the bacteria is modeled by the function $Q(t) = Q_0 e^{xt}$. Based on this information, what is the value of x?

A. $\dfrac{\ln 5}{10}$

B. $\ln 5$

C. $\ln 10 - \ln 5$

D. $\ln \dfrac{1}{5}$

43. Which of the following functions is the polynomial of lowest degree that has zeroes at -5, $\dfrac{1}{2}$, 4, and -3?

A. $P(x) = x(x+5)(x-\dfrac{1}{2})(x-4)(x+3)$

B. $P(x) = (x-5)(2x+1)(x+4)(x-3)$

C. $P(x) = (x+5)(2x-1)(x-4)(x+3)$

D. $P(x) = 2x(x+5)(x-\dfrac{1}{2})(x-4)(x+3)$

44. Which of the following sets is the domain of the function $y = \dfrac{3}{x^2-4}$?

A. $\{x \mid x$ is a real number such that $x \neq 2$ or $x \neq -2\}$

B. $\{x \mid x$ is a real number such that $x \neq 4$ or $x \neq -4\}$

C. $\{x \mid x$ is a real number such that $x > \pm 2\}$

D. $\{x \mid x$ is a real number$\}$

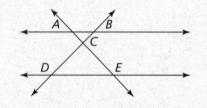

45. In the figure shown above, $\overleftrightarrow{AB} \parallel \overleftrightarrow{DE}$, which of the following geometric theorems would most likely be used in proving that $\triangle ABC \approx \triangle CDE$?

I. Corresponding sides of similar triangles are proportional.

II. If two parallel lines are cut by a transversal, then any pair of alternate interior angles is congruent.

III. If two angles of one triangle are congruent to two corresponding angles of another triangle, then the triangles are similar.

A. I and II only

B. I and III only

C. II and III only

D. I, II, and III

46. For what value of x is the matrix $\begin{bmatrix} 2x & -4 \\ 12 & 3 \end{bmatrix}$ NOT invertible?

A. -48

B. -8

C. 8

D. 48

47. What is the volume of a right hexagonal prism that is 30 centimeters in height and whose bases are regular hexagons that are 6 centimeters on a side?

A. 468 cm^3

B. 1080 cm^3

C. 2806 cm^3

D. 3240 cm^3

48. Which of the following vertex-edge graphs is a tree?

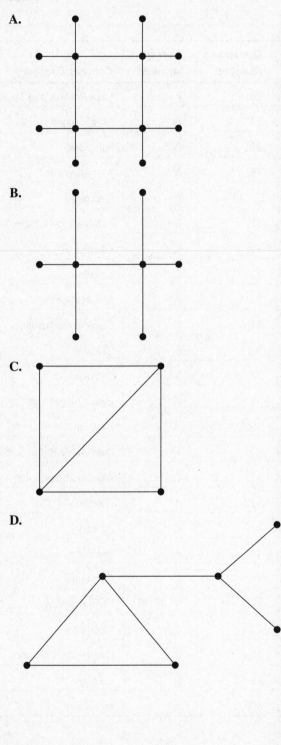

A.

B.

C.

D.

49. Find the area enclosed by the curves $y = 2x - x^2$ and $y = 2x - 4$.

A. $\dfrac{16}{3}$

B. $\dfrac{32}{3}$

C. 16

D. $\dfrac{64}{3}$

50. A civic club has 100 members. A committee of 3 members is to be selected to attend a national conference. If the committee members are selected at random, what is the probability a particular committee of three people is chosen to attend the national conference?

A. $\dfrac{1}{_{100}C_3}$

B. $\dfrac{1}{_{100}P_3}$

C. $\dfrac{1}{100^3}$

D. $\dfrac{1}{3!}$

IF YOU FINISH BEFORE TIME IS CALLED, CHECK YOUR WORK ON THIS SECTION ONLY. DO NOT WORK ON ANY OTHER SECTION IN THE TEST.

Practice Test 2

Mathematics: Content Knowledge Practice Test 2 Answer Key

Question Number	Correct Answer	Content Category	Question Number	Correct Answer	Content Category
1.	C	Algebra and Number Theory	26.	A	Data Analysis and Statistics
2.	A	Algebra and Number Theory	27.	B	Matrix Algebra
3.	B	Algebra and Number Theory	28.	B	Functions
4.	C	Functions	29.	B	Measurement
5.	C	Algebra and Number Theory	30.	C	Geometry
6.	C	Discrete Mathematics	31.	B	Algebra and Number Theory
7.	D	Measurement	32.	C	Calculus
8.	D	Geometry	33.	C	Calculus
9.	B	Geometry	34.	B	Matrix Algebra
10.	B	Data Analysis and Statistics	35.	C	Discrete Mathematics
11.	C	Algebra and Number Theory	36.	B	Calculus
12.	B	Functions	37.	B	Calculus
13.	A	Trigonometry	38.	C	Data Analysis and Statistics
14.	A	Trigonometry	39.	A	Functions
15.	D	Matrix Algebra	40.	A	Data Analysis and Statistics
16.	C	Discrete Mathematics	41.	D	Algebra and Number Theory
17.	A	Data Analysis and Statistics	42.	A	Functions
18.	C	Probability	43.	C	Functions
19.	B	Trigonometry	44.	A	Functions
20.	D	Measurement	45.	C	Geometry
21.	A	Algebra and Number Theory	46.	B	Matrix Algebra
22.	B	Functions	47.	C	Geometry
23.	B	Functions	48.	B	Discrete Mathematics
24.	D	Trigonometry	49.	B	Calculus
25.	C	Calculus	50.	A	Probability

Answer Explanations for Practice Test 2

1. **C.** The question asks you to identify the mathematical technique that is key for converting $y = ax^2 + bx + c$ into the form $y - k = a(x - h)^2$. The following procedure shows how you can achieve the conversion.

   First, write $y = ax^2 + bx + c$ as $y - c = a(x^2 + \frac{b}{a}x)$. Next, make the expression inside the parentheses on the right into a perfect square. You do this by "completing the square"; that is, take half the coefficient of x, square it, and add the result, which is $\frac{b^2}{4a^2}$, to the quantity inside the parentheses. Since there is a factor of a outside the parentheses, this is equivalent to adding $\frac{b^2}{4a}$ to the right side of the equation. To keep the equation balanced, you must add $\frac{b^2}{4a}$ to the left side of the equation as well, yielding the equation $y - c + \frac{b^2}{4a} = a(x^2 + \frac{b}{a}x + \frac{b^2}{4a^2})$, which can be rewritten as $y - c + \frac{b^2}{4a} = a\left(x + 2\frac{b}{a}\right)^2 \Rightarrow y - (c - \frac{b^2}{4a}) = a\left(x - \left(-\frac{b}{2a}\right)\right)^2 \Rightarrow y - k = a(x - h)^2$, where $k = c - \frac{b^2}{4a}$ and $h = -\frac{b}{2a}$. As you can see, the mathematical technique of "completing the square" is key to achieving the conversion of $y = ax^2 + bx + c$ into the form $y - k = a(x - h)^2$, so Choice C is the correct response. The techniques in the other answer choices are not useful for achieving the desired conversion.

2. **A.** This question is an example of a multiple-response set question. One approach to answering this type of question is to follow the following steps. First, read the question carefully to make sure you understand what the question is asking; next, identify choices that you know are incorrect from the Roman numeral options, and then draw a line through every answer choice that contains a Roman numeral you have eliminated; and then examine the remaining answer choices to determine which Roman numeral options you need to consider.

   Looking at the three properties given in the Roman numeral options, you can immediately eliminate Roman III because there are no parentheses in the computation sequence, meaning that the distributive property did not come into play. Draw a line through choices B, C, and D because each of these answer choices contains Roman numeral III. This leaves answer Choice A as the correct response. This choice includes commutativity (Roman I) and associativity (Roman II), both of which are used in the computation sequence.

3. **B.** Since the answer choices are given as exponential expressions, the best way to work this problem is to perform on x the sequence of operations indicated by the function machine, using the exponential form for the operation:

   $x \rightarrow \sqrt{x} = x^{\frac{1}{2}} \rightarrow \sqrt{x^{\frac{1}{2}}} = \left(x^{\frac{1}{2}}\right)^{\frac{1}{2}} = x^{\frac{1}{4}} \rightarrow \sqrt{x^{\frac{1}{4}}} = \left(x^{\frac{1}{4}}\right)^{\frac{1}{2}} = x^{\frac{1}{8}} \rightarrow \left(x^{\frac{1}{8}}\right)^6 = x^{\frac{6}{8}} = x^{\frac{3}{4}}$, Choice B. The other answer choices result if you fail to use the rules for exponents correctly.

4. **C.** The graph of the function $y = \dfrac{5}{16x^2 + kx + 9}$ will have vertical asymptotes at values of x for which the denominator, $16x^2 + kx + 9$, equals zero. The trinomial, $16x^2 + kx + 9$, will have exactly one zero when it is a perfect square. For $16x^2 + kx + 9$ to be a perfect square, the coefficient, k, of x needs to be $2 \cdot \sqrt{16} \cdot \sqrt{9}$, which is $2 \cdot 4 \cdot 3 = 24$, choice C. If k is 0 (Choice A) or 12 (Choice B), the graph of y does not have a vertical asymptote. If k is 48 (Choice D), the graph of y has two vertical asymptotes.

Tip: You can check your answer by substituting into the equation the values for _k_ given in the answer choices and graphing the resulting functions using your graphing calculator. However, it is best that you work out the problem analytically, rather than use only your graphing calculator to determine a solution because on a graphing calculator, the graphs of functions that have asymptotes are sometimes misleading.

5. **C.** Analyze the problem. When two lines are perpendicular, their slopes are negative reciprocals of each other. You can write the equation of a line when you know the slope of the line and a point on the line. Devise a plan. To find the equation of the line that is perpendicular to the line whose equation is $5x - 6y = 4$ and passes through the point $(3, 1)$ will take three steps. First, find the slope, m, of the line whose equation is $5x - 6y = 4$; next, find the negative reciprocal of m, which is $-\frac{1}{m}$; and then use the point-slope form to determine the equation of the line with slope $-\frac{1}{m}$ that passes through the point $(3, 1)$.

Step 1. Find the slope of the line whose equation is $5x - 6y = 4$.

Rewrite $5x - 6y = 4$ as $y = \frac{5}{6}x - \frac{2}{3}$, which shows the slope of this line is $\frac{5}{6}$.

Step 2. Find the negative reciprocal of $\frac{5}{6}$.

The negative reciprocal of $\frac{5}{6}$ is $-\frac{6}{5}$.

Step 3. Use the point-slope form to determine the equation.

$y - 1 = -\frac{6}{5}(x - 3) \Rightarrow 5y - 5 = -6x + 18 \Rightarrow 6x + 5y = 23$, Choice C.

Choice A results if you fail to do step 2 above. Choice B results if you use $\frac{6}{5}$ instead of $-\frac{6}{5}$, for the slope in step 3 above. Choice D results if you switch the x and y values for the point (3, 1) in the point-slope form.

6. **C.** For the recursive function given in the problem, you will need to find $f(3)$ and $f(4)$ before you can find $f(5)$. Since the problem tells you that $f(1) = 1$ and $f(2) = 2$ and that $f(n) = 2f(n - 1) + f(n - 2)$ for $n \geq 3$, then

$f(3) = 2f(2) + f(1) = 2(2) + 1 = 4 + 1 = 5$

$f(4) = 2f(3) + f(2) = 2(5) + 2 = 10 + 2 = 12$

$f(5) = 2f(4) + f(3) = 2(12) + 5 = 24 + 5 = 29$, Choice C.

Choice A is $f(3)$, not $f(5)$. Choice B is $f(4)$, not $f(5)$. Choice D is $f(6)$, not $f(5)$.

7. **D.** This is a unit analysis problem. Write your measurement as a fraction with denominator 1 and let unit analysis tell you which conversion fractions to multiply by, keeping in mind that you want cups as your final answer:
$\frac{5 \text{ gal}}{1} \times \frac{4 \text{ qt}}{1 \text{ gal}} \times \frac{2 \text{ pt}}{1 \text{ qt}} \times \frac{2 \text{ c}}{1 \text{ pt}} = 80$ cups, Choice D. The other answer choices result if you use incorrect conversion fractions.

8. **D.** Analyze the problem. You want to find the cost of the paint needed to cover the surface area of the sphere. Devise a plan. To determine the cost of the paint will take three steps. First, find the surface area of the sphere; next, find the number of gallons of paint needed; and then find the cost of the paint.

Step 1. Find the surface area (SA) of the sphere with $r = 12$ ft.

$SA = 4\pi r^2 = 4\pi(12 \text{ ft})^2 = 1809.5575 \ldots \text{ ft}^2$ (Tip: Don't round this answer.)

Note: The formula for the surface area of a sphere is provided in the Notation, Definitions, and Formulas pages at the beginning of the test booklet.

Step 2. Find the number of gallons needed.

$1809.5575 \ldots \text{ ft}^2 \div \frac{400 \text{ ft}^2}{1 \text{ gal}} = 4.5238 \ldots$ gallons, so 5 gallons will need to be purchased (since the paint is sold in gallon containers only).

Step 3. Find the cost of 5 gallons of paint.

5 gallons $\times \frac{\$22.40}{1 \text{ gal}} = \$112.00$, Choice D.

Choices A and B result if you calculate the surface area incorrectly. Choice C results if you fail to round up to 5 gallons in step 2.

9. B. First sketch a diagram to illustrate the problem.

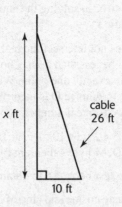

Analyze the problem. The pole, the cable, and the ground form a right triangle. From the diagram, you can see that the length of the cable, 26 feet, is the hypotenuse of a right triangle that has legs of 10 feet and x feet. You can use the Pythagorean theorem to find the missing leg. Devise a plan. To find the length of the missing leg, plug into the formula for the Pythagorean theorem and solve for the missing leg, denoted by x:

c = hypotenuse = 26 ft, a = 10 ft, and b = x ft

$c^2 = a^2 + b^2 \Rightarrow (26 \text{ ft})^2 = (10 \text{ ft})^2 + x^2 \Rightarrow 676 \text{ ft}^2 = 100 \text{ ft}^2 + x^2 \Rightarrow x^2 = 676 \text{ ft}^2 - 100 \text{ ft}^2 = 576 \text{ ft}^2 \Rightarrow x = 24$ feet, Choice B.

Choice A results if you mistakenly decide to solve the problem by subtracting the given lengths to find the length of the missing leg. Choice C results if you mistakenly treat the length of the cable as the length of a leg of the right triangle. Choice D results if you assume the cable is attached to the top of the pole.

10. B. Analyze the problem. You need to find the difference between Kathryn's median running time and her mean running time. Devise a plan. To find the difference between the median and the mean will take three steps: first, calculate the mean; next, calculate the median; and then find the difference between the two.

Method 1: The most efficient way to work the problem is to use the statistical features of your calculator. Enter the data set as a list into your calculator. Use the appropriate commands to find the mean, which is 31, and the median, which is 33. Subtract to find the difference: 33 minutes – 31 minutes = 2 minutes, Choice B.

Method 2: You can calculate the mean and median by using the appropriate formulas.

Step 1. Find the mean (omitting units for convenience).

$$\text{mean} = \frac{\text{the sum of the running times}}{\text{the number of running times recorded}} = \frac{20 + 25 + 28 + 30 + 32 + 34 + 35 + 35 + 35 + 36}{10} = \frac{310}{10} = 31 \text{ min.}$$

Step 2. Find the median.

Put the times in order: 20, 25, 28, 30, 32, 34, 35, 35, 35, 36. Average the two middle times: $\frac{32 + 34}{2} = 33$ min.

Step 3. Find the difference.

33 minutes – 31 minutes = 2 minutes, Choice B.

Choice A results if you mistakenly decide that the mean and median are equal. Choice C results if you fail to order the data values before finding the median. Choice D is the difference between the mode and the mean, not between the median and the mean.

11. C. Analyze the problem. Suppose x is the total number of minutes that the call lasted. Then x is the sum of the first minute and the total number of minutes talked after the first minute, which is $x - 1$. The charge for the first minute, \$3.75, plus the charge for the additional minutes, \$0.55($x - 1$), equals the total charge for the call, \$11.45. Devise a plan. Write an equation and solve for x.

$3.75 + $0.55(x − 1) = $11.45 ⇒ $3.75 + $0.55x − $0.55 = $11.45 ⇒ $0.55x = $8.25 ⇒ x = 15 minutes, Choice C. Choices A and D occur if you make an error in solving the equation. Choice B occurs if you fail to account for the first minute of conversation in the equation.

12. B. The graph of the quadratic function does not intersect the real axis, indicating the function has no real zeroes. Therefore, the discriminant, $b^2 − 4ac$, must be less than zero, Choice B. When $b^2 − 4ac = 0$ (Choice A), the quadratic function intersects the real axis in exactly one point. When $b^2 − 4ac > 0$ (Choice C), the quadratic function intersects the real axis in two points. Choice D is incorrect because the coefficients of the quadratic function are real numbers, meaning $b^2 − 4ac$ is a real number, so it is not undefined.

13. A. The expression $(2 \cos 10° + i2 \sin 10°)^3 = 2^3(\cos 10° + i \sin 10°)^3 = 8(\cos 10° + i \sin 10°)^3$. You can evaluate the second factor of this product by using DeMoivre's theorem (which is provided in the Notation, Definitions, and Formulas pages at the beginning of the test booklet), to obtain $8(\cos 30° + i \sin 30°) = 8(\frac{\sqrt{3}}{2} + i\frac{1}{2}) = 4\sqrt{3} + 4i$, Choice A. Choice B occurs if you evaluate cosine and sine of 30° incorrectly. Choice C occurs if you make an error using DeMoivre's theorem. Choice D occurs if you make an error using DeMoivre's theorem and you also switch cosine and sine in your answer.

14. A. Analyze the problem. The sum of the angles of a triangle is 180°. Devise a plan. To find the percent error of the student's sum will take two steps. First, find the absolute error by finding the difference between 180° and the student's sum, and then find the percent error by dividing the difference by 180°.

Step 1. Find the difference: $180° − 172° = 8°$.

Step 2. Find the percent error: $\frac{8°}{180°} = 0.0444 \ldots$ or approximately 4%, Choice A.

Choice B occurs if you divide by 172° in step 2, instead of 180°. Choices C and D occur if you make calculation errors.

15. D. In a reflection over the x-axis, the x-coordinates of the image will be the same as the x-coordinates of the pre-image, and the y-coordinates of the image will be the negatives of the y-coordinates of the pre-image. Thus, you are looking for a matrix multiplication that will yield the product matrix $\begin{bmatrix} 2 & −3 & 5 \\ −1 & −4 & 3 \end{bmatrix}$. A quick way to determine which product given in the answer choices will result in the matrix $\begin{bmatrix} 2 & −3 & 5 \\ −1 & −4 & 3 \end{bmatrix}$ is to perform the matrix multiplications in each of the answer choices using your graphing calculator. You can expedite the process by first entering the transformation matrix given in Choice A, entering the vertex matrix shown, and then premultiplying by the transformation matrix. Thereafter, you can use the edit feature of your graphing calculator and the recall entry feature to check the other answer choices. Only Choice D will yield the desired product matrix. The transformation matrix in Choice A will result in a reflection over the y-axis. The transformation matrix in Choice B will result in a 90-degree rotation about zero. The transformation matrix in Choice C will result in a reflection over the line $y = x$.

16. C. An equivalence relation is a reflexive, symmetric, and transitive relation. Note: The definitions for reflexive, symmetric, transitive, and equivalence relation are given in the Notation, Definitions, and Formulas pages at the beginning of the Mathematics CK test booklet. The relation in Choice C, "is perpendicular to" over the set of all lines in the Cartesian coordinate plane, is not an equivalence relation because this relation is neither reflexive nor transitive. The relations in the other answer choices are equivalence relations.

17. A. When a data set contains some extremely high values that are not balanced by corresponding extremely low values, the mean for the data set will be misleadingly high as an indication of a "typical" or "central" value for the data set. The median, which is not influenced by extreme values, is the preferred alternative to the mean when the situation of unbalanced extremely high values occurs in a data set. Since the data set in Choice B is somewhat symmetrical, there would be no particular reason to prefer the median over the mean as a measure of central tendency. For the data sets given in choices C and D, there is not enough information to "clearly" prefer the median over the mean.

18. C. Analyze the problem. The box contains 50 tiles numbered 1 through 50. Some of the numbers on the tiles are prime numbers. If one tile is drawn at random, to find the probability the number on the tile is prime will take two steps. First, count how many numbers between 1 and 50 are prime, and then divide this answer by 50 and simplify, if possible.

Step 1. Count how many numbers between 1 and 50 are prime.

The primes between 1 and 50 are 2, 3, 5, 7, 11, 13, 17, 19, 23, 29, 31, 37, 41, 43, 47, which is a total of 15 primes. (Remember, the number 1 is neither prime nor composite.)

Step 2. Divide by 50 and simplify.

$\frac{15}{50} = \frac{3}{10}$, Choice C.

Choices A and B result if you analyze the problem incorrectly. Choice D results if you mistakenly count the number 1 as a prime.

19. B. Sketch a diagram to help you understand the problem, letting d be the distance between the two houses.

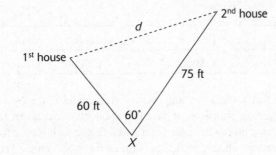

Analyze the problem. Looking at the diagram, you can see that you are given the measures of two sides and the included angle of an oblique triangle. Design a plan. To find the distance between the two houses, plug the given information into the law of cosines and solve for d. Note: The law of cosines is given in the Notation, Definitions, and Formulas pages at the beginning of the Mathematics CK test booklet.

$c^2 = a^2 + b^2 - 2ab(\cos C) \Rightarrow d^2 = (60 \text{ ft})^2 + (75 \text{ ft})^2 - 2(60 \text{ ft})(75 \text{ ft})(\cos 60°) = 3600 \text{ ft}^2 + 5625 \text{ ft}^2 - 4500 \text{ ft}^2 = 4725 \text{ ft}^2 \Rightarrow d = 68.7386 \ldots$ or approximately 69 feet, Choice B.

Tip: Be sure to check that your calculator is in degree mode when the angle given is in degrees.

Choice A results if you make a computation error. Choice C results if you work the problem as if the angle at X is a right angle. Choice D results if you fail to take the square root of 4725.

20. D. Analyze the problem. You are to find the mass, in grams, of the cube. The units for density are grams per cubic centimeter ($\frac{\text{g}}{\text{cm}^3}$), so unit analysis tells you that if you want to have grams as the units of your answer then you will need to "cancel" cm^3 from the denominator of the density quantity. Cubic centimeters are units of volume. Therefore, you need to find the volume of the cube. Devise a plan. To find the mass of the lead cube will take two steps. First, find the volume of the cube, and then multiply by the density of lead.

Step 1. Find the volume of the cube.

volume of cube $= (1.5 \text{ cm})^3 = 3.375 \text{ cm}^3$

Step 2. Multiply the volume of the cube by the density of lead.

$(3.375 \text{ cm}^3)(\frac{11.3 \text{ g}}{\text{cm}^3}) = 38.1375 \ldots$ or approximately 38.1 grams, Choice D.

Choice A results if you divide by the density quantity, instead of multiply. Choice B results if you multiply by the length of a side of the cube, instead of its volume. Choice C results if you multiply by the area of the cube, instead of its volume.

21. **A.** The number of people over age 65 who get a flu shot is $25\%N = 0.25N$. Of this number, 2% will have an adverse reaction. Thus, the estimated number of people over age 65 who will have an adverse reaction after getting flu shots is $(0.02)(0.25)N = 0.005N$, Choice A. Choice B is the estimated percent of the general population that will have an adverse reaction to the flu shot. Choice C is the estimated percent of the population over age 65 that will get flu shots. Choice D results if you mistakenly add the percents given in the problem, instead of multiplying them.

22. **B.** A function is a relation in which each first component is paired with *one and only one* second component. Only the relation in Roman numeral III satisfies this requirement, Choice B. In Roman I, the first component 4 is paired with two different second components, namely, 5 and 9. In Roman II, the first component 3 is paired with four different second components. In Roman numeral III, every first component has one and only one second component.

23. **B.** A good way to analyze this problem is to make a chart, showing the growth of the deer population as a function of time, t.

Time in years	$t = 0$	. . .	$t = 8$	. . .	$t = 16$	. . .	$t = 24$	. . .
Deer population	2500	. . .	$(2500)2$	. . .	$(2500)2^2$	. . .	$(2500)2^3$	. . .

From your table, you can see that at eight year intervals, you are multiplying by a power of 2. Therefore, the function that models the population growth must have an exponential factor that has base 2 in it, so you can eliminate choices A and C, which do not have an exponential factor with base 2. Now you must decide whether the exponent for 2 in the expression should be $0.125t$ (Choice B) or $8t$ (Choice D). Again, use your table to help you decide. When $t = 0$, $(2500)2^{0.125t} = (2500)2^{8t} = (2500)2^0 = (2500)1 = 2500$, which matches the table. When $t = 8$, $(2500)2^{0.125t} = (2500)2^{0.125(8)} = (2500)2^1 = 2500$, which matches the table; but $(2500)2^{8t} = (2500)2^{8(8)} = (2500)2^{64} = 4.6 \ldots \times 10^{22}$, which does not match the table. Therefore, Choice B is the correct response.

24. **D.** Since $\csc\theta = \dfrac{1}{\sin\theta}$, the expression $\cos\theta\csc\theta$ can be rewritten as $\cos\theta \cdot \dfrac{1}{\sin\theta} = \dfrac{\cos\theta}{\sin\theta} = \cot\theta$, Choice D.

The other answer choices result if you use an incorrect trigonometric identity.

25. **C.** You are asked to find the numerical derivative of a function.

Method 1: A fast and efficient way to calculate this numerical derivative is with your graphing calculator. Here are the steps using a TI-83 calculator. Before you enter functions, you must select Func mode, from the MODE menu. Enter the function $y = -x^{\wedge}(-2)$ into the Y = editor, which is where you define functions. As a precaution, clear any previously entered functions before you enter the function. Check the viewing WINDOW to make sure that the value 2 falls between Xmin and Xmax. If not, change Xmin and/or Xmax, as needed. Select 6: dy/dx from the CALC (calculate) menu. Type 2 as the X value and then press ENTER. The derivative value is displayed as .25000013 or approximately 0.25, which is the same as Choice C.

Method 2: Find the numerical derivative using methods of calculus.

$f(x) = -x^{-2} \Rightarrow f'(x) = 2x^{-3} \Rightarrow f'(2) = 2(2)^{-3} = 2 \cdot \dfrac{1}{8} = \dfrac{1}{4}$, Choice C.

The other answer choices occur if you make an error finding $f'(x)$.

26. **A.** Correlation values very close to either -1 or $+1$ indicate very *strong* correlations. The closer $|r|$ is to 1, the stronger is the relationship. Thus, Choice A indicates the strongest relationship between the two variables because $|-0.88|$ is greater than the absolute values of any of the correlation coefficients in the other answer choices.

27. **B.** On the set of $n \times n$ matrices containing elements that are real numbers only, matrix multiplication is closed (eliminate Choice A), associative (eliminate Choice C), and the distributive property holds (eliminate Choice D); but, in general, matrix multiplication is not commutative, Choice B.

28. B. Everywhere you have x in $f(x) = \dfrac{2x+6}{x+2}$, you must substitute $x+2$, and then simplify, if possible:

$$(f \circ g)(x) = f(g(x)) = f(x+2) = \frac{2(x+2)+6}{(x+2)+2} = \frac{2x+4+6}{x+2+2} = \frac{2x+10}{x+4}, \text{ Choice B.}$$

Choice A is the result of finding $(g \circ f)(x) = g(f(x))$ instead of $(f \circ g)(x) = f(g(x))$. Choice C results if you make the mistake of finding $(g \circ f)(x)$, instead of $(f \circ g)(x)$, and you make a simplifying error. Choice D results if you make a simplifying error when finding $(f \circ g)(x)$.

29. B. This is a unit analysis problem. Plug the units into the formula and simplify as you would for variable quantities.

$$Y = \frac{Adv}{t} = \frac{\left(\text{cm}^2\right)\left(\dfrac{\text{g}}{\text{cm}^3}\right)\left(\dfrac{\text{cm}}{\text{s}}\right)}{\text{s}} = \frac{\dfrac{\text{g}}{\text{s}}}{\text{s}} = \frac{\text{g}}{\text{s}^2}, \text{ Choice B.}$$ The other answer choices occur if you make an error manipulating the units.

30. C. Analyze the problem. Looking at the diagram of the figure, you can see that the distance around the figure can be broken into three portions: (one-half the circumference of a circle with radius 1 cm) plus (the hypotenuse of a right triangle with legs of 1 cm and 2 cm) plus (1 cm). Devise a plan. To find the perimeter of the figure will take three steps. First, find one-half the circumference of a circle with radius 1 cm; next, find the hypotenuse of a right triangle with legs of 1 cm and 2 cm; and then add 1 cm to the results of the first two steps to find the perimeter of the figure.

Step 1. Find one-half the circumference of a circle with radius 1 cm.

$\frac{1}{2} \cdot 2\pi r = \frac{1}{2} \cdot 2 \cdot \pi \cdot 1 \text{ cm} = \pi \text{ cm}$ (Don't evaluate yet.)

Step 2. Find the hypotenuse of a right triangle with legs of 1 cm and 2 cm.

$c^2 = a^2 + b^2 \Rightarrow c^2 = 1^2 + 2^2 = 5 \Rightarrow c = \sqrt{5}$ cm (Don't evaluate yet.)

Step 3. Find the perimeter.

$1 \text{ cm} + \pi \text{ cm} + \sqrt{5} \text{cm} = 6.3776 \ldots$ or approximately 6.4 cm, Choice C.

Choice A occurs if you omit the 1 cm in step 3. Choice B occurs if you calculate the hypotenuse of the right triangle to be $\sqrt{3}$cm, instead of $\sqrt{5}$cm. Choice D occurs if you omit the factor of $\frac{1}{2}$ in step 1.

31. B. $(2+3i)(2-3i) = 4 - 9i^2 = 4 - 9(-1) = 4 + 9 = 13$, Choice B. Choice A occurs if you evaluate i^2 as 1, instead of -1. Choices C and D occur if you make sign errors when multiplying.

32. C. Substituting 3 into the numerator and denominator yields the indeterminate form $\frac{0}{0}$.

Method 1: Since the $\lim\limits_{x \to 3}(2x-6) = \lim\limits_{x \to 3}(x^2-9) = 0$, you can use *L'Hôpital's* rule to evaluate the limit by taking the derivatives of the numerator and denominator before evaluating the limit.

Thus, you have $\lim\limits_{x \to 3}\dfrac{2x-6}{x^2-9} = \lim\limits_{x \to 3}\dfrac{2}{2x} = \dfrac{2}{6} = \dfrac{1}{3}$, Choice C.

Method 2: Both the numerator and denominator of the algebraic fraction $\dfrac{2x-6}{x^2-9}$ are polynomials. The expression $(x-3)$ is a factor of each of these polynomials because $x = 3$ makes each of them sum to zero. Therefore, you have $\lim\limits_{x \to 3}\dfrac{2x-6}{x^2-9} = \lim\limits_{x \to 3}\dfrac{2(x-3)}{(x-3)(x+3)} = \lim\limits_{x \to 3}\dfrac{2}{(x+3)} = \dfrac{2}{6} = \dfrac{1}{3}$, Choice C.

Choice A is incorrect because the limit does exist. Choices B and D occur if you make simplification errors.

33. C. Analyze the problem. Recall that the first derivative of a position function is the velocity function. Devise a plan. To find the distance traveled after 5 seconds find the numerical integral of the velocity function between 0 and 5 seconds. That is, evaluate the following definite integral: $\int_0^5 1.8t^2\,dt$.

Method 1: The fastest and most efficient way to calculate this numerical integral is with your graphing calculator. Here are the steps using a TI-83 calculator. Before you enter functions, you must select Func mode, from the MODE menu. Enter the function $y = 1.8x^2$ into the Y = editor, which is where you define functions. Notice that you must use y and x for the variables instead of v and t. As a precaution, clear any previously entered functions before you enter the function. Check the viewing WINDOW to make sure that the interval between 0 and 5 falls between Xmin and Xmax. If not, change Xmin and/or Xmax, as needed. Select 7: $\int f(x)\,dx$ from the CALC (calculate) menu. Type 0 as the lower limit and then press ENTER. Type 5 as the upper limit and then press ENTER. The integral value is displayed as 75. Therefore, the distance the car has traveled after 5 seconds is 75 feet, Choice C.

Method 2: Integrate the function using methods of calculus.

$\int_0^5 1.8t^2\,dt = \left.\dfrac{1.8t^3}{3}\right|_0^5 = \left.0.6t^3\right|_0^5 = 0.6(5)^3 - 0.6(0)^3 = 0.6(125) - 0.6(0) = 75 - 0 = 75.$ Therefore, the distance the car has traveled after 5 seconds is 75 feet, Choice C. Choice A results if you make a calculation error. Choice B results if you fail to integrate the function. Choice D results if you fail to integrate the function, and you make a calculation error.

34. B. Using the rules for matrix subtraction, you can write 4 equations.

$a - 3a = -8$, $4b + 6 = b$, $5 - 2c = 7$, and $d + 2d = 9$

From the first equation, you have $a - 3a = -8 \Rightarrow -2a = -8 \Rightarrow a = 4$; eliminate Choices A and D because these answer choices have $a = -4$, which is incorrect. Since both of the remaining answer choices have $b = -2$, go on to the next equation. You have $5 - 2c = 7 \Rightarrow -2c = 2 \Rightarrow c = -1$; eliminate Choice C. Thus, Choice B is the correct response.

35. C. Since there are six places to be filled, so to speak, on a license plate, you can work this problem by extending the Fundamental Counting Principle to six events. There are 26 possible values for each of the four letters and 10 possibilities for each of the two digits, which means the total number of possible license plates is $26 \cdot 26 \cdot 26 \cdot 26 \cdot 10 \cdot 10 = 26^4 \cdot 10^2$, Choice C. The other answer choices result if you analyze the problem incorrectly.

36. B. Analyze the problem. The y-value at the point where $x = 1$ equals $f(1)$. The slope, m, of the tangent line at the point $(1, f(1))$ is given by $f'(1)$. Devise a plan. To find the equation of the line tangent to the graph of $y = 2x^3 - x + 3$ at the point where $x = 1$ will take three steps. First, find $y = f(1)$; next, find $m = f'(1)$; and then use the point-slope form to find the equation of the tangent line.

Step 1. Find $y = f(1)$.

$y = 2x^3 - x + 3 = 2(1)^3 - (1) + 3 = 4$

Step 2. Find $m = f'(1)$.

$f'(x) = 6x^2 - 1 \Rightarrow f'(1) = 6(1)^2 - 1 = 5$

Tip: You can use your graphing calculator to evaluate this numerical derivative.

Step 3. Use the point-slope form to find the equation of the tangent line at the point $(1, 4)$.

$y - 4 = 5(x - 1) \Rightarrow y - 4 = 5x - 5 \Rightarrow 1 = 5x - y$, which is the same as Choice B.

Choice A results if you make a mistake determining the slope. Choices C and D occur if you make simplification errors.

37. B. Make a quick sketch of the graph.

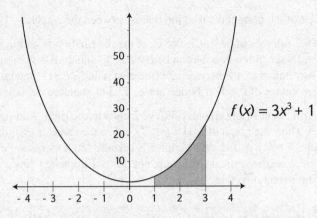

The area of the region bounded by the graph of $f(x) = 3x^2 + 1$, the x-axis, and the vertical lines $x = 1$ and $x = 3$ is given by: Area $= \int_1^3 (3x^2 + 1)\, dx$.

Method 1: The fastest and most efficient way to calculate this numerical integral is with your graphing calculator. Here are the steps using a TI-83 calculator. Before you enter functions, you must select Func mode, from the MODE menu. Enter the function $y = 3x^2 + 1$ into the Y = editor, which is where you define functions. As a precaution, clear any previously entered functions before you enter the function. Check the viewing WINDOW to make sure that the interval between 1 and 3 falls between Xmin and Xmax. If not, change Xmin and/or Xmax, as needed. Select 7: $\int f(x)\, dx$ from the CALC (calculate) menu. Type 1 as the lower limit and then press ENTER. Type 3 as the upper limit and then press ENTER. The graph is shaded and the integral value is displayed as 28, Choice B.

Method 2: Integrate the function using methods of calculus.

$\int_1^3 (3x^2 + 1)\, dx = (x^3 + x)\Big|_1^3 = (3^3 + 3) - (1^3 + 1) = 30 - 2 = 28$, Choice B. The other answer choices result if you make a mistake integrating the function.

38. **C.** Analyze the problem. According to the 68-95-99.7 rule, approximately 68 percent of the values of a random variable that is normally distributed falls within 1 standard deviation of the mean, about 95 percent falls within 2 standard deviations of the mean, and about 99.7 percent falls within 3 standard deviations of the mean. The mean height, μ, of the plants is 24 inches with standard deviation, σ, of 3.5 inches. Devise a plan.

Method 1: Using the statistical features of your graphing calculator is an efficient and time-saving way to work problems involving the normal distribution. Consult your owner's manual for detailed instructions on how to find percentages and probabilities using areas under a normal curve. Here are the steps, using a TI-83 calculator, to find the approximate probability that a randomly chosen plant from a distribution with mean of 24 inches and standard deviation of 3.5 inches will be between 20.5 inches and 27.5 inches tall. Select 2:normalcdf() from the DISTR (distributions) menu to paste normalcdf() to the home screen. Type 20.5, 27.5, 24, 3.5 inside the parentheses. Close the parentheses and press ENTER. The display will show .6826 . . . or approximately 68%, Choice C.

Method 2: To find the approximate probability that a randomly chosen plant will be between 20.5 inches and 27.5 inches tall will take two steps. First, determine the z-scores for 20.5 inches and 27.5 inches, and then find the percentage of the normal distribution that is between those two z-scores.

Step 1. Find the z-scores for 20.5 inches and 27.5 inches.

$z\text{-score} = \dfrac{x\text{-value} - \mu}{\sigma} = \dfrac{20.5 - 24}{3.5} = -1$. Therefore, 20.5 is 1 standard deviation below the mean.

$z\text{-score} = \dfrac{x\text{-value} - \mu}{\sigma} = \dfrac{27.5 - 24}{3.5} = 1$. Therefore, 27.5 is 1 standard deviation above the mean.

Step 2. Find the percentage of the normal distribution that is between the z-scores –1 and 1.

According to the 68-95-99.7 rule, about 68%, Choice C, of the distribution is within 1 standard deviation of the mean. Choice A is the percentage of the distribution below 20.5 (1 standard deviation below the mean). Choice B is the percentage of the distribution that is between 24 (the mean) and 27.5 (1 standard deviation above the mean). Choice D is the percentage of the distribution above 27.5 (1 standard deviation above the mean).

39. A. Subtracting 2 from x will result in a horizontal shift of 2 units to the right. Adding 5 to $f(x)$ will result in a vertical shift of 5 units up. Thus, the graph of $g(x) = (x - 2)^3 + 5$ is the same as the graph of $f(x) = x^3$ shifted right by 2 units and up by 5 units, Choice A. Eliminate choice B because the horizontal shift is to the right, not to the left. Eliminate Choice C because the vertical shift is up, not down. Eliminate Choice D because in this answer choice both shifts are in the wrong direction.

Tip: If you are unsure whether the shift is to the right or left or up or down, graph the two functions on your graphing calculator to check.

40. A. A good way to compare the student's performance on the four exams relative to the performance of the student's classmates is to compute the student's z-score for each of the four exams.

Exam 1: z-score $= \dfrac{x\text{–value} - \mu}{\sigma} = \dfrac{65 - 55}{5} = 2$. Therefore, the student scored 2 standard deviations above the mean on Exam 1.

Exam 2: z-score $= \dfrac{x\text{–value} - \mu}{\sigma} = \dfrac{87 - 88}{2} = -0.5$. Therefore, the student scored 0.5 standard deviation below the mean on Exam 2.

Exam 3: z-score $= \dfrac{x\text{–value} - \mu}{\sigma} = \dfrac{92 - 86}{4} = 1.5$. Therefore, the student scored 1.5 standard deviations above the mean on Exam 3.

Exam 4: z-score $= \dfrac{x\text{–value} - \mu}{\sigma} = \dfrac{70 - 60}{10} = 1$. Therefore, the student scored 1 standard deviation above the mean on Exam 4.

Since the student's z-score for Exam 1 is greater than any of the z-scores for the other exams, the student's best performance was on Exam 1 (Choice A) relative to that of the student's classmates.

41. D. Solve the inequality: $\dfrac{2-x}{5} < 1 \Rightarrow 2 - x < 5 \Rightarrow -x < 3 \Rightarrow x > -3$. **Tip:** Remember to reverse the inequality when you multiply both sides by a negative quantity. The graph for this inequality will be a ray extending to the right from the point –3 with an open-dot at the point –3, Choice D. Eliminate Choices A and B because these graphs have solid dots at –3. Choice C occurs if you fail to reverse the inequality when multiplying both sides by –1.

42. A. Analyze the problem. You are given two points (0, 1000) and (10, 5000) that satisfy the function $Q(t) = Q_0 e^{xt}$. Devise a plan. To find the value of x will take two steps. First, plug the values for the two points into $Q(t) = Q_0 e^{xt}$, and then solve the resulting system of equations for x.

Step 1: Plug the values for the two points into $Q(t) = Q_0 e^{xt}$.

$1000 = Q_0 e^{x(0)} = Q_0 e^0 = Q_0 \cdot 1 = Q_0$

$5000 = Q_0 e^{x(10)} = Q_0 e^{10x} = 1000 e^{10x}$ (using the results from the first equation) $\Rightarrow 5000 = 1000 e^{10x} = \Rightarrow 5 = e^{10x} \Rightarrow \ln 5 = \ln(e^{10x}) = 10x\ln e = 10x \Rightarrow x = \dfrac{\ln 5}{10}$, Choice A. The other answer choices result if you make an error solving for x.

43. C. Analyze the problem. You are given the zeroes of the desired polynomial. If r is a zero of a polynomial, $P(x)$, then $x - r$ is a factor of $P(x)$. Looking at the answer choices and using the previous statement, you can see that choices A and D have the desired zeroes; however, Choice C also has the desired zeroes because the factor $(2x - 1)$ would yield a zero of $\dfrac{1}{2}$. Of the answer choices A, C, and D, Choice C is the polynomial of lowest degree. Therefore, Choice C is the correct response.

44. A. The domain of $y = \frac{3}{x^2 - 4}$ excludes any value for x that makes the denominator equal zero. Set $x^2 - 4 = 0$ and solve for x: $x^2 - 4 = 0 \Rightarrow x = \pm 2$. Thus, the domain is the set of all real numbers except $x = 2$ and $x = -2$, choice A. Choice B results if you fail to take the square root of 4. Choice C is incorrect because this set includes only the two values for which $y = \frac{3}{x^2 - 4}$ is undefined. Choice D is incorrect because it includes the values $x = 2$ and $x = -2$, for which $y = \frac{3}{x^2 - 4}$ is undefined.

45. C. This question is an example of a multiple-response set question. One approach to answering this type of question (as shown in a previous answer explanation) is to follow the following steps. First, read the question carefully to make sure you understand what the question is asking; next, identify choices that you know are incorrect from the Roman numeral options, and then draw a line through every answer choice that contains a Roman numeral you have eliminated; and then examine the remaining answer choices to determine which Roman numeral options you need to consider.

The question asks which theorems most likely would be used to prove $\triangle ABC$ is similar to $\triangle CDE$. Looking at the three theorems given in the Roman numeral options, Roman I would be eliminated from the proof because the lengths of the sides of the triangle are not given. Eliminate Choices A, B, and D because these choices contain Roman I. A simple way to show two triangles are similar is to show that two angles of one triangle are congruent to two corresponding angles of the other triangle (Roman III). You could proceed by showing that $\angle ABC$ is congruent to $\angle EDC$ and $\angle BAC$ is congruent to $\angle DEC$ because these angles form pairs of alternate-interior angles of two parallel lines cut by a transversal (Roman II).

46. B. Analyze the problem. The matrix $\begin{bmatrix} 2x & -4 \\ 12 & 3 \end{bmatrix}$ is not invertible if its determinant is equal to zero. Devise a plan. Set the determinant of the matrix equal to zero and solve for d.

$6x - (-4)(12) = 6x + 48 = 0 \Rightarrow 6x = -48 \Rightarrow x = -8$, Choice B. The other answer choices result if you make a calculation error.

47. C. Analyze the problem. The volume of a right prism is given by $V = Bh$. (Note: This formula is provided in the Notation, Definitions, and Formulas pages at the beginning of the test booklet.) Devise a plan. To find the volume of the right hexagonal prism will take two steps. First, find the area, B, of one of the regular hexagonal bases, and then find the volume by multiplying B by the height of the prism, h.

Step 1. Find the area of one of the regular hexagonal bases.

Sketch a diagram.

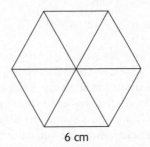

6 cm

A regular hexagon with side 6 cm can be divided into six equilateral triangles with each side equal to 6 cm. The area of an equilateral triangle with sides of 6 cm is given by: Area $= \frac{\sqrt{3}}{4} s^2 = \frac{\sqrt{3}}{4}(6 \text{ cm})^2 = 9\sqrt{3} \text{ cm}^2$.

Tip: If you forget the formula for the area of an equilateral triangle, you can derive it by using the Pythagorean theorem or trigonometric functions to determine the height (altitude) of the triangle, and then using the formula, area $= \frac{1}{2}bh$, to find the area of the equilateral triangle.

Thus, the area of the regular hexagonal base of the prism is given by: $B = 6(9\sqrt{3} \text{ cm}^2) = 54\sqrt{3} \text{ cm}^2$.

Step 2. find the volume by multiplying B by the height of the prism, h.

Volume $= (54\sqrt{3} \text{ cm}^2)(30 \text{ cm}) = 2805.9223 \ldots$ or approximately 2806 cm³, Choice C. Choice A results if you forget to multiply the area of the equilateral triangle by 6 to obtain the area of the hexagonal base. Choice B results if you use an incorrect formula for the volume of the prism. Choice D results if you use an incorrect formula for an equilateral triangle.

48. B. A **tree** is a connected vertex-edge graph that contains no simple circuits. Only the vertex-edge graph in Choice B is a tree. The vertex-edge graphs in the other answer choices contain simple circuits, so these graphs are not trees.

49. B. Make a quick sketch of the two graphs.

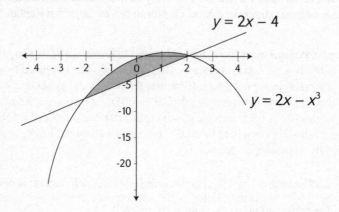

Analyze the problem. The two graphs intersect at two points, and the graph of $y = 2x - x^2$ lies above $y = 2x - 4$ between the points of intersection. Devise a plan. To find the area of the region bounded by the two graphs will take three steps. First, find the x-values for the points of intersection of the two graphs; next, find the difference between the two functions, being sure to subtract the equation of the lower graph from the equation of the upper graph; and then evaluate the definite integral of the difference of the two graphs, between the two x-values of their intersection.

Step 1. Find the x-values for the points of intersection of the two graphs.

Using substitution, you have $2x - x^2 = 2x - 4 \Rightarrow -x^2 = -4 \Rightarrow x^2 = 4 \Rightarrow x = \pm 2$

Step 2. Find the difference between the two graphs.

Difference $= (2x - x^2) - (2x - 4) = 2x - x^2 - 2x + 4 = -x^2 + 4$

Step 3. Evaluate the definite integral $\int_{-2}^{2} (-x^2 + 4)\, dx$.

Method 1: The fastest and most efficient way to calculate this numerical integral is with your graphing calculator. Here are the steps using a TI-83 calculator. Before you enter functions, you must select Func mode, from the MODE menu. Enter the function $y = -x^2 + 4$ into the Y = editor, which is where you define functions. As a precaution, clear any previously entered functions before you enter the function. Check the viewing WINDOW to make sure that the interval between –2 and 2 falls between Xmin and Xmax. If not, change Xmin and/or Xmax, as needed. Select 7: $\int f(x)\, dx$ from the CALC (calculate) menu. Type –2 as the lower limit and then press ENTER.

Type 2 as the upper limit and then press ENTER. The integral value is displayed as 10.666667 and the graph is shaded (Note: the graph and the shaded region will not look like what you've sketched above because you entered the difference of the two functions into the function editor). Since the answer choices are given as fractions, select 1:Frac from the MATH menu. The display will show Ans▶Frac. Press ENTER. The display shows 32/3, Choice B.

Method 2: Integrate the function using methods of calculus.

$$\int_{-2}^{2}\left(-x^2+4\right)dx = \left(-\frac{x^3}{3}+4x\right)\bigg|_{-2}^{2} = \left(-\frac{2^3}{3}+4\cdot 2\right)-\left(-\frac{(-2)^3}{3}+4\cdot -2\right) = \left(-\frac{8}{3}+8\right)-\left(\frac{8}{3}+-8\right) = -\frac{8}{3}+8-\frac{8}{3}+8 =$$

$16-\frac{16}{3}=\frac{32}{3}$, Choice B. The other answer choices result if you make a mistake integrating the function.

50. A. Analyze the problem. If the members of the committee are selected at random, then every committee of three people that can be formed for this purpose is equally likely. To find the probability that a particular committee of three people will be chosen will take two steps. First, find the number of different committees of size three that can be selected, and then find the probability that a particular committee of three will be selected.

Step 1. Find the number of different committees of size three that can be selected.

Since the order in which committee members are chosen does not make a difference as regards the composition of the committee, the number of different committees of size three that can be selected from the 100 members is the combination of 100 members taken 3 at a time, which is $_{100}C_3$.

Step 2. Find the probability that a particular committee of 3 will be selected.

The particular committee of 3 has 1 chance in $_{100}C_3$ of being selected $= \dfrac{1}{_{100}C_3}$, Choice A. Choice B is incorrect because this answer counts different orders of selection of the same committee members as different committees. Choices C and D result if you analyze the problem incorrectly.

Answer Grid for Practice Test 3

(Remove This Sheet and Use It to Mark Your Answers)

1 Ⓐ Ⓑ Ⓒ Ⓓ		26 Ⓐ Ⓑ Ⓒ Ⓓ
2 Ⓐ Ⓑ Ⓒ Ⓓ		27 Ⓐ Ⓑ Ⓒ Ⓓ
3 Ⓐ Ⓑ Ⓒ Ⓓ		28 Ⓐ Ⓑ Ⓒ Ⓓ
4 Ⓐ Ⓑ Ⓒ Ⓓ		29 Ⓐ Ⓑ Ⓒ Ⓓ
5 Ⓐ Ⓑ Ⓒ Ⓓ		30 Ⓐ Ⓑ Ⓒ Ⓓ
6 Ⓐ Ⓑ Ⓒ Ⓓ		31 Ⓐ Ⓑ Ⓒ Ⓓ
7 Ⓐ Ⓑ Ⓒ Ⓓ		32 Ⓐ Ⓑ Ⓒ Ⓓ
8 Ⓐ Ⓑ Ⓒ Ⓓ		33 Ⓐ Ⓑ Ⓒ Ⓓ
9 Ⓐ Ⓑ Ⓒ Ⓓ		34 Ⓐ Ⓑ Ⓒ Ⓓ
10 Ⓐ Ⓑ Ⓒ Ⓓ		35 Ⓐ Ⓑ Ⓒ Ⓓ
11 Ⓐ Ⓑ Ⓒ Ⓓ		36 Ⓐ Ⓑ Ⓒ Ⓓ
12 Ⓐ Ⓑ Ⓒ Ⓓ		37 Ⓐ Ⓑ Ⓒ Ⓓ
13 Ⓐ Ⓑ Ⓒ Ⓓ		38 Ⓐ Ⓑ Ⓒ Ⓓ
14 Ⓐ Ⓑ Ⓒ Ⓓ		39 Ⓐ Ⓑ Ⓒ Ⓓ
15 Ⓐ Ⓑ Ⓒ Ⓓ		40 Ⓐ Ⓑ Ⓒ Ⓓ
16 Ⓐ Ⓑ Ⓒ Ⓓ		41 Ⓐ Ⓑ Ⓒ Ⓓ
17 Ⓐ Ⓑ Ⓒ Ⓓ		42 Ⓐ Ⓑ Ⓒ Ⓓ
18 Ⓐ Ⓑ Ⓒ Ⓓ		43 Ⓐ Ⓑ Ⓒ Ⓓ
19 Ⓐ Ⓑ Ⓒ Ⓓ		44 Ⓐ Ⓑ Ⓒ Ⓓ
20 Ⓐ Ⓑ Ⓒ Ⓓ		45 Ⓐ Ⓑ Ⓒ Ⓓ
21 Ⓐ Ⓑ Ⓒ Ⓓ		46 Ⓐ Ⓑ Ⓒ Ⓓ
22 Ⓐ Ⓑ Ⓒ Ⓓ		47 Ⓐ Ⓑ Ⓒ Ⓓ
23 Ⓐ Ⓑ Ⓒ Ⓓ		48 Ⓐ Ⓑ Ⓒ Ⓓ
24 Ⓐ Ⓑ Ⓒ Ⓓ		49 Ⓐ Ⓑ Ⓒ Ⓓ
25 Ⓐ Ⓑ Ⓒ Ⓓ		50 Ⓐ Ⓑ Ⓒ Ⓓ

CUT HERE

Mathematics: Content Knowledge Practice Test 3

Directions: Each of the questions or incomplete statements is followed by four suggested answers or completions. Select the one that is best in each case, and then fill in the corresponding lettered space on the answer sheet.

1. In order to estimate the population of fish in a lake, a parks and recreation team captures and tags 300 fish, and then releases the tagged fish back into the lake. One month later, the team returns and captures 75 fish from the lake, 15 of which bear tags that identify them as being among the previously captured fish. If all the tagged fish are still active in the lake when the second group of fish is captured, what is the best estimate of the fish population in the lake based on the information obtained through this capture-recapture strategy?

   A. 60 fish
   B. 1500 fish
   C. 1800 fish
   D. 2000 fish

$$
\begin{array}{r}
3012 \\
\times\ \ 23 \\
\hline
9036 \\
60240 \\
\hline
69276
\end{array}
$$

2. The application of the multiplication algorithm shown in the above computation illustrates which of the following properties of the real numbers?

   I. commutativity
   II. associativity
   III. distributive property

   A. I only
   B. II only
   C. III only
   D. I, II, and III

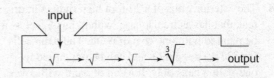

3. If x^6, where x is a positive number, is used as the input for the function machine shown above, which of the following is equivalent to the output?

   A. $x^{\frac{11}{6}}$
   B. $x^{\frac{1}{4}}$
   C. $x^7 \cdot x^{\frac{1}{6}}$
   D. x^{11}

4. For what value of k will the function $y = 25x^2 - kx + 16$ have exactly one real zero?

   A. $40i$
   B. -20
   C. 20
   D. 40

5. What is the distance from the point $(-3, 7)$ to the line that has equation $4x + 3y = 5$?

   A. 0.6 unit
   B. 0.8 unit
   C. 2.0 units
   D. 2.8 units

6. A baseball diamond is a square that is 90 feet on a side. What is the approximate length of the diagonal of the baseball diamond in a scale model in which 9 feet = 1 inch?

   A. 13 in
   B. 14 in
   C. 15 in
   D. 20 in

GO ON TO THE NEXT PAGE

7. For disaster relief in a hurricane-damaged area, $2.5 billion is needed. This amount of money is approximately equivalent to spending one dollar per

   A. second for 80 years
   B. hour for 1000 years
   C. day for 20,000 years
   D. month for 1 million years

8. The exterior walls of a 20-foot high right cylindrical tank that has a circular base, with radius 5 feet, is to be painted with one coat of paint. The paint sells for $23.40 per gallon and can be purchased in one-gallon cans only. If a can of paint will cover approximately 400 square feet, what is the cost of the paint needed to paint the exterior walls of the tank?

   A. $23.40
   B. $36.75
   C. $46.80
   D. $93.60

9. A length of cable is attached to the top of a 30-foot pole. The cable is anchored 16 feet from the base of the pole. What is the length of the cable?

   A. 23 feet
   B. 25 feet
   C. 34 feet
   D. 46 feet

10. Donna scored at the 75th percentile on a multiple-choice history exam. The best interpretation of this information is that

   A. Donna answered 75 percent of the questions on the test correctly.
   B. only 25 percent of the other students did worse on the test than did Donna.
   C. Donna answered 75 questions correctly.
   D. Donna did as well as or better than 75% of the students who took the exam.

11. If $\sin \theta = -\frac{5}{13}$ and $\pi < \theta < \frac{3\pi}{2}$, then $\tan \theta$ is

   A. $-\frac{12}{5}$
   B. $-\frac{5}{12}$
   C. $\frac{12}{5}$
   D. $\frac{5}{12}$

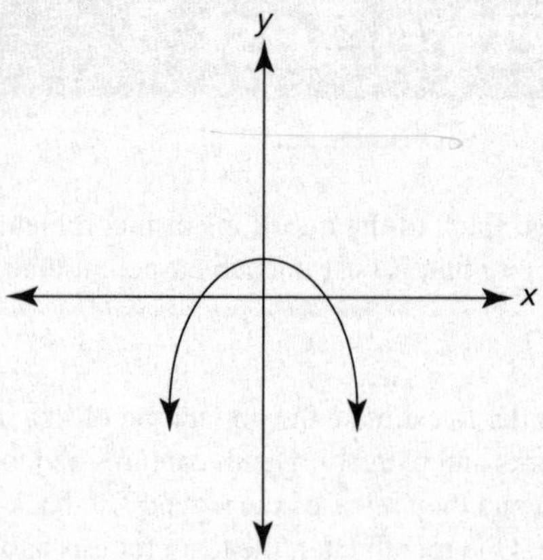

12. A quadratic function $y = ax^2 + bx + c$ has the graph shown above. Which of the statements about the discriminant of the function is true?

   A. $b^2 - 4ac = 0$.
   B. $b^2 - 4ac < 0$.
   C. $b^2 - 4ac > 0$.
   D. $b^2 - 4ac$ is undefined.

13. If $y - 2.8 = 4 \sin x$, what is the minimum value of y?

   A. -6.8
   B. -1.2
   C. 1.2
   D. 6.8

14. Which of the following expressions is an identity for $\frac{\tan\theta + \cot\theta}{\sec\theta\csc\theta}$?

   A. $\sin^2 \theta + \cos^2 \theta$
   B. $2 \cos^2 \theta$
   C. $2 \sin \theta \cos \theta$
   D. $1 - 2 \sin^2 \theta$

15. Triangle ABC has vertices $(3, -1)$, $(-5, 7)$, and $(2, -4)$. Which of the following matrix multiplications would result in a reflection of $\triangle ABC$ over the y-axis?

   A. $\begin{bmatrix} -1 & 0 \\ 0 & 1 \end{bmatrix}\begin{bmatrix} 3 & -5 & 2 \\ -1 & 7 & -4 \end{bmatrix}$

   B. $\begin{bmatrix} 0 & 1 \\ -1 & 0 \end{bmatrix}\begin{bmatrix} 3 & -5 & 2 \\ -1 & 7 & -4 \end{bmatrix}$

   C. $\begin{bmatrix} 0 & 1 \\ 0 & 0 \end{bmatrix}\begin{bmatrix} 3 & -5 & 2 \\ -1 & 7 & -4 \end{bmatrix}$

   D. $\begin{bmatrix} 1 & 0 \\ 0 & -1 \end{bmatrix}\begin{bmatrix} 3 & -5 & 2 \\ -1 & 7 & -4 \end{bmatrix}$

16. On the set of $n \times n$ matrices, the relation "is conformable for multiplication" satisfies which of the following properties?

   I.   reflexive

  II.   symmetric

 III.   transitive

  A.   I only

  B.   III only

  C.   I and III only

  D.   I, II, and III

Mean Score	65
Median Score	73
Modal Score	77
Range	52
Standard Deviation	15
Number of Students	50

17. The data in the table summarize the scores on a chemistry exam. Which of the following statements best describes the distribution of the scores?

  A.   The distribution is positively skewed.

  B.   The distribution is negatively skewed.

  C.   The distribution is symmetric.

  D.   The distribution is bimodal.

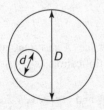

18. In the picture shown, the diameter, d, of the smaller circle is one-fourth the diameter, D, of the larger circle. If a point inside the larger circle is chosen at random, what is the probability that the point will also be inside the smaller circle?

  A. $\dfrac{1}{16}$

  B. $\dfrac{1}{8}$

  C. $\dfrac{1}{4}$

  D. $\dfrac{1}{2}$

19. $i^{218} =$

  A. -1

  B. $-i$

  C. 1

  D. i

20. Using a graduated cylinder, a chemist measures the volume of a chemical solution and uses the appropriate number of significant figures to record the volume as 40.6 milliliters (mL). Which of the following ways most accurately expresses the range of possible values of the volume of the solution?

  A.   40.6 mL $\pm$ 0.005 mL

  B.   40.6 mL $\pm$ 0.05 mL

  C.   40.6 mL $\pm$ 0.5 mL

  D.   40.6 mL $\pm$ 0.1 mL

21. Which of the following expressions is equivalent to the expression $\log_{10}\left(\dfrac{x^3}{20}\right)$?

  A. $(\log_{10}x)^3 - 2$

  B. $3\log_{10}x - 2$

  C. $(\log_{10}x)^3 - \log_{10}20$

  D. $3\log_{10}x - \log_{10}2 - 1$

22. Which of the following matrices are nonsingular?

  I. $\begin{bmatrix} -3 & 5 \\ -6 & 10 \end{bmatrix}$

  II. $\begin{bmatrix} 4 & 0 \\ 0 & 4 \end{bmatrix}$

 III. $\begin{bmatrix} 2 & -5 & 3 \\ 6 & 1 & -4 \\ 0 & 0 & 0 \end{bmatrix}$

 IV. $\begin{bmatrix} 1 & 0 & 0 \\ 0 & 1 & 0 \\ 0 & 0 & 1 \end{bmatrix}$

  A.   I and II only

  B.   I and III only

  C.   II and IV only

  D.   III and IV only

GO ON TO THE NEXT PAGE

23. The research department for sales at an Internet bookseller company finds that the relationship between total sales and the number of telephone orders that it receives is modeled by the function $S(x) = 5000\ln x + 1500$, where $S(x)$ is the total sales represented in thousands of dollars and x is the number of telephone orders received. Based on this model, approximately how many telephone orders should the bookseller expect to fill for projected sales of $20 million?

   A. 40
   B. 54
   C. 4000
   D. 5012

24. Which of the following sets is the domain of the function $y = \tan x$?

   A. $\{x \in \text{reals}, x \neq \frac{\pi}{2} + k\pi\}$
   B. $\{x \in \text{reals}, x \neq k\pi\}$
   C. $\{x \in \text{reals}, -\frac{\pi}{2} < x < \frac{\pi}{2}\}$
   D. $\{x \in \text{reals}\}$

25. If $f(x) = -16x^{-4}$, then $f'(2)$ is

   A. -2
   B. $-\frac{\pi}{2}$
   C. $\frac{1}{2}$
   D. 2

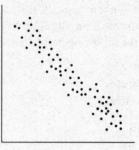

26. The graph shown is a scatterplot for a set of bivariate data, paired values of data from two variables. What does the shape of the scatterplot indicate about the relationship between the two variables?

   A. There is little relationship between the two variables.
   B. There is a linear, negative relationship between the two variables.
   C. There is a linear, positive relationship between the two variables.
   D. There is a strong exponential relationship between the two variables.

27. Given $A = \begin{bmatrix} 0 & 2 \\ 1 & 3 \end{bmatrix}$ and $B = \begin{bmatrix} -2 & 3 \\ 2 & 0 \end{bmatrix}$, then BA is

   A. $\begin{bmatrix} 0 & 6 \\ 2 & 0 \end{bmatrix}$
   B. $\begin{bmatrix} 3 & 5 \\ 0 & 4 \end{bmatrix}$
   C. $\begin{bmatrix} 4 & 0 \\ 4 & 3 \end{bmatrix}$
   D. The matrices A and B are not conformable for multiplication.

28. If $f(x) = x^2 - 4$ and $g(x) = 3x + 2$, then $(f \circ g)(x) = f(g(x)) =$

   A. $(x^2 - 4)(3x + 2)$
   B. $(3x + 2)(x^2 - 4)$
   C. $3x(3x + 4)$
   D. $3x^2 - 10$

29. What are the units of the quantity $m_2 = \dfrac{gr^2}{kP}$, where g is given in meters per second squared ($\dfrac{\mathrm{m}}{\mathrm{s}^2}$), r is measured in meters (m), k has units of meters squared per kilogram squared ($\dfrac{\mathrm{m}^2}{\mathrm{kg}^2}$), and P is given in kilogram-meters per second squared ($\dfrac{\mathrm{kg-m}}{\mathrm{s}^2}$)?

A. kg

B. $\dfrac{1}{\mathrm{kg}}$

C. $\dfrac{\mathrm{kg}}{\mathrm{s}^4}$

D. $\dfrac{\mathrm{kg-m}^3}{\mathrm{s}^4}$

30. Suppose that the parents of a newborn child establish a trust fund account for the child with an investment of $10,000. Assuming no withdrawals and no additional deposits are made, approximately what interest rate compounded annually is needed to double the investment in 20 years?

A. 3.5%

B. 5.5%

C. 10.0%

D. 103.5%

31. What is the product of the complex numbers $4 + 5i$ and $4 - 5i$?

A. -9

B. 41

C. $41 - 40i$

D. $41 + 40i$

32. A manufacturing company purchases a robotic machine that can produce $Q(h)$ components per hour, where $Q(h) = \dfrac{10(4h + 25)}{2h + 5}$. Assuming the machine continues to work efficiently, approximately how many components is the machine able to produce per hour after being in operation for a long extended period of time?

A. 5 components

B. 20 components

C. 40 components

D. 50 components

33. Water is running into a right cylindrical tank, which has a radius of 5 feet, at a constant rate of 30 cubic feet per minute $\left(\dfrac{\mathrm{ft}^3}{\mathrm{min}}\right)$. What is the instantaneous rate of change of the height of water after the water starts running?

A. $0.38\dfrac{\mathrm{ft}}{\mathrm{min}}$

B. $0.95\dfrac{\mathrm{ft}}{\mathrm{min}}$

C. $1.05\dfrac{\mathrm{ft}}{\mathrm{min}}$

D. $2.6\dfrac{\mathrm{ft}}{\mathrm{min}}$

$$2x + 5y - z = 5$$
$$-4x + 3y + 5z = 13$$
$$8x + 10y = -4$$

34. Solve the system of equations above for z.

A. -3

B. -1

C. 0

D. 2

35. A small town has three prefixes available—560, 564, and 569—for the seven-digit telephone numbers in the town. How many different telephone numbers are possible if all three prefixes are used?

A. $3 \cdot \left({}_{10}C_4\right)$

B. $3 \cdot 10^4$

C. 10^7

D. 10^{12}

GO ON TO THE NEXT PAGE

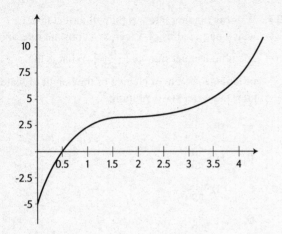

36. The graph shown is the graph of $y = x^3 - 6x^2 + 12x - 5$; which of the following statements is true about the rate of change of y with respect to x?

   A. The rate of change is constant between 0 and 0.5.

   B. The rate of change is increasing between 0.5 and 1.5.

   C. The rate of change is decreasing between 2 and 3.

   D. The rate of change is increasing between 3 and 3.5.

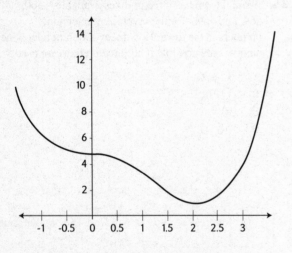

37. The graph shown is the graph of $f(x) = x^4 - 3x^3 + x^2 + 5$. What is the area of the region bounded by the graph of f and the x-axis over the closed interval $[0, 2]$?

   A. 1 square unit

   B. 5 square units

   C. $\dfrac{32}{5}$ square units

   D. $\dfrac{106}{15}$ square units

38. The gas mileage in miles per gallon (mpg) for automobiles of a certain luxury model is normally distributed with a mean of 29 mpg and a standard deviation of 4 mpg. What is the approximate probability that an automobile of this type chosen at random has gas mileage less than 25 mpg?

   A. 16%

   B. 34%

   C. 68%

   D. 84%

39. Given the trigonometric function $f(x) = \tan x$, which of the following best describes the function $g(x) = \tan(4x - \pi) + 3$?

   A. the same as the graph of $f(x) = \tan x$ shifted right by $\dfrac{\pi}{4}$ units and up by 3 units

   B. the same as the graph of $f(x) = \tan x$ shifted left by $\dfrac{\pi}{4}$ units and down by 3 units

   C. the same as the graph of $f(x) = \tan x$ shifted right by π units and up by 3 units

   D. the same as the graph of $f(x) = \tan x$ shifted left by π units and down by 3 units

40. For which of the following studies would the results most likely establish a cause-effect relationship?

   A. An experimental study investigating the effect of a new type of fertilizer on plant growth.

   B. A survey of teachers' opinions about standardized testing of students.

   C. An observational study investigating factors related to delinquent behavior in teenagers.

   D. A correlational study investigating the relationship between college GPA and birth order.

41. Which of the following sets is the solution to $2x^2 - x < 1$?

   A. $\{x \in \text{reals}, x < -1 \text{ or } x > \frac{1}{2}\}$

   B. $\{x \in \text{reals}, x < -\frac{1}{2} \text{ or } x > 1\}$

   C. $\{x \in \text{reals}, -\frac{1}{2} < x < 1\}$

   D. $\{x \in \text{reals}, -1 < x < \frac{1}{2}\}$

Time (in years)	Population
0	500
5	1500

42. The table above gives the population of a deer herd at two different times in years. The growth of the population is modeled by the function $P(t) = P_0 e^{xt}$. Based on this information, what is the value of x?

A. $\dfrac{\ln 3}{5}$

B. $\ln 3$

C. $\ln 3 - \ln 5$

D. $\ln \dfrac{3}{5}$

43. A ball is dropped from a height of 120 feet. If each rebound is $\dfrac{3}{4}$ the height of the previous bounce, which of the following functions would best model the height of the ball as a function of rebound number n?

A. quadratic

B. polynomial

C. linear

D. exponential

44. The function $y = \dfrac{2x^3 + 3x - x + 1}{x^2 - 8x + 16}$ has how many asymptotes?

A. 0

B. 1

C. 2

D. 3

45. An interior decorator wants to replace a rectangular table that measures 3 feet by 4.5 feet with a circular table that has a diameter of 4 feet. Approximately how much less area will the circular table require as compared to the area of the square table?

A. 0.93 ft²

B. 12.57 ft²

C. 26.07 ft²

D. 36.77 ft²

46. A sequence is defined recursively by

$a_1 = 1$,
$a_n = a_{n-1} + 2n + 3$ for $n \geq 2$

The closed-form representation of the sequence is best modeled as

A. arithmetic

B. geometric

C. quadratic

D. exponential

47. What is the volume of a right triangular prism that is 25 inches in height and whose bases are equilateral triangles that are 4 inches on a side?

A. 7 in³

B. 100 in³

C. 173 in³

D. 200 in³

48. An experiment consists of flipping a coin 6 times. How many different outcomes are in the sample space for this experiment?

A. $_6P_2$

B. 2^6

C. 6^2

D. 6^6

49. Find the area enclosed by the curves $y = \dfrac{1}{4}x^2$ and $y = x^2 + 3x - 9$.

A. 64 square units

B. 118 square units

C. 172 square units

D. It cannot be determined from the information given.

50. A bag contains 10 blue marbles, 7 red marbles, 5 green marbles, and 3 yellow marbles. If two marbles are randomly drawn from the bag without replacement after the first draw, what is the probability that both marbles will be yellow?

A. $\dfrac{3}{25} \cdot \dfrac{3}{25}$

B. $\dfrac{3}{25} \cdot \dfrac{2}{24}$

C. $\dfrac{3}{25}$

D. $\dfrac{2}{24}$

IF YOU FINISH BEFORE TIME IS CALLED, CHECK YOUR WORK ON THIS SECTION ONLY. DO NOT WORK ON ANY OTHER SECTION IN THE TEST.

Practice Test 3

Mathematics: Content Knowledge
Practice Test 3 Answer Key

Question Number	Correct Answer	Content Category	Question Number	Correct Answer	Content Category
1.	B	Algebra and Number Theory	26.	B	Data Analysis and Statistics
2.	C	Algebra and Number Theory	27.	B	Matrix Algebra
3.	B	Algebra and Number Theory	28.	C	Functions
4.	D	Functions	29.	A	Measurement
5.	B	Algebra and Number Theory	30.	A	Discrete Mathematics
6.	B	Geometry	31.	B	Algebra and Number Theory
7.	A	Measurement	32.	B	Calculus
8.	C	Geometry	33.	A	Calculus
9.	C	Geometry	34.	B	Matrix Algebra
10.	D	Data Analysis and Statistics	35.	B	Discrete Mathematics
11.	D	Trigonometry	36.	D	Calculus
12.	C	Functions	37.	D	Calculus
13.	C	Trigonometry	38.	A	Data Analysis and Statistics
14.	A	Trigonometry	39.	A	Functions
15.	A	Matrix Algebra	40.	A	Data Analysis and Statistics
16.	D	Discrete Mathematics	41.	C	Algebra and Number Theory
17.	B	Data Analysis and Statistics	42.	A	Functions
18.	A	Probability	43.	D	Functions
19.	A	Algebra and Number Theory	44.	C	Functions
20.	B	Measurement	45.	A	Geometry
21.	D	Algebra and Number Theory	46.	C	Discrete Mathematics
22.	C	Matrix Algebra	47.	C	Geometry
23.	A	Functions	48.	B	Probability
24.	A	Trigonometry	49.	A	Calculus
25.	D	Calculus	50.	B	Probability

Answer Explanations for Practice Test 3

1. **B.** Analyze the problem. If all the tagged fish are still active in the lake when the second group of fish is captured, the proportion of tagged fish in the second group should be equal to the proportion of tagged fish in the whole population, P, of fish in the lake. Devise a plan. Set up an equation and solve for P.

$\frac{15}{75} = \frac{300}{P} \Rightarrow P = \frac{75 \cdot 300}{15} = 1500$ fish, Choice B. Choice A occurs if you set up the proportion incorrectly. Choices C and D occur if you make a computation error when solving the proportion.

2. **C.** This question is an example of a multiple-response set question. One approach to answering this type of question is to follow the following steps. First, read the question carefully to make sure you understand what the question is asking; next, identify choices that you know are incorrect from the Roman numeral options, and then draw a line through every answer choice that contains a Roman numeral you have eliminated; and then examine the remaining answer choices to determine which Roman numeral options you need to consider.

Looking at the Roman numeral options, you can eliminate Roman I because the order of the factors is not changed in the multiplication shown. Draw a line through choices A and D because these answer choices include Roman I. The remaining answer choices, B and C, each contain only one Roman numeral option. You can eliminate Roman II because there are only two factors in the multiplication problem shown, so different groupings are not an option. Draw a line through Choice B because this answer choice contains Roman II. This leaves answer Choice C as the correct response because it includes every Roman numeral option that is correct and no incorrect Roman numeral options.

3. **B.** Since the answer choices are given as exponential expressions, the best way to work this problem is to perform on x^6 the sequence of operations indicated by the function machine, using the exponential form for the operations: $x^6 \rightarrow \sqrt{x^6} = x^3 \rightarrow \sqrt{x^3} = \left(x^3\right)^{\frac{1}{2}} = x^{\frac{3}{2}} \rightarrow \sqrt{x^{\frac{3}{2}}} = \left(x^{\frac{3}{2}}\right)^{\frac{1}{2}} = x^{\frac{3}{4}} \rightarrow \sqrt[3]{x^{\frac{3}{4}}} = \left(x^{\frac{3}{4}}\right)^{\frac{1}{3}} = x^{\frac{1}{4}}$, Choice B. The other answer choices result if you fail to use the rules for exponents correctly.

4. **D.** The function $y = 25x^2 - kx + 16$ will have exactly one real zero when the trinomial, $25x^2 - kx + 16$, is a perfect square. For $25x^2 - kx + 16$ to be a perfect square, the coefficient, k, of x needs to be $\pm(2 \cdot \sqrt{25} \cdot \sqrt{16})$, which is $\pm(2 \cdot 5 \cdot 4) = \pm 40$. Since Choice D contains 40, it is the correct response. The other answer choices would not result in exactly one real zero.

5. **B.** The formula for the distance from point (x_1, y_1) to line $Ax + By + C = 0$ is given by $d = \frac{|Ax_1 + By_1 + C|}{\sqrt{A^2 + B^2}}$. Note: This formula is provided in the Notation, Definitions, and Formulas pages at the beginning of your test booklet. First, rewrite $4x + 3y = 5$ as $4x + 3y - 5 = 0$, and then apply the formula using the point $(-3, 7)$.

$d = \frac{|Ax_1 + By_1 + C|}{\sqrt{A^2 + B^2}} = \frac{|4(-3) + 3(7) - 5|}{\sqrt{4^2 + 3^2}} = \frac{|-12 + 21 - 5|}{\sqrt{25}} = \frac{|4|}{5} = \frac{4}{5}$ or 0.8 unit, Choice B.

Choice A results if you calculate the denominator incorrectly. Choice C results if you fail to rewrite the equation as $4x + 3y - 5 = 0$ before using the formula, and you calculate the denominator incorrectly. Choice D results if you fail to rewrite the equation as $4x + 3y - 5 = 0$ before using the formula.

6. **B.** Analyze the problem. The diagonal of the baseball diamond is the hypotenuse of a right isosceles triangle with legs of 90 feet each. The scale for the length of the diagonal in the actual baseball diamond to the length of the diagonal in the model is $\frac{9 \text{ ft}}{1 \text{ in}}$. Devise a plan. To find the length of the diagonal in the model will take two steps. First, find the length, D, of the diagonal in the actual baseball diamond, and then set up and solve a proportion to find the length of the diagonal, d, in the model.

Step 1. Find the length of the diagonal in the actual model.

$D^2 = (90)^2 + (90)^2 = 8100 + 8100 = 16,200 \Rightarrow D = \sqrt{16,200}$ ft

Step 2. Set up a proportion and solve for d.

$\frac{D}{d} = \frac{9 \text{ ft}}{1 \text{ in}} \Rightarrow \frac{\sqrt{16,200}}{d} = \frac{9 \text{ ft}}{1 \text{ in}} \Rightarrow d = \frac{\sqrt{16,200}}{9} = 14.1421\ldots$ or approximately 14 inches, Choice B. The other answer choices occur if you analyze the problem incorrectly or you make a computation error.

149

7. A. Analyze the problem. You want to know how many years it would take to spend $2.5 billion per second, hour, day, or month. Devise a plan. The best way to determine which answer is correct is to check each answer choice. Each is a unit analysis problem. Write $2.5 billion as a fraction with denominator 1 and let unit analysis tell you which conversion fractions to multiply by, keeping in mind that you want years as your final answer.

Checking A: $\dfrac{\$2,500,000,000}{1} \times \dfrac{1\cancel{s}}{\$1} \times \dfrac{1\cancel{\text{min}}}{60\cancel{s}} \times \dfrac{1\cancel{h}}{60\cancel{\text{min}}} \times \dfrac{1\cancel{d}}{24\cancel{h}} \times \dfrac{1\,\text{yr}}{365\cancel{d}} = 79.2744$ or approximately 80 years, indicating Choice A is the correct response.

In a test situation, you should go on to the next question since you have obtained the correct answer. You would not have to check the other answer choices; but for your information, the number of years given in each of the other answer choices falls short of the number of years needed to spend $2.5 billion.

8. C. Analyze the problem. You need to find the cost of the paint needed to cover the lateral surface area of the cylinder. Devise a plan. To determine the cost of the paint will take three steps. First, find the lateral surface area of the cylinder; next, find the number of gallons of paint needed; and then find the cost of the paint.

Step 1. Find the lateral surface area (*SA*) of the cylinder with $r = 5$ ft.

$SA = 2\pi rh = 2\pi(5\text{ ft})(20\text{ ft}) = 628.3185 \ldots \text{ ft}^2$ (Tip: Don't round this answer.)

Step 2. Find the number of gallons needed.

$628.3185 \ldots \text{ ft}^2 \div \dfrac{400\text{ ft}^2}{1\text{ gal}} = 1.5707 \ldots$ gallons, so 2 gallons of paint need to be purchased.

Step 3. Find the cost of 2 gallons of paint.

$2\text{ gallons} \times \dfrac{\$23.40}{1\text{ gal}} = \$46.80$, Choice C.

Choice A results if you round down to 1 gallon, instead of rounding up to 2 gallons in step 2. Choice B results if you do not round up to 2 gallons in step 2. Choice D occurs if you use an incorrect formula for the surface area of the cylinder.

9. C. First sketch a diagram to illustrate the problem.

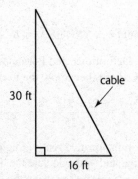

Analyze the problem. The pole, the cable, and the ground form a right triangle. From the diagram, you can see that the length of the cable is the hypotenuse of a right triangle that has legs of 30 feet and 16 feet. You can use the Pythagorean theorem to find the hypotenuse. Devise a plan. To find the length of the cable, plug into the formula for the Pythagorean theorem and solve for the hypotenuse, denoted by *c*.

c = hypotenuse = ?, $a = 30$ ft, and $b = 16$ ft.

$c^2 = a^2 + b^2 = (30\text{ ft})^2 + (16\text{ ft})^2 = 900\text{ ft}^2 + 256\text{ ft}^2 = 1156\text{ ft}^2 \Rightarrow c = 34$ ft, Choice C. Choice A results if you make a calculation error. Choice B results if you mistakenly decide that 30 feet is the length of the hypotenuse, instead of the length of a leg of the right triangle. Choice D results if you mistakenly decide to solve the problem by adding the lengths of the two legs to find the length of the hypotenuse.

10. D. The 75th percentile is a value at or below which 75 percent of the data fall. Therefore, the best interpretation of Donna's score is that she did as well as or better than 75% of the students who took the exam, Choice D. The statements in the other answer choices are not good interpretations for the concept of percentile.

11. D. Make a sketch to illustrate the problem.

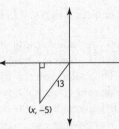

Because the Mathematics CK is a multiple-choice test, for problems of this type a clever approach is to eliminate answer choices based on the information provided. From the sketch, you can see that the $\tan \theta = \frac{y}{x} = \frac{-5}{x}$ and that $x < 0$. Therefore, $\tan \theta > 0$ because it is the quotient of two negative numbers. This allows you to eliminate choices A and B because these answer choices contain negative values. Looking at the two remaining answer choices, you can see that only Choice D has a 5 in the numerator for the tangent, meaning that Choice D must be the correct response. Of course, a more conventional way to work the problem is to use the formulas, $r^2 = x^2 + y^2$ and $\tan \theta = \frac{y}{x}$ (which are provided in the Notation, Definitions, and Formulas pages at the beginning of your test booklet), to determine that $x = \sqrt{13^2 - (-5)^2} = \sqrt{144} = \pm 12$. Since x is to the left of the origin, $x = -12$. Thus, $\tan \theta = \frac{y}{x} = \frac{-5}{-12} = \frac{5}{12}$, Choice D. Choices A and B are incorrect because the tangent is positive in the third quadrant, not negative. Choice C is the $\cot \theta$, not $\tan \theta$.

Tip: Be careful of using the inverse trigonometric function keys on your graphing calculator to work problems of this type. You might get an answer that has the wrong sign.

12. C. The graph of the quadratic function intersects the real axis at two points, indicating the function has two real zeroes. Therefore, the discriminant, $b^2 - 4ac$, must be greater than zero, Choice C. When $b^2 - 4ac = 0$ (Choice A), the graph of the quadratic function intersects the real axis in exactly one point. When $b^2 - 4ac < 0$ (Choice B), the graph of the quadratic function does not intersect the real axis. Choice D is incorrect because the coefficients of the quadratic function are real numbers, meaning $b^2 - 4ac$ is a real number, so it is not undefined.

13. C. First, rewrite $y - 2.8 = 4 \sin x$ as $y = 4 \sin x + 2.8$. The minimum value of the sine function is -1, so the minimum value of $4 \sin x$ is -4. Thus, the minimum value of $y = 4 \sin x + 2.8 = -4 + 2.8 = 1.2$, Choice C. Choices A and B result if you make a sign error. Choice D results if you mistakenly use 4 as the minimum value for $4 \sin x$.

14. A. Method 1: Since all the answer choices are given in terms of sine and cosine, rewrite $\frac{\tan \theta + \cot \theta}{\sec \theta \csc \theta}$ as $\frac{\frac{\sin \theta}{\cos \theta} + \frac{\cos \theta}{\sin \theta}}{\frac{1}{\cos \theta} \cdot \frac{1}{\sin \theta}} = \frac{\frac{\sin^2 \theta + \cos^2 \theta}{\cos \theta \sin \theta}}{\frac{1}{\cos \theta \sin \theta}} = \sin^2 \theta + \cos^2 \theta$, Choice A.

Method 2: Rewrite $\frac{\tan \theta + \cot \theta}{\sec \theta \csc \theta}$ as $\frac{\tan \theta + \frac{1}{\tan \theta}}{\frac{1}{\cos \theta} \cdot \frac{1}{\sin \theta}}$, so that you can use the trigonometric function keys on your graphing calculator to evaluate the expression for a convenient value of θ, say $30°$. When you evaluate $\frac{\tan 30° + \frac{1}{\tan 30°}}{\frac{1}{\cos 30°} \cdot \frac{1}{\sin 30°}}$, you get 1 for an answer. You should recognize that Choice A is an identity that equals 1 for all values of θ, so Choice A is the correct response. In a test situation, you should go on to the next question since you have obtained the correct answer. You would not have to check the other answer choices; but for your information, Choice B yields 1.5, Choice C yields .8660 . . . , and Choice D yields 0.5.

15. A. In a reflection over the *y*-axis, the *x*-coordinates of the image will be the negatives of the *x*-coordinates of the preimage, and the *y*-coordinates of the image will be the same as the *y*-coordinates of the preimage. Thus, you are looking for a matrix multiplication that will yield the product matrix $\begin{bmatrix} -3 & 5 & -2 \\ -1 & 7 & -4 \end{bmatrix}$. A quick way to determine which product given in the answer choices will result in the matrix $\begin{bmatrix} -3 & 5 & -2 \\ -1 & 7 & -4 \end{bmatrix}$ is to perform the matrix multiplications shown in each of the answer choices using your graphing calculator. You can expedite the process, by first entering the transformation matrix given in Choice A, entering the vertex matrix shown, and then premultiplying by the transformation matrix. Thereafter, you can use the edit feature of your graphing calculator and the recall entry feature to check the other answer choices. Only Choice A will yield the desired product matrix. The transformation matrix in Choice B will result in a 90-degree rotation about zero. The transformation matrix in Choice C will result in a reflection over the line *y = x*. The transformation matrix in Choice D will result in a reflection over the *x*-axis.

16. D. This question is an example of a multiple-response set question. One approach to answering this type of question is to follow the following steps. First, read the question carefully to make sure you understand what the question is asking; next, identify choices that you know are incorrect from the Roman numeral options, and then draw a line through every answer choice that contains a Roman numeral you have eliminated; and then examine the remaining answer choices to determine which Roman numeral options you need to consider.

Two matrices, *A* and *B*, are conformable for matrix multiplication in the order *AB*, only if the number of columns of matrix *A* is equal to the number of rows of matrix *B*. For the set of $n \times n$ matrices, the number of columns will equal the number of rows for any two matrices. Therefore, looking at the Roman numeral options, none would be eliminated because on the set of $n \times n$ matrices the relation "is conformable for multiplication" is reflexive because an $n \times n$ matrix is conformable for multiplication with itself; is symmetric because if an $n \times n$ matrix *A* is conformable for multiplication with an $n \times n$ matrix *B*, then matrix *B* is conformable for multiplication with matrix *A*; and is transitive because if an $n \times n$ matrix *A* is conformable for multiplication with an $n \times n$ matrix *B* and matrix *B* is conformable for multiplication with an $n \times n$ matrix *C*, then matrix *A* is conformable for multiplication with matrix *C*. Thus, Choice D is the correct response because it includes every Roman numeral option that is correct and no incorrect Roman numeral options.

17. B. If the data were represented using a histogram, the mean would lie to the left of both the median and the mode on the horizontal axis, indicating that the data are skewed, with a tail on the left. Thus, the distribution is negatively skewed, Choice B. None of the statements in the other answer choices accurately describes the distribution.

18. A. Analyze the problem. The probability that a point chosen at random in the larger circle will also be in the smaller circle is equal to the ratio of the area of the smaller circle to the area of the larger circle. Devise a plan. To find the probability will take three steps. First, determine the area of the smaller circle; next, determine the area of the larger circle; and then find the ratio of the area of the smaller circle to the larger circle.

Step 1. Find the area of the smaller circle.

The diameter *d* of the smaller circle is $\frac{1}{4}D$, so its radius is $\frac{1}{8}D$. Thus, the area of the smaller circle in terms of *D* is given by: area = $\pi(\frac{1}{8}D)^2 = \frac{\pi D^2}{64}$.

Step 2. Find the area of the larger circle.

The radius of the larger circle is $\frac{1}{2}D$. Thus, the area of the larger circle in terms of *D* is given by: area = $\pi(\frac{1}{2}D)^2 = \frac{\pi D^2}{4}$.

Step 3. Find the ratio of the area of the smaller circle to the larger circle.

The probability that a point chosen at random in the larger circle will also be in the smaller circle = $\dfrac{\frac{\pi D^2}{64}}{\frac{\pi D^2}{4}} = \frac{1}{16}$,

Choice A. The other answer choices result if you fail to compare areas or you make a computation error.

19. A. Since $i = i$, $i^2 = -1$, $i^3 = -i$, $i^4 = 1$, $i^5 = i$, $i^6 = -1$, $i^7 = -i$, $i^8 = 1$, $i^9 = -1$, and so on. You can see that the powers of the complex number i are cyclic, such that $i^{4k+1} = i$, $i^{4k+2} = i^2 = -1$, $i^{4k+3} = i^3 = -i$, and $i^{4k+4} = i^4 = 1$. So to evaluate a power of i, you divide its exponent by 4 and use the remainder as the exponent for i. Thus, $i^{218} = i^2 = -1$, Choice A.

20. B. The maximum possible error of a measurement is half the magnitude of the smallest measurement unit used to obtain the measurement. The most accurate way of expressing the measurement is as an interval. Thus, a measurement of 40.6 mL should be reported as 40.6 mL $\pm$ 0.05 mL, Choice B. Choice A is incorrect because this interval indicates an error that is less than should be indicated. Choices C and D are incorrect because these intervals indicate an error that is more than what should be indicated.

21. D. Method 1: Using the properties for logarithms, $\log_{10}\left(\dfrac{x^3}{20}\right) = \log_{10}x^3 - \log_{10}20 = 3\log_{10}x - \log_{10}(2 \cdot 10) =$
$3\log_{10}x - (\log_{10}2 + \log_{10}10) = 3\log_{10}x - \log_{10}2 - \log_{10}10 = 3\log_{10}x - \log_{10}2 - 1$, Choice D. The other answer choices occur if you make an error using the properties of logarithms.

Method 2: Select a convenient value for x, say 5, and evaluate $\log_{10}\left(\dfrac{5^3}{20}\right)$, which is $0.79588\ldots$, and then evaluate each of the expressions given in the answer choices for x equal to 5. Choice A yields $1.65851\ldots$, Choice B yields $.09691\ldots$, Choice C yields $-.95954\ldots$, and Choice D yields $0.79588\ldots$. Thus, Choice D is the correct response.

22. C. This question is an example of a multiple-response set question. One approach to answering this type of question is to follow the following steps. First, read the question carefully to make sure you understand what the question is asking; next, identify choices that you know are incorrect from the Roman numeral options, and then draw a line through every answer choice that contains a Roman numeral you have eliminated; and then examine the remaining answer choices to determine which Roman numeral options you need to consider.

A matrix that has an inverse is said to be nonsingular. A matrix has an inverse if and only if its determinant does *not* equal zero. Therefore, to determine which of the matrices are nonsingular, you can compute the determinant for each. If the determinant is *not* equal to zero, the matrix is nonsingular.

You can eliminate Roman III because the matrix $\begin{bmatrix} 2 & -5 & 3 \\ 6 & 1 & -4 \\ 0 & 0 & 0 \end{bmatrix}$ has a row of zeroes. If a square matrix has a row or column consisting of only zeroes, the determinant of the matrix equals zero. Therefore, $\begin{bmatrix} 2 & -5 & 3 \\ 6 & 1 & -4 \\ 0 & 0 & 0 \end{bmatrix}$ is *not* a nonsingular matrix. Draw a line through choices B and D because these answer choices contain Roman III. The remaining answer choices, A and C, both contain Roman II, so you need check only the matrices in Roman I and Roman IV.

Starting with the 2×2 matrix in Roman I, the determinant is computed as follows.

$\begin{vmatrix} -3 & 5 \\ -6 & 10 \end{vmatrix} = (-3 \cdot 10) - (5 \cdot -6) = -30 - (-30) = -30 + 30 = 0$, so $\begin{bmatrix} -3 & 5 \\ -6 & 10 \end{bmatrix}$ is *not* a nonsingular matrix.

Eliminate Choice A because it contains Roman I. This leaves answer Choice C as the correct response because it includes every Roman numeral option that is correct and no incorrect Roman numeral options.

23. A. Analyze the problem. You need to find the value of x for a given value of $S(x)$. Devise a plan. Set $S(x) = 20{,}000$ (Notice that total sales are represented in thousands of dollars) in $S(x) = 5000\ln x + 1500$, and then solve for x.

$20{,}000 = 5000\ln x + 1500 \Rightarrow 20{,}000 - 1500 = 5000\ln x \Rightarrow 18{,}500 = 5000\ln x \Rightarrow 3.7 = \ln x \Rightarrow e^{3.7} = x \Rightarrow x = 40.4473\ldots$ or approximately 40 telephone orders, Choice A. Choices B and D occur if you make a computation error. Choice D results if you mistakenly use base 10 logarithm instead of base e logarithm in the problem.

24. A. The tangent function is undefined at odd multiples of $\dfrac{\pi}{2}$. One way to write odd multiples of $\dfrac{\pi}{2}$ is $(2k+1)\dfrac{\pi}{2} = k\pi + \dfrac{\pi}{2} = \dfrac{\pi}{2} + k\pi$, Choice A. Choice B is incorrect because the domain given in this answer choice excludes real numbers for which the tangent function is defined and fails to exclude real numbers for which the tangent function is undefined. Choice C is incorrect because the set given in this answer choice is a subset of the domain of the tangent function. Choice D is incorrect because the domain given in this answer choice fails to exclude real numbers for which the tangent function is undefined.

25. D. You are asked to find the numerical derivative of a function.

Method 1: A fast and efficient way to calculate this numerical derivative is with your graphing calculator. Here are the steps using a TI-83 calculator. Before you enter functions, you must select Func mode from the MODE menu. Enter the function $y = -16x\char94(-4)$ into the Y = editor, which is where you define functions. As a precaution, clear any previously entered functions before you enter the function. Check the viewing WINDOW to make sure that the value 2 falls between Xmin and Xmax. If not, change Xmin and/or Xmax, as needed. Select 6: dy/dx from the CALC (calculate) menu. Type 2 as the X value and then press ENTER. The derivative value is displayed as 2.0000 . . . , Choice D.

Tip: Be sure to use the negative key, not the subtraction key, when you enter negative numbers into the calculator.

Method 2: Find the numerical derivative using methods of calculus.

$f(x) = -16x^{-4} \Rightarrow f'(x) = 64x^{-5} \Rightarrow f'(2) = 64(2)^{-5} = 64 \cdot \frac{1}{32} = 2$, Choice D. The other answer choices occur if you make an error finding $f'(x)$.

26. B. From the scatterplot, it appears that a linear relationship exists between the two variables. Since the line of best fit would slant to the left, the relationship is negative. Thus, Choice B is the correct response. None of the statements in the other answer choices is an accurate interpretation of the shape of the scatterplot.

27. B. Method 1: A quick and reliable way to work this problem is to use the matrix features of your graphing calculator. Enter the two matrices into the calculator, then perform the multiplication, being sure to put B on the left in the multiplication. The display will show $\begin{bmatrix} 3 & 5 \\ 0 & 4 \end{bmatrix}$ (Choice B) as the product.

Method 2: Using the definition for matrix multiplication, compute the product BA, which is given by

$\begin{bmatrix} -2 & 3 \\ 2 & 0 \end{bmatrix}\begin{bmatrix} 0 & 2 \\ 1 & 3 \end{bmatrix} = \begin{bmatrix} -2\cdot0+3\cdot1 & -2\cdot2+3\cdot3 \\ 2\cdot0+0\cdot1 & 2\cdot2+0\cdot3 \end{bmatrix} = \begin{bmatrix} 3 & 5 \\ 0 & 4 \end{bmatrix}$, Choice B.

Choice A results if you perform the matrix multiplication incorrectly. Choice C is the product AB, not BA. Choice D is incorrect because the two matrices are conformable for multiplication.

28. C. Everywhere you have x in $f(x) = x^2 - 4$, you must substitute $(3x + 2)$, and then simplify, if possible:

$(f \circ g)(x) = f(g(x)) = f(3x + 2) = (3x + 2)^2 - 4 = 9x^2 + 12x + 4 - 4 = 9x^2 + 12x = 3x(3x + 4)$, Choice C. Choice A is $(f \cdot g)(x)$, not $(f \circ g)(x)$. Choice B is $(g \cdot f)(x)$, not $(f \circ g)(x)$. Choice D is $(g \circ f)(x)$, not $(f \circ g)(x)$.

29. A. This is a unit analysis problem. Plug the units into the formula and simplify as you would for variable quantities.

$m_2 = \frac{gr^2}{kP} = \frac{\left(\frac{m}{s^2}\right)(m)^2}{\left(\frac{m^2}{kg^2}\right)\left(\frac{kg-m}{s^2}\right)} = \frac{\frac{m^3}{s^2}}{\frac{m^3}{kg-s^2}} = \frac{1}{\frac{1}{kg}} = kg$, Choice A. The other answer choices occur if you make an error manipulating the units.

30. A. Analyze the problem. The compound interest formula is $P = P_0(1 + r)^t$, where r is the rate, compounded annually, and P is the value after t years of an initial investment of P_0. You need to find the rate, compounded annually, that will double an investment of $10,000 in 20 years. In other words, you need to find the rate, compounded annually, that will yield a value of $20,000 for P in 20 years. Devise a plan.

Method 1: Plug into the formula (omitting the units) and solve for r.

$P = P_0(1 + r)^t \Rightarrow 20{,}000 = 10{,}000(1 + r)^{20} \Rightarrow 2 = (1 + r)^{20} \Rightarrow \ln 2 = \ln(1 + r)^{20} \Rightarrow \ln 2 = 20\ln(1 + r) \Rightarrow \frac{\ln 2}{20} =$ $\ln(1 + r) \Rightarrow 1 + r = e^{\frac{\ln 2}{20}} \Rightarrow r = e^{\frac{\ln 2}{20}} - 1 = .03526\ldots$ or approximately 3.5%, Choice A. Choices B and D occur if you make a mistake in solving for r. Choice C occurs if you use the simple interest formula instead of the formula for compound interest.

Method 2: You can work this problem by checking the answer choices.

Checking A: $10{,}000(1 + 0.035)^{20} = 19{,}897.8886\ldots$ or approximately 20,000, indicating Choice A is the correct response.

In a test situation, you should go on to the next question since you have obtained the correct answer. You would not have to check the other answer choices; but for your information, Choice B yields $29{,}177.5749\ldots$, Choice C yields $67274.9994\ldots$, and Choice D yields $1.4835\ldots \cdot \text{E}10$.

31. B. $(4 + 5i)(4 - 5i) = 16 - 25i^2 = 16 - 25(-1) = 16 + 25 = 41$, Choice B. Choice A occurs if you evaluate i^2 as 1, instead of -1. Choices C and D occur if you make sign errors when multiplying.

32. B. Analyze the problem. The phrase "a long extended period of time" is a clue that this is a calculus problem in which you need to find the limit of a function as the variable approaches infinity. Devise a plan. To answer the question, you will need to find the limit of the function $Q(h) = \dfrac{10(4h + 25)}{2h + 5}$ as h approaches infinity:

$$\lim_{h\to\infty}\frac{10(4h + 25)}{2h + 5} = \lim_{h\to\infty}\frac{40h + 250}{2h + 5} = \lim_{h\to\infty}\frac{40 + \dfrac{250}{h}}{2 + \dfrac{5}{h}} = \frac{40 + 0}{2 + 0} = \frac{40}{2} = 20 \text{ components, Choice B. Choices A and}$$

C result if you evaluate the limit as h approaches infinity incorrectly. Choice D results if you find the limit as h approaches zero, instead of the limit as h approaches infinity.

33. A. Analyze the problem. At any time t after the water starts running, let $h(t)$ be the height of the water in the tank. Using the formula for the volume of a right cylinder, which is provided in the Notation, Definitions, and Formulas pages at the beginning of the test booklet, you have $V = \pi r^2 h(t) = \pi(5)^2 h(t) = 25\pi h(t)$. The volume of water at any time t is $30\dfrac{\text{ft}^3}{\text{min}}t$. Thus, omitting the units, $30t = 25\pi h(t) \Rightarrow h(t) = \dfrac{30t}{25\pi}$. The instantaneous rate of change of the height of the water at any time t is $h'(t) = \dfrac{30}{25\pi} = 0.3819\ldots$ or approximately $0.38\dfrac{\text{ft}}{\text{min}}$, Choice A. Choices B and C occur if you use an incorrect formula for the volume of a cylinder. Choice D occurs if you make a computation error.

34. B. The augmented matrix for the system is

$$\begin{bmatrix} 2 & 5 & -1 & 5 \\ -4 & 3 & 5 & 13 \\ 8 & 10 & 0 & -4 \end{bmatrix}.$$

Notice that you must enter a zero for the coefficient when a variable does not appear in an equation.

Although you can work this problem by using operations on the rows to transform the matrix so that the solution to the system is easily obtainable, the process is tedious and time-consuming. Since the Mathematics CK is a timed test, you should use your graphing calculator to find the solution. Enter the elements of the augmented matrix into the calculator, and then have the calculator produce the reduced row-echelon form of the augmented matrix. The display will show the following.

$$\begin{bmatrix} 1 & 0 & 0 & -3 \\ 0 & 1 & 0 & 2 \\ 0 & 0 & 1 & -1 \end{bmatrix}. \text{ Thus, } x = -3, y = 2, \text{ and } z = -1 \text{ is the solution to the system.}$$

Since $z = -1$, Choice B is the correct response. Choice A is the value of x in the solution set. Choice D is the value of y in the solution set. Choice C occurs if you make an error when determining the solution.

35. B. You can extend the Fundamental Counting Principle to determine the number of possible telephone numbers for each prefix as follows. After the prefix, there are four slots, so to speak, to fill. For each slot, 10 digits are available, which means the number of possible telephone numbers for each prefix is $10 \cdot 10 \cdot 10 \cdot 10 = 10^4$. By the Addition Principle, the total number of possible telephone numbers if all three prefixes are used is $10^4 + 10^4 + 10^4 = 3 \cdot 10^4$, Choice B. The other answer choices result if you analyze the problem incorrectly.

36. D. The rate of change of a curve at a point is described by the slope of the tangent to the curve at the point. The best way to work this problem is to check each statement against the behavior of the graph of the function. Choice A is incorrect because the slope of the tangent line is decreasing between 0 and 0.5, not constant. Choice B is incorrect because the slope of the tangent line is decreasing between 0.5 and 1.5. Choice C is incorrect because the slope of the tangent line is increasing between 2 and 3. Choice D is correct because the slope of the tangent line is increasing between 3 and 3.5.

37. D. The area of the region bounded by the graph of $f(x) = x^4 - 3x^3 + x^2 + 5$, the x-axis, and the vertical lines $x = 0$ (y-axis) and $x = 2$ is given by: Area $= \int_0^2 \left(x^4 - 3x^3 + x^2 + 5 \right) dx$.

Method 1: The fastest and most efficient way to calculate this numerical integral is with your graphing calculator. Here are the steps using a TI-83 calculator. Before you enter functions, you must select Func mode from the MODE menu. Enter the function $y = x^4 - 3x^3 + x^2 + 5$ into the Y = editor, which is where you define functions. As a precaution, clear any previously entered functions before you enter the function. Check the viewing WINDOW to make sure that the interval between 0 and 2 falls between Xmin and Xmax. If not, change Xmin and/or Xmax, as needed. Select 7: $\int f(x) dx$ from the CALC (calculate) menu. Type 0 as the lower limit and then press ENTER. Type 2 as the upper limit and then press ENTER. The graph is shaded and the integral value is displayed as 7.06666 . . . . Since the answer choices are given as fractions, select 1: Frac from the MATH menu. The display will show Ans▶Frac. Press ENTER. The display shows 106/15, Choice D.

Method 2: Integrate the function using methods of calculus.

$$\int_0^2 \left(x^4 - 3x^3 + x^2 + 5 \right) dx = \left(\frac{x^5}{5} - \frac{3x^4}{4} + \frac{x^3}{3} + 5x \right) \Big|_0^2 = \left(\frac{2^5}{5} - \frac{3 \cdot 2^4}{4} + \frac{2^3}{3} + 5 \cdot 2 \right) - \left(\frac{0^5}{5} - \frac{3 \cdot 0^4}{4} + \frac{0^3}{3} + 5 \cdot 0 \right) =$$

$\frac{32}{5} - \frac{48}{4} + \frac{8}{3} + 10 = \frac{106}{15}$, Choice D. The other answer choices result if you make a mistake integrating the function.

38. A. Analyze the problem. According to the 68-95-99.7 rule, approximately 68 percent of the values of a random variable that is normally distributed falls within 1 standard deviation of the mean, about 95 percent falls within 2 standard deviations of the mean, and about 99.7 percent falls within 3 standard deviations of the mean. The mean miles per gallon, μ, of the automobiles is 29 mpg with standard deviation, σ, of 4 mpg. Devise a plan.

Method 1: Using the statistical features of your graphing calculator is an efficient and time-saving way to work problems involving the normal distribution. Consult your owner's manual for detailed instructions on how to find percentages and probabilities using areas under a normal curve. Using a TI-83 calculator, here are the steps to find the approximate probability that a randomly selected automobile of this type will have gas mileage less than 25 mpg from a distribution with mean of 29 mpg and standard deviation of 4 mpg. Select 2:normalcdf(from the DISTR (distributions) menu to paste normalcdf(to the home screen. Type –1E99, 25, 29, 4 inside the parentheses. (Note: –1E99 is used as a proxy for –∞.) Close the parentheses and press ENTER. The display will show .1586 . . . or approximately 16%. Thus, the approximate probability that an automobile of this type chosen at random has gas mileage less than 25 mpg is 16 percent, Choice A.

Method 2: To find the approximate probability that a randomly chosen automobile will have gas mileage less than 25 mpg will take two steps. First, determine the z-score for 25 mpg, and then find the percentage of the normal distribution that is below this z-score.

Step 1. Find the z-score for 25 mpg.

z-score $= \dfrac{x\text{-value} - \mu}{\sigma} = \dfrac{25 - 29}{4} = -1$. Therefore, 25 is 1 standard deviation below the mean.

Step 2. Find the percentage of the normal distribution that is below a z-score of -1.

You know that about 68% of the distribution is within standard deviation of the mean. Make a sketch to illustrate the problem.

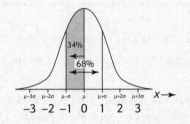

Since the normal curve is symmetric, about 34 percent ($\frac{1}{2}$ of 68 percent) of the distribution is between the mean and a z-score of -1. Again, due to symmetry, 50 percent of the total distribution is to the left of the mean. Thus, approximately $50 - 34 = 16$ percent of the distribution is below a z-score of -1. Thus, the approximate probability that an automobile of this type chosen at random has gas mileage less than 25 mpg is 16 percent, Choice A. Choice B is the probability the gas mileage will be between 25 and 29 mpg. Choice C is the probability the gas mileage will be between 25 and 33 mpg (1 standard deviation above the mean). Choice D is the probability that the gas mileage will be more than 25 mpg.

39. A. Analyze the problem. The tangent function, $y = \tan(bx - c) + k$, has a horizontal shift of $\frac{c}{b}$ units (to the right of the origin if $\frac{c}{b}$ is positive; to the left of the origin if $\frac{c}{b}$ is negative), and a vertical shift of $|k|$ units (up from the origin if k is positive; down from the origin if k is negative). Thus, $g(x) = \tan(4x - \pi) + 3$ has a horizontal shift to the right of $\frac{\pi}{4}$ units and a vertical shift up of 3 units, Choice A. Choice B is incorrect because neither shift is in the correct direction. Choice C occurs if you fail to divide π by 4. Choice D is incorrect because neither shift is in the correct direction in this answer choice, and the magnitude of the horizontal shift is also incorrect.

Tip: If you are unsure whether the shift is to the right or left or up or down, graph the two functions on your graphing calculator to check.

40. A. Establishing cause-and-effect relationships is most likely when investigators conduct well-designed experimental studies, so Choice A is the correct response. Choices B and C are incorrect because cause-effect relationships are not established with the types of studies given in these answer choices. Choice D is incorrect because establishing cause-effect relationships in observational studies is problematic given that the investigators are unable to manipulate variables of interest.

41. C. Analyze the problem. Rewrite $2x^2 - x < 1$ as $2x^2 - x - 1 < 0$. Factor the left side of the inequality to obtain $(2x + 1)(x - 1) < 0$. You need to determine when the product $(2x + 1)(x - 1)$ is negative. Devise a plan. To solve the inequality will take two steps. First, find the values for x at which the factors change sign; that is, find the zero for each factor. Next, make an organized chart to determine when the product of the two factors will be negative.

Step 1. Find the values for x at which the factors change sign.

Set each factor equal to zero and solve for x.

$2x + 1 \Rightarrow x = -\dfrac{1}{2}$ and $x - 1 = 0 \Rightarrow x = 1$.

Step 2. Make a chart to determine when $(2x + 1)(x - 1)$ is negative.

The two values $-\dfrac{1}{2}$ and 1 divide the number line into three intervals: $(-\infty, -\frac{1}{2})$, $(-\frac{1}{2}, 1)$, and $(1, 0)$. Make an organized chart to determine the sign of $(2x + 1)(x - 1)$ for each of these intervals.

Interval	Sign of (2x + 1)	Sign of (x – 1)	Sign of (2x + 1)(x – 1)
$(-\infty, -\frac{1}{2})$	negative	negative	positive
$(-\frac{1}{2}, 1)$	positive	negative	negative
$(1, 0)$	positive	positive	positive

From your chart, you can see that the $(2x +1)(x - 1)$ is negative only in the interval $(-\frac{1}{2}, 1)$, Choice C. Answer choices A and D occur if you make a mistake finding the zeroes for the factors. Choice B occurs if you make a mistake in your sign chart.

42. A. Analyze the problem. You are given two points $(0, 500)$ and $(5, 1500)$ that satisfy the function $P(t) = P_0e^{xt}$. Devise a plan. To find the value of x will take two steps. First, plug the values for the two points into $P(t) = P_0e^{xt}$, and then solve the resulting system of equations for x.

Step 1. Plug the values for the two points into $P(t) = P_0e^{xt}$.

$500 = P_0e^{x(0)} = P_0e^0 = P_0 \cdot 1 = P_0$

$1500 = P_0e^{x(5)} = P_0e^{5x} = 500e^{5x}$ (using the results from the first equation) $\Rightarrow 1500 = 500e^{5x} = \Rightarrow 3 = e^{5x} \Rightarrow \ln 3 = \ln(e^{5x}) \Rightarrow \ln 3 = 5x \ln e \Rightarrow \ln 3 = 5x \Rightarrow x = \frac{\ln 3}{5}$, Choice A. The other answer choices result if you make an error solving for x.

43. D. Make a chart showing the height of the ball as a function of rebound number.

Height of Ball (in feet)	120	$120 \cdot \frac{3}{4}$	$120 \cdot \frac{3}{4} \cdot \frac{3}{4}$	$120 \cdot \frac{3}{4} \cdot \frac{3}{4} \cdot \frac{3}{4}$	. . .
Rebound Number n	0	1	2	3	. . .

Examination of the table leads to a general term for the nth bounce, which is $120 \cdot \left(\frac{3}{4}\right)^n$. Thus, an exponential function (Choice D) would best model the height of the ball as a function of rebound number n. None of the functions in the other answer choices works as well as an exponential model.

44. C. The function $y = \dfrac{2x^3 + 3x - x + 1}{x^2 - 8x + 16}$ will have vertical asymptotes at any value for x that makes the denominator equal zero. Set $x^2 - 8x + 16 = 0$ and solve for x: $x^2 - 8x + 16 = 0 \Rightarrow (x - 4)^2 = 0 \Rightarrow x = 4$. Thus, y has one vertical asymptote at $x = 4$. Since the degree of the numerator of y exceeds the degree of the denominator of y by exactly 1, y will have one oblique asymptote. Thus, y has a total of 2 asymptotes, Choice C. The other answer choices do not contain the correct number of asymptotes.

45. A. Analyze the problem. You need to find the difference in the areas of the two tables. You are given the dimensions of the rectangular table and the diameter of the circular table. Devise a plan. Three steps are needed to solve the problem. First, find the area of the rectangular table; next, find the area of the circular table; and then find the difference between the two areas.

Step 1. Find the area of the rectangular table.

$A = lw = (4.5 \text{ ft})(3 \text{ ft}) = 13.5 \text{ ft}^2$

Step 2. Find the area of the circular table.

You are given that the diameter of the circular table is 4 feet. The radius is half the diameter, or 2 feet.

$A = \pi r^2 = \pi(2 \text{ ft})^2 = 12.5663 \ldots \text{ft}^2$ (Don't round this number.)

Step 3. Find the difference between the two areas:

13.5 ft^2 – 12.5663 . . . ft^2 = 0.9336 . . . or approximately 0.93 ft^2, Choice A.

Tip: Use the recall answer feature of your calculator to find the difference without rounding until the final computation.

Choice B is the area of the circular table, not the difference in the two areas. Choice C is the sum of the two areas, not the difference. Choice D results if you use 4 feet for the radius in finding the area of the circular table.

46. C. Analyze the problem. To determine the closed form for a sequence requires looking for a pattern in the terms of the sequence or in the first and second differences between terms. Devise a plan. Make a table that includes the terms of the sequence and the first and second differences between terms, and then look for a pattern.

n	a_n	1st **Difference**	2nd **Difference**
1	1		
2	8	8 – 1 = 7	
3	17	17 – 8 = 9	9 – 7 = 2
4	28	28 – 17 = 11	11 – 9 = 2
5	41	41 – 28 = 13	13 – 11 = 2
6	56	56 – 41 = 15	15 – 13 = 2

The table shows that the second differences are constant. When the second difference is constant, the relationship between terms of the sequence is quadratic, Choice C. The models given in the other answer choices do not describe the closed-form representation of the sequence.

47. C. Analyze the problem. The volume of a right prism is given by $V = Bh$. (Note: This formula is provided in the Notation, Definitions, and Formulas pages at the beginning of the test booklet.) Devise a plan. To find the volume of the right triangular prism will take two steps. First, find the area, B, of one of the equilateral triangular bases, and then find the volume by multiplying B by the height of the prism, h.

Step 1. Find the area of one of the regular equilateral triangular bases.

The area of an equilateral triangle with sides of 4 in is given by: Area $= \frac{\sqrt{3}}{4}s^2 = \frac{\sqrt{3}}{4}(4\text{ in})^2 = 4\sqrt{3}\text{ in}^2$

Tip: If you forget the formula for the area of an equilateral triangle, you can derive it by using the Pythagorean theorem or trigonometric functions to determine the height (altitude) of the triangle, and then using the formula, area $= \frac{1}{2}bh$, to find the area of the equilateral triangle.

Step 2. Find the volume by multiplying B by the height of the prism, h.

Volume $= (4\sqrt{3}\text{in}^2)(25\text{ in}) = 173.2050 . . .$ or approximately 173 in^3, Choice C. Choice A results if you fail to do step 2. Choice B results if you use an incorrect formula for the volume of the prism. Choice D results if you use an incorrect formula for the area of an equilateral triangle.

48. B. Analyze the problem. Since the coin is to be flipped six times, you can work this problem by extending the Fundamental Counting Principle to six events. There are 2 possibilities for each of the 6 coin flips, which means the total number of possible outcomes in the sample space is $2 \cdot 2 \cdot 2 \cdot 2 \cdot 2 \cdot 2 = 2^6$, Choice B. The other answer choices result if you analyze the problem incorrectly.

49. A. Make a quick sketch of the two graphs.

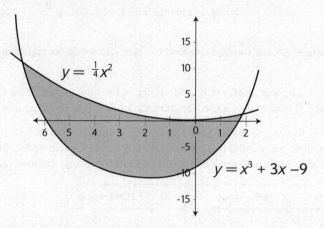

Analyze the problem. The two graphs intersect at two points, and the graph of $y = \frac{1}{4}x^2$ lies above $y = x^2 + 3x - 9$ between the points of intersection. Devise a plan. To find the area of the region bounded by the two graphs will take three steps. First, find the x-values for the points of intersection of the two graphs; next, find the difference between the two functions, being sure to subtract the equation of the lower graph from the equation of the upper graph; and then evaluate the definite integral of the difference of the two graphs between the two x-values of their intersection.

Step 1. Find the x-values for the points of intersection of the two graphs.

Using substitution, you have $\frac{1}{4}x^2 = x^2 + 3x - 9 \Rightarrow 0 = \frac{3}{4}x^2 + 3x - 9 \Rightarrow 0 = 3x^2 + 12x - 36 \Rightarrow 0 = x^2 + 4x - 12 \Rightarrow 0 = (x + 6)(x - 2) \Rightarrow x = -6$ and $x = 2$.

Step 2. Find the difference between the two graphs.

Difference $= (\frac{1}{4}x^2) - (x^2 + 3x - 9) = \frac{1}{4}x^2 - x^2 - 3x + 9 = -\frac{3}{4}x^2 - 3x + 9$

Step 3. Evaluate the definite integral $\int_{-6}^{2} \left(-\frac{3}{4}x^2 - 3x + 9\right) dx$.

Method 1: The fastest and most efficient way to calculate this numerical integral is with your graphing calculator. Here are the steps using a TI-83 calculator. Before you enter functions, you must select Func mode from the MODE menu. Enter the function $y = -3/4x^2 - 3x + 9$ into the Y = editor, which is where you define functions. (Note: Check your manual to make sure your calculator treats $-3/4x^2$ as $(3/4)x^2$. If not, include the parentheses around 3/4 when you enter the function.) As a precaution, clear any previously entered functions before you enter the function. Check the viewing WINDOW to make sure that the interval between -6 and 2 falls between Xmin and Xmax. If not, change Xmin and/or Xmax, as needed. Select 7: $\int f(x)\, dx$ from the CALC (calculate) menu. Type -6 as the lower limit and then press ENTER. Type 2 as the upper limit and then press ENTER. The integral value is displayed as 64 (Choice A) and the graph is shaded. (Note: The graph and the shaded region will not look like what you've sketched above because you entered the difference of the two functions into the function editor.)

Method 2: Integrate the function using methods of calculus.

$$\int_{-6}^{2} \left(-\frac{3}{4}x^2 - 3x + 9\right) = \left(-\frac{x^3}{4} - \frac{3x^2}{2} + 9x\right)\Big|_{-6}^{2} = \left(-\frac{2^3}{4} - \frac{3 \cdot 2^2}{2} + 9 \cdot 2\right) - \left(-\frac{(-6)^3}{4} - \frac{3 \cdot (-6)^2}{2} + 9 \cdot -6\right) =$$

$(-2 - 6 + 18) - (54 - 54 - 54) = 10 + 54 = 64$, Choice A. The other answer choices result if you make a mistake integrating the function.

50. B. By the Multiplication Rule, to find the probability that an event A occurs on the first trial and an event B occurs on the second trial, multiply the probability of event A times the probability of event B, where you have determined the probability of B by taking into account that the event A has already occurred. The probability that a yellow marble is drawn on the first draw is given by: $P(\text{yellow on first draw}) = \dfrac{\text{Number of yellow marbles in bag}}{\text{Total number of marbles}} = \dfrac{3}{25}$. After this event occurs, since the first yellow marble is not put back in the bag, the probability that a yellow marble will be drawn on the second draw is given by: $P(\text{yellow on second draw given first draw is yellow}) = \dfrac{2}{24}$. Thus, the probability that both marbles will be yellow when two marbles are randomly drawn from the bag without replacement is given by: $\dfrac{3}{25} \cdot \dfrac{2}{24}$, Choice B. Choice A is the probability of drawing two yellow marbles with replacement. Choice C is the probability of drawing a yellow marble on the first draw. Choice D is the probability of drawing a yellow marble on the second draw if the first yellow marble is not put back in the bag.

Simplifying Radicals

A radical is **simplified** when

    a.   the radicand contains no variable factor raised to a power equal to or greater than the index of the radical.

    b.   the radicand contains no constant factor that can be expressed as a power equal to or greater than the index of the radical.

    c.   the radicand contains no fractions.

    d.   no fractions contain radicals in the denominator.

    e.   the index of the radical as reduced to its lowest value.

For example,

- $\sqrt[3]{24a^5 b^6} = \left(\sqrt[3]{8a^3 b^6}\right)\left(\sqrt[3]{3a^2}\right) = 2ab^2\left(\sqrt[3]{3a^2}\right)$ is simplified.

- $\sqrt{12} = \left(\sqrt{4}\right)\left(\sqrt{3}\right) = 2\left(\sqrt{3}\right)$ is simplified.

- $\dfrac{\sqrt{54}}{\sqrt{6}} = \sqrt{\dfrac{54}{6}} = \sqrt{9} = 3$ is simplified.

- $\dfrac{1}{\sqrt{2}} = \left(\dfrac{1}{\sqrt{2}}\right)\dfrac{\sqrt{2}}{\sqrt{2}} = \dfrac{\sqrt{2}}{2}$ is simplified.

- $\sqrt[4]{a^2} = \sqrt{a}$ is simplified.

Since square roots occur so frequently, the remainder of the examples will use only square root radicals.

Radicals that have the same index and the same radicand are **like radicals.** To add or subtract like radicals, combine their coefficients and write the result as the coefficient of the common radical factor. Indicate the sum or difference of unlike radicals.

$$5\sqrt{3} + 2\sqrt{3} = 7\sqrt{3}$$

You may have to simplify the radical expressions before combining them.

$$5\sqrt{3} + \sqrt{12} = 5\sqrt{3} + \left(\sqrt{4}\right)\left(\sqrt{3}\right) = 5\sqrt{3} + 2\sqrt{3} = 7\sqrt{3}.$$

To multiply radicals that have the same index, multiply their coefficients to find the coefficient of the product. Multiply the radicands to find the radicand of the product. Simplify the results.

$$(5\sqrt{3})(2\sqrt{3}) = 10\sqrt{9} = 10(3) = 30.$$

For a sum or difference, treat the factors as you would binomials, being sure to simplify radicals after you multiply.

- $(2\sqrt{3} + 5\sqrt{7})(\sqrt{3} - 3\sqrt{6}) = 2\sqrt{9} - 6\sqrt{18} + 5\sqrt{21} - 15\sqrt{42} =$
  $2(3) - 6\sqrt{9}\sqrt{2} + 5\sqrt{21} - 15\sqrt{42} = 6 - 18\sqrt{2} + 5\sqrt{21} - 15\sqrt{42}.$

- $(1 - \sqrt{3})(1 + \sqrt{3}) = 1 - \sqrt{3} + \sqrt{3} - \sqrt{9} = 1 - 3 = -2.$

A technique called **rationalizing** is used to remove radicals from the denominator of a fraction. For square root radicals, if the denominator contains a single term, multiply the numerator and denominator by the smallest radical that will produce a perfect square in the denominator. For example,

$$\frac{5}{\sqrt{3}} = \left(\frac{5}{\sqrt{3}}\right)\left(\frac{\sqrt{3}}{\sqrt{3}}\right) = \frac{5\sqrt{3}}{3}.$$

If the denominator contains a sum or difference of square roots, multiply the numerator and denominator by a difference or sum that will cause the middle term to sum to zero when you multiply. For example,

$$\frac{5}{1-\sqrt{3}} = \left(\frac{5}{1-\sqrt{3}}\right)\left(\frac{1+\sqrt{3}}{1+\sqrt{3}}\right) = \left(\frac{5\left(1+\sqrt{3}\right)}{1-3}\right) = -\frac{5+5\sqrt{3}}{2}.$$